"This witty, incisive memoir delves into white privilege, identity, and intersectionality, as Maxfield reflects on her childhood growing up in a Jewish household and sharply reported moments as an adult pushing back against stereotypes and misjudgments. Her candid account blends crack comic storytelling with dead-serious considerations of what it's like to be Jewish in America. ... This layered narrative will resonate with readers trying to define themselves in a world of mislabels, and her ability to transform childhood insecurities into superpowers as an adult inspires, though she never discounts how devastating it is to be 'othered.'"

—*BookLife Reviews*

"Follow this hilarious, feisty heroine as she infuses humor and wit into what it was like growing up a *JewGirl* and now at a time when antisemitism is on the rise and women's rights are at risk. Learn how she endeavors to 'fix the things that were wrong with your childhood' and ultimately learns to love the woman she's become."

—Ruthie Marlenée,
And Still Her Voice, Agave Blues

"In this deeply personal yet socially illuminating memoir, Maxfield navigates her Jewish American experience, tracing the tension between assimilation and exclusion. ... From her family lore—which includes bootleggers, a Hungarian grandfather, and a relative nicknamed 'King David' of McKeesport—to contemporary tragedies like the Tree of Life massacre, the author situates her story in both intimate and historical frames. The memoir is rich in self-reflection, exploring guilt, empathy, and responsibility; Maxfield challenges readers to consider how social justice movements often overlook Jewish women when grappling with histories like slavery and the Holocaust. The author is unflinching about her own complicity, struggles, and ambivalence—she reflects on her reluctance to finally include her maiden name, Blumberg (thus claiming her Jewishness professionally), until after the 2016 presidential election. ... A fearless, witty memoir about being both privileged and perpetually at risk."

—*Kirkus Reviews*

"Reading this book felt like sitting across from a friend who's decided to tell you everything without a filter. I loved the way Maxfield blends humor with pain. One moment I was laughing at her sharp one-liners, the next I felt a knot in my stomach from the ugliness of the prejudice she describes. What I liked most was her honesty. She doesn't pretend to have neat answers, and that made the book feel real. ... She writes with urgency, as if she knows these stories need to be told now, before they're forgotten or drowned out by louder voices. ... It's not a book that holds your hand. It's a book that looks you in the eye and says, This is how it is."

—*Literary Titan*

"*JewGirl* is a brave memoir about being a Jewish woman in today's society. But it's also about destructive relationships, the loss of innocence, casual antisemitism, and simply wanting to be seen and understood as a member of a tiny tribe that has withstood thousands of years of persecution. Maxfield tells it all through her personal lens of sensitivity and biting humor. *JewGirl* will remind you of the difficulties all girls face and open your eyes to the struggle and courage of the Jewish people."

—Meredith Berlin, author of *Friends with Issues*

"Marcie Blumberg Maxfield has succeeded in writing a brave, thoughtful, original, relatable, often irreverent, and much-needed book about what it's like to be othered as both a Jew and a woman. If you're a Jewish woman, you'll find yourself nodding in recognition. If you're not, this book is also for you—I think you'll find it eye-opening."

—Deborah K. Shepherd, author of *So Happy Together*

"*Jewgirl* by Marcie Maxfield is the book all Jews and non-Jews alike should read. It's part memoir, part historical, and beautifully written. She describes her experiences and challenges as a Jewish person, yet she has expertly crafted a book of stories that are relatable to everyone, regardless of their background."

—Leslie A. Rasmussen, award-winning author of *When People Leave*

Jew Girl

On Being and Belonging

MARCIE MAXFIELD

Published October 1, 2025
Print ISBN: 979-8-9925390-1-1
E-ISBN: 979-8-9925390-0-4
Library of Congress Control Number: 2025902167

For information, contact:
Desert Canyon Books, LLC, PO Box 4084, Palm Springs, CA 92262

Book and Cover Design by Dearly Creative
Printed in the United States of America

Author's Note

JewGirl is a work of nonfiction. Names and identifying characteristics of individuals and settings have been changed, and some dialogue has been re-created. This book represents my recollections of experiences over time. Additionally, I relied on personal journals, interviews, feedback, and questionnaires to supplement my memory of certain events. Others who were present might recall things differently, but this is my story to tell.

Contents

Boxes

SOMEWHERE IN THE DESERT, in the parking lot of a strip mall, adjacent to a CVS, amidst sweltering heat, about to give blood, my identity came into focus.

"White?" the big burly guy filling out the computer intake form asked me.

"No," I replied.

This was not premeditated. I didn't wake up and say to myself, *Today's the day I stop checking the box "White."* It had been a long time coming. I guess you could say it had been on the back burner of my consciousness, simmering. Maybe because of the excessive heat, which tends to slow the pace of life here in Palm Springs, a calm came over me, my voice quiet but firm. It was a decisive "no."

"Caucasian?" Burly Guy asked. As if it were a simple matter of terminology. As if, maybe, I just didn't like the word "white," but I'd be cool with "Caucasian." This time I shook my head no, my hair a mess of curls. Because even in the desert, even in dry heat, when it's sweat-dripping hot outside, there's enough humidity in the air to make my hair frizz.

Burly Guy scratched his head. It was his job to process donors quickly and efficiently, and here I was mucking up the system. Me, clearly *to him*, a white lady.

For years, I accepted this unconscious default to skin color. No big deal. But it no longer feels comfortable to be lumped in the "White" box along with the alt-right, far right, white supremacists, Christian nationalists, neo-Nazis—all the groups, too numerous to list—that collectively make up the white power movement in the United States, many of whom want to wipe my people, Jewish people, off the face of the earth. In a way, we're siloed, neither a People of Color nor white enough for a white Christian world.

There are boxes I freely check: Female, Jewish, Married, American. But there's one box I won't check anymore, and it's not about skin color. It's about the growing fundamentalist vision of a white Christian America that does not include Jews. If I check a box, I want it to come with a sense of belonging. Peace, love, and harmony. Shared history or perspective. I know this may sound naïve, but a sense of belonging is important to me. I've struggled to find it my whole life. The expectation that I should go along with the ruse, that I should smile, and say, *sure, okay, put me in the "White" box with the antisemites* is no longer okay with me.

Plus, Caucasian?

That isn't even a thing. It's an outdated racist term that has come to be synonymous with white, even though, geographically speaking, not all Caucasians are white-skinned. And, not to nitpick, but my ancestors weren't from the Caucasus: an area between the Black Sea and the Caspian Sea that includes parts of Southern Russia, Georgia, Armenia, and Azerbaijan. Had to google *the Caucasus* because I had no idea where it was. My ancestors were from Hungary and Lithuania, that much I do know. More to the point, though, the term "white" is often conflated with Christianity in the U.S., and I'm not feeling a kinship with this idea of a white Christian country. I was happier with the melting pot.

"Jewish," I told him.

"That's not a race," he responded.

Well, that's a chicken-or-egg sort of statement. I mean, scholars way smarter than me have debated the question of race for ages because, as it turns out, the entire concept of race has no biological validity, whereas my DNA defines me as Jewish: ninety-eight percent Ashkenazi. The missing two percent could be due to intermarriage. Or, just as likely, it could be the result of rape somewhere along the Diaspora trail. That happened a lot. What does it mean to be Jewish anyway? Is it a religion? Ethnicity?

Am I a rat?

JAP.

Dirty.

Kike.

Pushy.

Greedy.

Power-hungry-media-controlling-secret-caballer.

"White or Caucasian?" Burly Guy said, laying out my options, frustration beginning to crack at the seams of his professional demeanor. Sometimes clerks talk so fast, slurring their words together, I find myself saying, *What?* Like I'm hard of hearing, or they're speaking another language. But Burly Guy wasn't like that. On the contrary, he was being conscientious.

Having started with "white" and switched to "Caucasian," now he was presenting them both as a *one or the other* alternative. Like an A/B test to determine which version of an ad campaign pulls better, the dancing bear or the kid with balloons. It was a bit of a stalemate, and I wasn't about to give in. I was planting a flag in the dirt, which was really a mobile blood unit. In the desert, natch. I mean, where else would a Jew roam but Palm Springs to hide out from the virus? That's why I was at this blood bank in the first place. My sister Chicky said the sky was falling.

"The vaccine may not work!" she screamed into the phone. "You need to get tested for antibodies!" So, there I was, having my blood tested just to appease my big sister Chicky, and Burly Guy couldn't seem to get past this question of race.

No hurry, I thought, smiling to myself. *I've got all day.*

Lady, his eyes seemed to say. *I just process intake forms. Help a guy out.*

But I was digging my heels in. Sandals, actually. Birkenstocks. Super comfortable. It was scorching outside. Desert heat. Over a hundred and ten degrees. The doors to the van were open, fans circulating hot air in a futile attempt at a breeze. Burly Guy wiped the sweat from his brow, his massive arms straining against the short sleeves of his standard-issue med-tech V-neck. The laminated photo ID clipped to his shirt pocket stated his name, Michael, and his job title. This is a guy who knew exactly who he was. I was just beginning to reclaim my identity, and unfortunately for him, my "aha" moment was happening on his watch. We were trying to come to terms: which box to check?

Here's the thing—it's not just a box on a form. It's a tacit agreement that says: *Yes, you can categorize me, put me in that column. Add me to the count.* This is what society does. It organizes things. Cities, counties, streets on a grid. ZIP codes.

And people.

It creates boxes and then it puts people in them. Whole swaths of people in a box. If you're lucky, you identify with your box; you get cozy with the corrugated cardboard and nest like a bird. Hatch eggs. But what if the box doesn't fit? It's too small, you feel cramped. You push against the top and kick the sides, trying to make more space. Or maybe it's too big; you feel lost and all alone, swiping left and right, looking for love. Sometimes it can feel like you're in the wrong box altogether and it makes you want to scream.

I'M NOT WHITE!

Just ask my in-laws, who are as WASPy as it gets. They'll tell you I'm Jewish. They whisper that my voice is too nasal when I call on the phone. *I talk too fast, too loud, with my hands. And that hair!* I admit my hair can be unmanageable, and it might not just be my hair. *You're too animated,* my boss at the animal rescue summed it up. *Tone it down, girl.* So I went into the bathroom, flipped my hair over my head, tousled it a little more and gave myself a wild animal mane, like a lioness. Only on me, it was more Jewess. I've been compared to rats, scurrying. Unclean. Well, not me personally. My people. The other ones, a colleague at a magazine once pointed out: the ones who wear weird hats and have strings hanging outside their pants. We were driving past Fairfax on our way to meet with a client of mine in West Hollywood at the time. That's when, referring to Orthodox Jews crossing the street, she said, "Look at them scurrying like rats."

"I'm Jewish, you know," I responded.

"Yes," she said, "but you're not like them." *You get a pass,* she implied.

This was not in the way-back 20th century. This was in the oughts, as in, you ought not to talk like that anymore. She was tall, with red hair, her wrists stacked with gold bangles that jangled in meetings. She was always conspiring, reducing everyone to stereotypes, not just Jews. She hired a guy with no sales experience to work in the design district just because he was gay.

"The gays will love him!" she said.

When that didn't pan out, she fired him. Later, she banished me to the Valley. "You'll do great in the Valley," she insisted. "They're all Jewish." Then she said something about how I could sell ice to an Eskimo, and I stopped listening. I also stopped working so hard. It's called quiet quitting. I did not file a report with HR; I just didn't do what she asked me to do: use my ethnicity to bring business into the magazine.

I don't differentiate between the insults people say to my face or whisper behind my back, and the ones they spew at Jewish people in general—the endless tropes about money and power. Hollywood and the media. I lived in Los Angeles and worked in media and entertainment for years—in marketing, advertising, public relations, and sales. Worked my way up from coordinator to manager to assistant director or associate publisher at this-or-that magazine or organization. It's a comfortable career, but still, paycheck to paycheck. Meanwhile, billionaire rappers complain about all the money and power Jews have.[1]

"Where's the money?" my sister Chicky always jokes. "Cuz I'd really like to get my hands on some of it."

"Me too," I say.

---

1   Kanye West

It's not about how much money we have, the color of my skin, or even my religious beliefs. The Nazis did not stop to ask anyone's thoughts on God when they branded Jews with yellow stars and sent them to death camps. It was all about the percentage of Jewish blood running through your veins, which brings me back to the blood bank.

Just outside the door to the van a line of potential donors was forming. People standing in relentless heat. "It's oppressive out there," I said.

Michael was staring at his computer screen trying to find a suitable label, one that I would accept, so he could check the box and move on down the form, then hand me off to a nurse, turn to the line outside the open van door, and say, *Next, please.* I smiled at him to let him know that I appreciated his time, but in hindsight, I doubt he could tell through the mask.

"Other?" He sighed, massaging his temples with his fingers.

"That works for me, Michael," I responded, because I've been othered my whole life. I was relieved that we had come to a resolution of sorts. A compromise position. If not an understanding, at least an acknowledgment of my point of view. After we got past the issue of which box to check, Michael sped through the rest of the questions: medical history, allergies, that type of thing, and then passed me off to the technician, who moved me to a bed and hooked me up to an IV. Her nails were long, acrylic, and painted like a Pantone color wheel.

"Those are fancy," I commented.

"Well, when you wear a uniform every day, you gotta jazz it up somehow."

"Makes sense."

When it was over, Fancy Nails offered me apple juice and a small bag of yogurt-covered raisins, cranberries, and peanuts. The kind you put in a kid's lunchbox. The snack—melted and liquefied from the heat—had decomposed into a messy concoction of fruit and nuts drowning in sugar syrup that belonged in the trash, but I tore into that bag with urgency. My body needed every drop of energy I could consume.

"May I have another?" I asked, licking my fingers like a five-year-old.

"You're white as a sheet!" Fancy Nails said.

And there it was, that other reality. My skin is white. Medium light with pinkish undertones. That's the description I use when purchasing cosmetics. But when I'm blood-sapped, it turns a milky shade of pale. I wanted to ask Fancy Nails what box she checked. Her skin was medium-dark with gold undertones. She looked like she could be Black or Latina, biracial perhaps, I couldn't tell. But I decided against asking, as it could be construed as an invasive question.

"You're not driving yourself home, are you?" asked Fancy Nails, whose name tag said *Betty*.

My husband was in the parking lot waiting for me. "I'll be okay," I assured her, standing up, ignoring the woozy feeling in my head, wobbling my way to the exit. Before I was two steps outside of the van, weaving like a day-drunk, Betty appeared at my side. She wrapped her arm around my back to support me, her fancy nails pressing into my waist as she escorted me to the car. Leaning into Betty's shoulder to steady myself, I told her, on repeat, that I could not have made it to the car without her help. Harry drove me home, put me to bed, and brought me sliced turkey and cheese, my go-to protein snack when I'm sick. Then I called Chicky to complain.

I could barely sit up!

I almost passed out!

I needed assistance walking to the car!

Chicky yelled at me for not eating something before giving blood. "No one told me to eat first," I wailed. Whenever the lab draws blood, they make you fast in advance. How was I supposed to know? "Marcelle," she said, "you are such an idiot! That's to check your cholesterol. Those tests don't require nearly as much blood as a donation does." Back and forth like that, until I was too tired to tell her about the big to-do over my refusing to check the box "White."

It seems a simple thing to choose "other," but it's not as easy as it sounds. My original plan had been to hide out in Palm Springs during COVID, but then we fell in love with the mountains, clean air, and the absence of traffic. So Harry and I sold our house in L.A. and moved to the desert. It occurred to me that I should find a local doctor. My new doctor's office emailed an online form to fill out and requested that I attach a copy of my photo ID. When they returned the executed paperwork, under race or ethnicity, they had changed "Other" to "White."

"They can't do that!" Chicky screamed into the phone when I told her they had edited my personal information. "It's illegal. You need to call them up and make them change it back." Chicky is more of a fighter than I am, always putting out little fires. I tend to let things go until they pile up, then I explode. She ends up being slightly disgruntled most of the time, which may not be healthy, and I appear easygoing until I turn into a crazy lady. Definitely not healthy.

My identifying as "other" makes some people uncomfortable. They act like I'm trying to slide out of being white. Skip the whole moment of reckoning for white people that's happening right now in the United States. Or maybe they think I'm trying to tag on to Black Lives Matter and somehow muddy the waters. That's not my intention. I have white skin and acknowledge the privilege that comes with it. I'm also Jewish and have experienced antisemitism. My issue is with the white power/Christian fundamentalist movement and the box system, not racial justice.

There are, it should be noted, many Jewish people who hold fierce to a "white" identity—possibly an existential reaction to what happened when the Nazis vilified Jews for being not just a different race, but subhuman. Vermin. Throughout history, Jews have been blamed for everything from the Black Death to global migration. So, I understand the urge to define oneself as white, to slip into that safety zone, but aligning ourselves along racial color lines in an attempt at assimilation isn't working.

To complicate matters, it feels as if the racial reckoning happening in this country has been largely limited to People of Color. Jewish people are left out of the conversation because many American Jews have white skin, ignoring the fact that Jews come in all colors. There are Jews from Europe and Russia, Mexico, and the Middle East. Ethiopia. And South America. My point is: Jews are not white, brown, or black. We're Jewish, and we have been targeted as such.

Some Ashkenazi American Jews jokingly refer to themselves as white-*ish*. White-*light*. Or white-*adjacent*. People sometimes say we're next in line to become white—a cute, jokey colloquialism for assimilation. An Italian acquaintance suggested to me over coffee that Jewish people just need to bide their time. Wait it out, she implied, and eventually you'll be full members of the white club. The gist of the conversation was that we had to pay our dues, like the Irish and Italian immigrants who came before us. It's not as simple as that, though. Although many Jews have white skin, none of us are Christian, and that is what's known in sales as a "deal-breaker."

If it makes people uncomfortable that I don't check the box "White," that's okay with me. I'm uncomfortable, too. I'm uncomfortable with the rise of antisemitism in the United States. And that was before the war between Israel and Hamas broke out, which, as I edit this book, is still ongoing. It concerns me that this kind of humorous, kind of fed-up, somewhat confessional book about my life as a Jewish American woman could be made null and void, overshadowed, by the brutality of the Hamas attack on Israeli citizens, the scale of Israel's relentless retaliation against Hamas and its devastating impact on Palestinians. The unconscionable loss of lives on both sides. How can my relatively cushy life have any relevance in a post–October 7th world?

And yet, how can it not?

Jews are tribal. What happens in Israel impacts Jewish people all over the world. It bleeds into the streets of New York and Washington, London and Paris, in the form of protests and peace rallies. It polarizes college campuses and spreads like a cancer on social media platforms. Jewish writers are becoming pariahs, storytellers finding it difficult to get their work published or produced. Blacklisted. Still, there persists this idea that Jews are privileged, meaning that we have white skin and are, therefore, not subject to systemic racism.

That way of thinking doesn't acknowledge the existential threat that Jews endure. Not just in Israel, but in the United States. Jews represent slightly more than two percent of the

American population, yet a significant and disproportionate 15 percent of hate crimes committed in the U.S. target Jews.[2] To characterize Jews simply as "oppressors" ignores the history of oppression experienced by Jewish people. Jews are both privileged and persecuted. The two concepts are not mutually exclusive.

Here's what happens when you're Ashkenazi Jewish. You get put in the "White" box because of the color of your skin. But the self-described "real" white people, the so-called "fringe" groups, don't want us in their box. They worry we're trying to replace them, which is a joke. We haven't even replaced ourselves since the Holocaust. When you think about it, even Replacement Theory is at odds with the whole "box" system. How can Jews be both white *and* responsible for a global plot to replace white people with nonwhite minorities? It doesn't make sense. None of this makes sense. White boys in prep-school clothes chanting *Jews Will Not Replace Us* in Charlottesville. Wearing red caps and flaunting the American flag. The ones who show up at rallies with guns or shoot up a synagogue in Pittsburgh. Kill a bunch of old people who could've been my relatives.

I mean that literally—people who could have been *my* relatives.

My maternal grandmother, Molly, grew up in a suburb of Pittsburgh. She had dark hair, alabaster skin, and delicate features. Molly's father, our great-grandfather, was a big muckymuck in McKeesport, Pennsylvania. His name was David.

"They called him King David!" Chicky told me over the phone. My other sister, Trish, said he was the mayor. My sisters and I haven't lived in the same state for decades, but we spend

---

2   Callum Sutherland, "The Rise of Antisemitism and Political Violence in the U.S.," Time magazine, June 2, 2025

hours on the phone dissecting our family history. Chicky takes much pride in this piece of information, like we're descendants of the real King David, the boy who fought Goliath with a slingshot to become ruler of Israel. Not just run-of-the-mill Jewish immigrants who arrived from Europe, homeless and penniless, fleeing oppression, in search of a better life.

According to Chicky, our grandfather came to the U.S. from Hungary as a young man. Blond-haired and blue-eyed, he landed at Ellis Island by boat, eventually making his way to McKeesport, Pennsylvania, in search of a Hungarian immigrant named David Rosenberg, aka King David. I imagine this name written on a piece of paper, folded neatly, securely tucked into his wallet, the only thing of value in my grandfather's possession other than his travel papers, his one contact in all of America—King David—the guy who connected Jewish immigrants with jobs in American cities. King David sent the young man who would become my grandfather to Detroit to find work. There, Grandpa Joe, who used to call me *Pigeon* and pinch my cheeks so hard my knees buckled, got into real estate. Before that, Trish insists, correcting Chicky's version of our origin story, Grandpa Joe was a bootlegger!

Trish swears there was a trap door in our grandparents' house that led to a secret storage room loaded with liquor. And she tells me, he wasn't a young man, he was only a boy—twelve years old—when he made the trip to the United States. His family in Hungary pooled their money together to send him to New York. Grandpa Joe promised to bring his siblings over once he got settled, meaning, once he made some money. He made that money in booze during Prohibition, before investing his bootlegger profits into real estate. True to his word, he paid for every one of his siblings to immigrate to the United States. Then, once he was an upstanding citizen, Grandpa Joe went back to McKeesport to claim the hand of King David's daughter—our grandmother—the girl with dark hair, alabaster skin, and delicate features.

It's hard to imagine Grandma Molly this fetching. I remember her in sturdy shoes and support stockings rolled at the knees. As the story goes, though, Molly was a very pretty, kind of spoiled teenage girl who did not know her way around the kitchen. She used to tell me stories about her childhood, like how she never brushed her own hair as a girl or carried her own schoolbooks. So, you can imagine how she reacted when she got to Detroit and found out that she had to cook and clean for herself *and* her new husband. She threw a proper hissy fit. *This box will not do!*

"Please, please let me come home!" Grandma Molly went crying back to her daddy in McKeesport. King David, being patriarchal and monarchical, promptly returned Molly to Grandpa Joe in Detroit, this time accompanied by a kitchen helper named Erzsébet, a woman with pastry secrets from the Old Country. Grandma Molly never became much of a cook; her turkey was dry as crackers, but her desserts were amazing.

Erzsébet taught my grandma Molly to bake delicious Hungarian pastry called pogácsa, pronounced, in my family, *poogatches*. Dense buttery treats that took all day to bake, mixing the ingredients by hand. She didn't write the recipe down; it was all in her head. The outcome was always the same: perfect golden-brown cookies, the texture of scones, shaped like circles or triangles, glazed with powdered sugar.

Molly and Joe had four kids; the youngest was my mother, Lois. McKeesport is where Grandma Molly grew up, and where her siblings—my great-aunts and uncles—lived and raised families. It's a suburb of Pittsburgh, just sixteen miles away, or about a half hour's drive into the city, which is not an unusual distance to travel for temple.

See where I'm going here?

A white guy opened fire at the Tree of Life Synagogue in Pittsburgh, killing eleven Jewish people, many of them elderly. For all I know, they could have been related to my grandma.

The Friday night following the bloodbath, my husband, kids, and I went to temple in Los Angeles. It was standing room only. Jews all over the world flooded temples in support of #ShowUpForShabbat. After the service, we wrote postcards to the members of the Pittsburgh congregation, to the families of the victims, who may or may not have been descendants of my great-grandfather, King David.

We sent this message: *We are one.*

And we are.

We are one tribe. A diverse, geographically dispersed people originating in the land of Israel, linked by a shared sense of history, identity, culture, and an umbrella religion. Whether we're roaming the desert, freezing in camps, or sitting on cushy couches in great rooms clicking through the news, bearing witness to the shifting winds, the resurgence of ancient hatreds—we're in this box together.

JewGirl

GROWING UP I THOUGHT everyone was Black or Jewish. Not that I gave the subject much thought, we were just kids living in Detroit. South of 8 Mile, which Eminem rapped into America's collective music consciousness. My childhood, however, was shaped more by Motown than rap.

We lived in the city, walked to public school and went to temple on weekends. After school we'd hang out at each other's houses or ride our bikes to the ice-cream parlor. I was happy. Until, in sixth grade, my mom yanked me out of public school and sent me to private school in Grosse Pointe. This was presented as a no-choice solution to a problem I didn't yet know existed. That summer, riots erupted in Detroit. When I came home from camp the city was smoldering; streets littered with broken glass, stores boarded up, chained, and padlocked. You could taste ash in the air, the ice-cream parlor was closed, along with the hobby shop where we used to race toy cars, and the drugstore where we bought candy and gum. Come September, I carpooled to private school.

Being the new girl, nobody paid much attention to me. I sat by myself during lunch, eating lousy cafeteria food off a plastic tray. I missed my old school: sack lunch and kickball on the playground with my friends Jules and Delia. And Kenny, a boy we all had crushes on. During free time, we'd listen to music, and the Black girls would teach us how to dance.

"You move like white girls!" Vanessa howled, doubled over with laughter, shaking her head so hard that her braids jiggled.

"No, no, no!" Trena chimed in, pushing us to the side to clear some space. "It's like this," she insisted, demonstrating preadolescent hip swagger. Trena's family owned a Black radio station in Detroit, which was a bit like having insider information: She knew all the cool moves. I ended up studying jazz, modern, and ballet in college, but the foundation of my dance practice is grounded in those grade-school practice sessions with Vanessa and Trena.

In the afternoons, the teacher let Trena and me sit in the back of the room and read on our own; it was called a self-guided study.

"That's why we sent you to private school," my mother always said, adding that I needed more of a classroom challenge. Then, defending her position, she said that she wanted me to have a better education. It was such an innocuous statement, it almost seemed reasonable; the right thing to do. It wasn't about race at all, one parent might say to another, talking about quality education and student-teacher ratio.

Fall came and went like a blur, with me trying to adjust to my new surroundings. My first few papers were returned with a bold "E" marked in red ink at the top of the page. This prompted my mother, concerned that I might be struggling academically, to call the school. When my teacher explained that "E" was for "Excellent," Mom was relieved. I crumpled my papers and stuffed them in a drawer. I wasn't worried about grades, but I was struggling. Private school was like learning a whole new language. Plus, I had no friends, which, to a pre-teen, can feel life-threatening. Right after Halloween, my new school went full-tilt boogie into the holiday spirit, planning for the annual Christmas pageant, Christmas potluck, and Christmas dance.

"Starting next week," our teacher announced, "the girls are going to make Christmas tree ornaments in art class." Then, singling me out by name, she said, "Except Marcie. Because she's Jewish." You could hear the swish and swivel of butts on seats turning in unison. All of them staring at me, as if seeing me for the first time, their faces registering some sort of *otherness* about me I had never encountered before. Although I knew we were Jewish, this was the moment I first understood that being Jewish wasn't the same as being white like them.

That Christianity trumped skin color.

And that there were more of them than there were of us. This was news to me.

My parents' entire social life revolved around the Jewish community. The kids I'd hung out with at public school were the same kids I knew from temple. Or they were Black. Sure, the kids next door were Italian and behind us, Greek, but they attended parochial schools. And that's where I got the whole thing ass-backwards. I thought they went to private school because they had religious *special needs.* In my limited worldview, there were only two Christian neighbors; everyone else was either Jewish or Black, and we all went to public school together.

I had no sense of being a *minority* until my mom sent me to private school in Grosse Pointe, where my new teacher was standing in front of the whole class, telling everyone that I was Jewish, and they were all looking at me like I was some kind of freak. All those blond heads and blue eyes and button noses. Even the cute boy named Billy, who had shaggy brown hair and dark eyes, turned to stare at me with something that looked like animal curiosity. My cheeks flamed in embarrassment. I slid down low in my chair, as if to disappear. It was an instinctive response—if they couldn't see me, they would stop staring at me, the teacher would stop talking about me, and I could go back to being the new girl no one paid attention to.

Instead, I became the JewGirl.

In my head I was protesting, *but we celebrate Christmas. We have a tree. And ornaments. A real one, too—not like the ginormous pink tinsel tree they have next door, either. Why can't I make an ornament like everyone else? Santa comes to our house, too. One year, he brought coal for one of my siblings who had been very naughty. Every box they opened on Christmas morning, coal!*

My mother often referred to herself as a "straight shooter." She would have told that teacher all about how we celebrated Christmas in our house, as well as Hanukkah, that we had the best of both worlds. And she would have insisted on making an ornament with the rest of the girls in the class. But I didn't have my mom's self-confidence, nor did I want to engage in a conversation about being different just to prove that I wasn't. That would have been mortifying. Instead, I let my teacher drone on until she was done outing me as a Jew. Then, phew, it was over. When she changed the subject to math, I let out a huge sigh of relief.

Only, it wasn't over. It was just the beginning.

The day after the announcement that I would be taking shop with the boys and making a chessboard instead of an ornament, I sat in my usual seat at lunch, by myself, reading a book about wolves, when the three most popular girls picked up their lunch trays and surrounded me like a scene straight out of a PG coming-of-age Hollywood movie.

They had questions.

Jan, in the powder-blue zip-up jumper, with stick-straight wispy hair, was the alpha girl. Always the first one to raise her hand in class. Lisa, with the blonde ponytail perched high on her head, who rode horses on the weekend, put horse stickers on all her notebooks, and drew horses on her homework assignments, quietly followed her lead. And Tyler, in Lilly Pulitzer for Girls, a pink-and-green print shift, who was also blonde but not horsey. She might have been the only one who smiled at me.

So many questions. They wanted to know what it was like to be Jewish.

What kind of food did we eat? Did we go to church? Did we believe in God?

"And Jesus?" Tyler asked.

"Do you have horns?" Jan wanted to know.

"And a tail?" Lisa wondered.

And would I show them? My tail and horns.

The cool girls were bombarding me with questions, and although I had never heard the horns-and-tail myth before, about the Jew as Devil (kids can be so literal), I knew in my gut that what they were asking was derogatory. They thought I had a vestigial tail—like a thorny lizard—as if being Jewish was not just a different religion or ethnicity but a different species. Lower on the evolutionary chain, with residual body parts from prehistoric times. The conflicting part of this story is that I craved the attention. I wanted to belong—to be friends with the cool girls, have sleepovers, and share secrets.

An older version of me might have been stunned into glaring silence, my eyes narrowing, my face stone-cold. I'm often so caught off guard by microaggressions that I shut down completely, unable to address the statement or rejoin the conversation. Silence is my response: a cold, *you are dead to me*, silence. But my preteen social survival instinct was strong; I wanted to be accepted by these girls. Plus, I didn't take it personally. On some level, I understood that they were just repeating what they heard at home. Because what kid cares about which religion the other kid's family is? It's totally an adult preoccupation.

That's why in middle school, at the cafeteria table, struck by an onslaught of bizarre questions about being Jewish, I smiled and responded that I ate normal food, like chicken and pasta. We go to temple, I said. It's like church, I explained, only on Saturdays instead of Sundays. And, yes, I told them, we believe that Jesus existed, but no, we do not believe he was the son of God. Then, as if to clear up a slight misunderstanding, I informed the cool girls that I did not have a tail or horns. Adding what I hadn't had the nerve to say out loud in front of the whole class, that my family celebrated Christmas like everyone else.

We lit the candles and we had a tree, with loads of presents and lots of cookies for Santa on the fireplace mantel. I'm sure the reason we celebrated Christmas was connected to my mom's strong desire for us to fit in. Which is to say, that overriding the fact of our Jewishness was my mom's insistence that we shouldn't feel deprived of anything, not just the presents but the cultural hurricane that is Christmas: the tree, the decorations, the reindeer and sled, the reading of "Twas the Night Before..." the anticipation, waking at dawn, the magic of Christmas morning. And the music.

Especially the music! Music is a powerful secular bridge to the Christian world.

As an adult, I can take or leave most everything else about this holiday—the tree, the presents, the rampant commercialization—but the music continues to bring me joy. Everything from John and Yoko's "Happy Xmas (War Is Over)" to Stevie Wonder's "Someday at Christmas." There's nothing religious in those songs; they're about peace and freedom. And there was nothing religious whatsoever about Christmas in our house growing up. It was all about fully participating in the dominant, i.e., Christian American, experience. That is what was so wrong about what my teacher did. She made an assumption about my homelife, based on religion, without bothering to inquire. In so doing, she reinforced the stereotype about Jews being "other."

Just my luck, there was another Jewish kid in our class. A boy. On the spot, at the cafeteria table, the cool girls decided that I should go to the Christmas dance with him. I wanted to go with Billy, the boy with the shaggy brown hair. They gave me Ira as a consolation. A namby-pamby Jewish boy. Making it clear that we would not be allowed to mix it up with the other kids. Theirs was a closed-loop dating pool.

That's how I ended up going steady with Ira, a short, pale, humorless boy I did not even like. He was as lukewarm about me as I was about him. I knew this because he never gave me his ID bracelet. And, believe me, I straight up asked for it. The whole point of going steady is the ID bracelet. You get to look at it in class, it gets caught in your sweater, it makes noise jangling against your desk. It's a broadcast signal that says: A boy, some boy, that boy, *the* boy whose name is engraved on the sterling silver bracelet dangling from my wrist, likes me.

"I can't just give it to you," Ira whined. "It was a birthday present from my parents."

"You can't just *say* we're going steady," I complained. The ID bracelet needed to exchange wrists.

Sure, we talked on the phone every night, but only our mothers knew that. We never got together outside of school, or kissed on the lips, let alone with tongue, in a closet, as I had done in fifth grade with Kenny Boy. Kenny had a moon face and a mushroom-shaped hairstyle that looked like his mom had put a cereal bowl over his head and snipped around it. We hung out together on weekends, along with Jules and Delia. We all lived within walking distance of each other's houses. Grosse Pointe was clear across town on the other side of Detroit. I had no idea where Ira lived; I never went to his house or invited him to mine. Our phone calls were punctuated with dead air.

Him: Hi

Me: Hi

Him: So, um, whatcha doin'?

Me: Nothing.

Him: (silence)

Me: Well, I, uh, guess I'll see you tomorrow.

Him: Yeah, okay, bye.

Me: Bye.

Ira strung me along, promising that his mother was going to get him another ID bracelet, so he'd have two: one to wear and one to give to me. Like a double identity—one for yourself and one for social survival. We were connected by not particularly liking each other but enduring our prescribed dating status. Our relationship lasted eight months. We went to exactly two school dances together, Christmas and spring, which is to say, we met up at the dance and pretended to be going steady. He never did give me his ID bracelet. For years after that, whenever we ran into each other, at temple or a party, we never spoke—just a nod of recognition. Like, *yeah, that was weird, wasn't it?* The year we were the only two Jews in the class, and they made us go steady with each other.

Tyler, the cool girl in the Lilly Pulitzer dresses, and I became friends. It was a lot of work tamping down my ethnicity to approximate her effortless WASPy cool. Not only was I never going to look like Tyler, but I would never live like her, either. Tyler's house was huge. I recall going to the bathroom and getting lost on the way back to the kitchen, where we were baking cookies with the nanny. It was dark outside; her little brother was asleep, we were in middle school, and it seemed weird to be hanging out with a nanny.

"Doesn't she ever go home?" I asked.

"Oh," Tyler explained, as if it were the most obvious thing in the world. "She lives in a house in our backyard." My backyard was big enough for a swing set and a sandbox. In the winter my mom would bundle up in snow boots and a puffy coat, cigarette dangling from her lips, holding the garden hose, while making a skating rink. This was a whole other level of affluence. Grosse Pointe was the bastion of real wealth. The kids in my class had the kind of last names that were displayed on cars and splashed across department stores. Brand names. They were the children of the titans of Detroit—Ford Motor Company and Hudson's Department Store.

Hudson's downtown department store was massive, second only to Macy's in New York. It had thirty-two floors, fifty-one elevators, and an annual Thanksgiving parade. It's hard to overstate how big a cultural touchpoint in Detroit Hudson's was. Like Macy's, they were famous for their Maurice salad. My grandmother used to take me there for lunch. This was after WWII. By then, Hudson's had ceased running employment ads that read "Only Gentiles need apply." I didn't know about this when we ate there, but my grandmother must have known the history; she had lived through it. Which means she chose to overlook it. Maybe because the salads were so good. More likely it was born of a sense of *It is what it is.*

Antisemitism was out in the open in Detroit during my grandmother's life. In the years leading up to WWII, Henry Ford started a local newspaper called *The Dearborn Independent*, distributed nationally through Ford dealerships. Every week, splashed across the front page was a column written by Henry Ford himself called "The International Jew: The World's Problem." Ford and Hitler were so aligned on the ideology of antisemitism that Ford received a medal from Hitler, and Hitler hung a signed portrait of Ford in his office. Using his money and power to spread conspiracy theories about a global Jewish plot to run the world, Ford blamed Jews for provoking the violence directed at Jewish people. That may sound crazy, but the same sort of conspiracy theories circulate today.

It's no surprise that my classmates echoed the antisemitism espoused or condoned by the family business. That's how antisemitism takes root: at the dinner table, overhearing comments dropped by elders you are taught to respect. Notably, up until the early 1960s, Blacks and Asians were not allowed to buy property in Grosse Pointe. There existed a realtor "Pointe System" to screen homeowners based on complexion, occupation, dress, and country of origin. The maximum score possible was one hundred. White Christians only needed fifty points to be eligible. Jews needed an additional thirty-five points—a surtax for being Jewish. Eighty-five points. That might explain why I had only one sleepover and wasn't invited to any birthday parties the entire year.

For my birthday at the end of June, I had a pool party. Despite not receiving a single invitation to their parties, I insisted on inviting my new classmates. I rationalized this by saying I wasn't even friends with them until almost halfway through the school year. My mother was beside herself in embarrassment. It meant she would be throwing a party at The Club and not inviting her friends' children, the kids I had grown up with. Like Lily, my mom's friend Sylvie's daughter. It was a social faux pas of some magnitude on the Richter scale of club etiquette.

"I want to invite my school friends to my party," I insisted, crossing my arms, one hip jutting out in protest. I remember this as a declaration of independence. *My* birthday party, *my* friends. I was changing schools again in the fall, the second time in two years, and I thought I would miss my new class-mates *sooooooooooo* much. *Another new school. It's not fair. My parents are so selfish. I hate them!* Slam the door.

"You'll never see those kids again," my mother said. And she cautioned: they probably wouldn't come. It *was* a long drive. The Club was as far from our house as Grosse Pointe had been, but in the complete opposite direction. So, it was twice as far a drive for my classmates. Over an hour. That wasn't the issue; what my mom meant was that those kids' parents wouldn't bring them to a Jewish country club. She was wrong, though. They did come to my party, but I never saw them again, so she was right about that. For my birthday, my mom gave me an ID bracelet with my name engraved in sterling silver. And I broke up with Ira.

It seems like such a long time ago—the riots in Detroit, racism, and antisemitism. Yesterday's news. And it is yesterday's news. It's also today's news. It's an evergreen news story that never seems to go away.

While I was workshopping this story in a writers' group, a woman asked me about antisemitism in the United States. At least I think she was limiting the conversation to the U.S. She didn't specify. What she said was, "Why do you think antisemitism exists?" The question came during feedback after I shared this piece about middle school. It was an earnest question from a writer of earnest, uplifting female stories. Girls with superpowers who talk to plants. Girls with superpowers who communicate with animals. Girls with superpowers like astral projection. The kind of writer who seeks to change girls' realities by creating fantasy worlds for them to thrive in.

I loved fantasy fiction as a kid, but there's a difference between a fictional world created to inspire girls and the real world. Her question struck me as naïve. So innocent that I wondered if, perhaps, she wasn't asking a question at all but making a point instead, by implying that there must be some valid reason why Jews have been targeted, otherwise, antisemitism wouldn't exist. As if it were our own damn fault. *Own up to it. Aren't Jews themselves the root cause of antisemitism?* I didn't respond to her question because I heard, couched in its phrasing, a mainstream antisemitic trope—the one about Jews as oppressors, or perpetrators of a global conspiracy to rule the world: controlling media, entertainment, banking, and powerful government lobbies.

I believe the writer identified as Latinx; there was an ancestral *abuela* at the spiritual center of her book. Maybe if you aren't

Jewish, and you don't know any Jewish people, you wouldn't be predisposed to pay attention to what's going on: the uptick of antisemitic rhetoric on social media, the increase in hate crimes targeting Jewish people and organizations, such as the mass murder at a synagogue in Pittsburgh, and the shooting of a young Jewish couple outside a Jewish Museum in Washington DC. You might think, *oh, people don't like Jews. Why is that?*

I was taken aback by her question, not just as a Jew but also as a writer. As if she were saying that my experience of being othered in middle school was somehow trivial and that perhaps I was ignoring a bigger truth: *Why does antisemitism exist? Why the cultural backslide?* When, in fact, in middle school, being othered can be devastating. The personal is political. If I learned one thing during freshman year in college, it was that statement.

Just writing my story runs counter to the narrative that considers skin color to be the defining characteristic of systemic racism. And the discussions surrounding intersectional politics, such as race, class, and gender, typically leave Jews out of the conversation. I glanced at the yellow Post-it note stuck to the upper right-hand corner of my computer screen that said, Don't Respond. Placed there because I had already experienced much worse confrontations while workshopping this book, and I was trying to be a better listener. So, I didn't say anything. Instead, I wrote her question down in my notes and underlined it: *Why does antisemitism exist?* This question struck me as disingenuous, expecting me to sum up more than two thousand years of antisemitism in a one- or two-minute response. If I could do that, sum it up in a soundbite, maybe I wouldn't have had to write this book at all. It could have become an essay instead. Or a tweet. Be done with it.

#JewsMatter

#JewsToo

It bothered me that she felt comfortable questioning the history of antisemitism in a way that I doubt she would ever ask about racism. I can't imagine her saying to a Black writer: *Why do you think racism exists?* A question like that is enormous. Racism and antisemitism span centuries and travel the globe. If I had been feeling snarky, I might have answered that question by saying, *Because Jews are a demographic tragedy, a perpetual minority. And the Christian and Muslim worlds are on a crusade to eliminate each other, but first, they want to kill all the Jews.* It's a numbers game—we're the easiest to pick off in terms of population and property. All we have is Israel and a few million Jewish people scattered in the Diaspora. There are almost as many Latinos in California as there are Jews in the entire world.

But I said nothing. Unlike my middle-school self, I wasn't embarrassed. I just didn't feel the need to be friends with this woman. To curry favor. To condense the history of the Jewish people into a simple response for her. And I did not blow it off as man's inhumanity to man, which means everything and nothing at the same time. It's like offering thoughts and prayers after a mass shooting. Nor did I center my response on the issue of land, the conflict between Israel and Palestine, which is only the current iteration of international antisemitism. Or share my belief that it's possible to support the existence of Israel *and* Palestinian liberation. That the two ideas should not be incompatible or unattainable, and that peace is always a possibility.

Then, because my silence was awkward, I mumbled, "It's complicated," which is what I say when I don't want to be a spokesperson for all Jewish people.

Humanism

HERE'S WHAT I STRUGGLE with: Who am I to speak of, about, on behalf of, to presume to represent Jewish girls? My mother served Honey Baked Ham at her annual Xmas party. Jumbo shrimp, too. Two foods that are strictly forbidden by Jewish law. We did not keep kosher. We weren't exactly model Jews, nor were we lapsed Jews. We were Reform Jews. Anything-goes Jews. Meaning that we could drop what didn't fit into a modern Jewish life and add whatever did.

We celebrated Christmas *and* Hanukkah. We lit the candles *and* we had a tree. With loads of presents and lots of cookies for Santa on the fireplace mantel.

My mother loved a celebration!

You'd think she'd have put us on the bar or bat mitzvah circuit, but we weren't that religious. Instead, I was confirmed, which sounds almost Christian and was, in fact, lifted from Christian catechism as a move toward assimilation. In practical terms, meaning, to my reptilian teenage brain, it meant that I didn't have to learn a Torah section in Hebrew but still got lots of presents. And a party if I wanted one, which I didn't. At thirteen, when you get bar or bat mitzvahed, the idea of boy-girl parties is exciting—dressing up and slow dancing! Never mind that everyone's parents are standing there watching from the sidelines. It's a rite of passage whose over-the-top excess has been well-documented in film. Who's invited, who isn't. I once attended a Hollywood bar mitzvah party where a famous actor/rapper prerecorded a personalized message to the bar mitzvah boy. It was projected onto a jumbo screen, and when the video ended, dancers smashed through the screen for a choreographed *Welcome to Manhood* dance in top hats and tights.

That was so not my style.

Confirmation is more subdued; it marks one's graduation from religious school and occurs when you're around fifteen or sixteen. I was deep into teenage angst by then. The last thing I wanted was to be the center of attention. Or attend, let alone host, a party with my parents. My attitude was: *skip the party, bring on the presents.* The only thing required, aside from going to Sunday school for years and years and years, was to write an essay on "What God Means to Me."

It was this essay that prompted a family conference.

The rabbi sat behind an impressive mahogany desk—big and bulky, built like a fortress. He wore a black ceremonial robe for maximum impact. He had a deep theatrical voice, and after exchanging niceties with my mom, his smile turned serious. His gaze zeroed in on me, laser-focused, no more chit-chat. He point-blank insisted that I recant what I had written.

Rewrite or drop out. Those were my options.

"What would you like to do?" the rabbi asked me. His face was stern, his tone intimidating. It wasn't just that he had no idea how to converse with kids; he wasn't even trying.

There would be no discussion, which, in hindsight, seems very *un*-Jewish. Judaism prides itself on being a religion that encourages thought, dialectic, and interpretation, but even in the Reform temple, there were boundaries, and I had run into the big one: belief in God. Not just God, but *one* God.

Whether or not I believe in God is beside the point; I'm still Jewish. That's what I had written in my essay. It was a theoretical discussion on Jewish identity based largely on this premise: belief in God is not central to my being Jewish. Given some of the ridiculous things I thought as a teenager, like that I had a guardian angel, and if you got too high, drinking orange juice would bring you down. Or that antisemitism was *like, so over*—that essay was preternaturally spot-on. I had begun to separate being Jewish from practicing Judaism. Identity from religion. I had yet to become a feminist; to grasp that single-god theory—aka monotheism—was created by men to get rid of the goddesses. A bold-faced power grab that has lasted for centuries.

It may have looked like I was playing with the giant safety pin on my skirt, la-di-da, but I was doing some serious thinking, sitting there, staring at my feet in proper shoes. Meaning, not sneakers. I had to wear good shoes to temple. No Velcro or laces. And kilts. I had a red plaid one. A black checkered one. And a royal-blue tartan. The whole kilt thing was a huge source of discomfort for me. They itched bare legs and clung to tights. And they were *so not cool*, I complained.

"Nonsense," my mother said. "Kilts never go out of style."

"A thing cannot go *out of style* if it was never in style to begin with," was my snappy retort.

Put on a kilt, my mom had insisted that morning. As if wearing a hand-me-down kilt from my sisters would sway the rabbi in my favor.

So, there I was, kilted, sitting in the rabbi's office. I was calculating the number of years I'd submitted to the boredom of attending temple (including the annual watching of black-and-white WWII footage, walking skeletons falling dead on the street, bodies shoveled into the back of wagons and thrown into ditches, creating mass graves, images so heinous as to be incomprehensible to my adolescent mind) versus the number of months left until confirmation, and it all came down to this: the getting of the gifts.

I wish I could tell you that I stood my ground on principle, reiterating my point of view that being Jewish wasn't necessarily connected to a belief in God; that my being Jewish was based on shared history, heritage, culture, and family. Not language, though—I was clueless when it came to Yiddish. My sibs and I were discouraged from speaking Yiddish in our household. We were raised *not* to sound Jewish in public. We weren't even supposed to appear Jewish: we did not wear necklaces with Jewish stars; there was no mezuzah on our door. This may sound hypocritical, but these decisions reflected my mother's desire that her children be able to assimilate.

Given that three out of four of her kids married non-Jews, it seems she was, to some extent, successful, although having her children marry non-Jewish partners was not her goal. Her dream was that our world would include, but not be limited to, the Jewish community. That we would know who we were as a people *and* be able to traverse seamlessly in other cultures. This is not to say that she wanted us to pass as white Christians. What she wanted was for us not to stick out as Jews. Nice try, Mom! Even the last name Maxfield doesn't disguise my identity. Rarely has anyone said to me, *Oh! You're Jewish. I didn't know!* For some reason, my persona reads as Jewish. It could be my hair, my face, my tone of voice, and, by voice, I'm not limiting that to the sound of my voice but, rather, enlarging it to encompass my written voice; the way I use humor to track pain, my lack of propriety, that I don't whisper or circle around an issue but, instead, address it head-on.

I wish I could report that when my mom and I were called to the rabbi's study, we had a deep and thought-provoking conversation about God, and that we came to some sort of middle ground or understanding about Jewish identity. We did not. There was no discussion whatsoever. I have such an uncomfortable memory of that meeting—the power that came with his black robe and big desk. My inability to push back against authority. I doubt that my mother was concerned about what I had written. More likely, she was hoping I'd call the rabbi's bluff. After all, so many of my ideas about Judaism came from her. It didn't matter either way. I was a teenager.

I wanted the loot.

It was the pot at the end of the rainbow. It was back pay for years of attending services. Monogrammed stationery and costume jewelry, but that's not the only reason why I caved. I just didn't want to be the girl who got kicked out of religious school. I was worried about my reputation. I figured, *whatever,* I'd write some bullshit about God and get on with it.

What I wrote in that essay on God reflected my truth. As far back as I can remember, I have never believed in the existence of a supreme being. In grade school, having to say "under God" when reciting the Pledge of Allegiance upset me. As an adult, I might use the term "conflicted" instead of "upset" because I was all-in on being American, just not so much the God part. "Don't make a big deal about it," my mom told me.

"You don't have to say those words. No one will know." That became an important, although silent, act of resistance for me, and I love that my mom empowered me in that way.

It's worth noting that "under God" was added to the Pledge of Allegiance in 1954 by President Eisenhower, motivated by the Red Scare and increasingly anti-communist sentiments. There were no religious references in the original version, written in 1892. Later, "In God We Trust" was added to our paper money. These moves toward solidifying the United States as a Christian nation are relatively recent, and the notion that the United States was always intended to be a Christian country is not accurate. The United States was intended to be a secular nation. If the Constitution didn't make that clear enough, the Treaty of Tripoli, begun by George Washington, signed by John Adams, and ratified by the Senate, states clearly that: "the Government of the United States of America is not, in any sense, founded on the Christian religion."

In not believing in God, I was at odds with both the Christian and Jewish communities. If my mom was disappointed in me for not standing my ground with the rabbi, she never let on. She did, however, quit the Reform temple after I was confirmed, and we joined the first Humanistic Jewish congregation.

Secular Humanistic Judaism was founded in Detroit by Sherwin Wine, a brilliant and innovative thinker who did not believe in God. So, I was predisposed to liking him. A lot. Rabbi Wine was an intellectual who staked his entire career and life's work on a controversial position that I had intuitively arrived at on my own and then been strong-armed into disavowing. If it weren't for Rabbi Wine and the Birmingham Temple[3], which he established, I might have left Judaism al-

---

3   Now called the Congregation for Humanistic Judaism of Metro Detroit

together. Humanistic Judaism sidesteps the whole God thing and focuses instead on the richness of Jewish tradition, culture, humor, and holidays. Its premise is that we're one great big international family, connected through history, ancestry, and, sadly, a shared sense of impending doom. Hence, the need for humor.

Rabbi Wine used to come to dinner whenever my mom thought my dad needed a political or social reset. In general, we were a liberal family; other than my conservative father, which meant family dinners were a battleground. Women's rights, racism, and war. Sex and drugs. My sister Chicky was the trailblazer. My sister, Trish, was a daddy's girl who could do no wrong. My brother was the prince. Being the youngest of the four siblings, it was easy to fly under the radar: My dad wasn't paying attention to me. Our father, Bert, was a traditional thinker, *my country right or wrong*, a guy who did what he was supposed to do. He joined the army, went off to war, came home, took over the family business, got married, and had some kids. He was an electrical engineer: great with math but not so good on social issues.

Whenever there was a problem, my mother, Lois, would summon Sherwin. He'd sit at one end of the table, always next to my mom, their alliance palpably clear. Pressing both hands together, fingertips interlaced, he would tilt his head and stare down the table at my dad, saying, *Now, Bert*. Then Sherwin would politely, with wit and understanding, knock some sense into our father. Rabbi Wine could command a room; he was charming and funny, tall, slender, and impeccably tailored. Gay. It must have just blown my dad's mind to be repeatedly course-corrected by Sherwin. I debated whether to mention his sexual orientation and decided that, as this book is all about *my* identity, it would seem wrong to skip over *his*. Because on top of being Jewish and having had to create a new sect of Judaism just to square his religious beliefs with his chosen career path, Sherwin was a gay man in Detroit in the eighties. Talk about trailblazers; Rabbi Wine was the living embodiment of change.

Secular Judaism provides a launchpad for discussion, as opposed to a set of rules to live by. It promotes the belief that, as humans, we have the ability to form opinions and conclusions that meet the needs of a dynamic modern world. It's all about how we, as Jewish people, walk on earth in this lifetime. No heaven or hell, no parting of the Red Sea unless it can be attributed to a tsunami. We support inclusivity and equality, and believe it is our calling to help repair the world. Knowledge, power, and responsibility, only the power is not vested in the robes or desk or a mythical godlike figure; it's people who have the power. There aren't a lot of us. By the numbers: 2.2 percent of adults in the United States identify as Jewish, and less than 4 percent of those who identify as Jews are secular Humanistic Jews. We're a small percentage of a minority population. I'm pretty sure some Jews don't recognize Humanistic Judaism as legitimate, and many Jews have not even heard of it.

Even my husband, Harry, has doubts about the validity of Humanistic Judaism, and he's an atheist. Harry has an entire bookshelf devoted to the negation of God. *The God Delusion* by Richard Dawkins. *God is Not Great* by Christopher Hitchens. Everything Sam Harris. He's scientific when it comes to spirituality. But Humanistic Judaism is not the same thing as atheism. The foundational core of atheism is that God does not exist. That's it, there is no God, okay ... deal with it. Whereas Humanistic Jews are more like, *eh, so there's no God, but there's a lot more to being Jewish than belief in a supernatural power. Join us for a nosh, we'll talk about it.*

"You're not really Jewish," Harry said one Sunday morning. This was because I didn't know the answer to the crossword clue: Jewish bogeyman—a humanlike creature in Jewish folklore representing good and evil. Harry was sitting at the kitchen table, wearing a blue Dodgers sweatshirt, drinking black coffee, doing the *New York Times* crossword puzzle. I guessed George Soros.

"Five letters," he replied.

"*Soros* has five letters," I said.

"Never mind," he said. "I got it. It's *golem.*"

"I thought golems were those scary statues on Notre Dame."

"That's a gargoyle!"

"Well, that's why you're better at crossword puzzles than me," I said, without looking up from the Opinion section. That's when Harry accused me of not being Jewish. My head snapped in his direction. I had been joking about George Soros, but he wasn't joking when he said I wasn't *really* Jewish. So, I pressed in on him.

"How could you say such a thing?"

"Well," he continued, without looking up from the Sunday magazine, "you don't believe in God, you don't belong to a temple, and you call yourself a Humanist Jew, which most people have never even heard of. You don't know what a *golem* is," he shrugged. "What's the big deal? Why be Jewish at all?"

That was a lot to unpack.

My husband was raised Christian, with the kind of white privilege that allows him to overlook identity as an issue. He walked away from his Christian upbringing with his whiteness intact. To him, religion is all about God, and because he's an atheist, he has no use for it. What he, and so many people, don't get is that even if I walked away from Judaism, I would still be Jewish. I was born Jewish. I was brought up Jewish; it's who I am at the core of my being. It's not just how I view myself, it's also how the world sees me.

It's in my DNA.

I was saying that bit about DNA metaphorically, but the last time I went for a mammogram, the technician asked me if any of my relatives were Ashkenazi Jews. "Yes!" I exclaimed. I felt so seen! Then, remembering I was naked from the top down, wearing a paper kimono that tied in the front, I asked, "Why?"

"Because Ashkenazi women have a much higher than average risk of breast cancer due to the BRCA1 and BRCA2 genes," she told me.

"Oh," I said, deflated. So now there's that to worry about. On top of everything else. Like the never-ending war in Israel. And my husband, with whom I have two children, who still doesn't understand what it means to be married to a Jewish woman.

"Practicing Judaism is a choice," I told Harry, slowly, as if I were talking to a child who couldn't seem to grasp this simple concept. "*Being* Jewish is not."

"I was just saying," he grumbled, "you're not very Jewish, so why are you so uptight about antisemitism?"

"What are you talking about?" I screamed. "We were married by Rabbi Wine, our kids went to Jewish preschool, Jewish sleepover camp, and temple. We light the candles on Hanukkah, we host an annual Passover Seder, and on Yom Kippur we invite friends and family to break the fast with bagels and lox. I make homemade chicken soup! You make latkes! What about our being Jewish is not computing with you?"

"That's food," he said. "It's not religion."

"It's family, community, tradition, and culture," I responded. "It's everything."

That's when I googled *Secular Judaism* and spun my laptop around to face him. Then I threw on my camo sweatshirt and went to yoga. When I got back, my laptop was sitting on the kitchen table, with a Post-it note that said "sorry" and a heart. Also, the kitchen had been cleaned.

This is a hard concept for my husband to grasp. Like many people, he views Judaism through a Christian lens. And, because he is a science guy, he applies a logical mindset to the equation: Christians are people who believe in Christianity, therefore, Jews are people who practice Judaism. It's a reductive thought process that focuses solely on a belief system. But Jews are tribal: We trace our history back to the ancient Hebrews in the land of Canaan, now called Israel. Our religious beliefs and practices are not uniform.

Also, Harry thinks antisemitism is nothing more than crazy talk on the fringe right. He doesn't get that it's on the right *and* the left, that it's always been hiding in the shadows, but it's moving into mainstream discourse. He doesn't take it seriously because it doesn't impact him personally, which is strange, since he's married to a Jewish woman, has two Jewish kids, a bunch of Jewish relatives, and he leads our annual Passover Seder. But it's one thing to lead the Seder, say a prayer and hide the matzah—to play the good Jewish patriarch once a year. I'm Jewish every day of my life. God or no God. Even with ham on Christmas.

Related

MY EARLIEST CHILDHOOD MEMORY is of my sister Trish dangling me over the banister. It was a winding staircase that connected the first and second floors of our home; there were windows on the landing where the stairs changed directions. I must have been around four, which means Trish would have been about ten. She was standing behind me, holding me by the waist, my butt seated on the banister, legs hanging over the railing. We were just outside the door to my parents' bedroom. Where they were, I have no idea. Probably at The Club, golfing. To my left, lined up along the stairway, were my siblings and cousins. Watching. My sister lifted me up and held me in the air suspended over the first floor for a few seconds before I slipped through her hands.

She caught me by my ponytail.

Now this is retold as a funny anecdote—the time Trish almost dropped Marcie over the stairway. Like the game "Deeper," a variation of playing doctor, only it was a pretend classroom, not a hospital, and I was the butt of the joke, bent over the desk with my pants pulled down. Pants *and* underwear. There were kids sitting on beds in the room Chicky and I shared, watching.

Neither of my sisters deny that these things happened, although some people have tried to dissuade me from writing this book, which begs the question: Why bring these events forward? Because family is a microcosm of society. There are the most vulnerable, in this case, me: the littlest girl. There's power in numbers—them. There's resistance when the weak one develops strength. All of it mirrors the Jewish dilemma: We're a minority with a history of being traumatized, and people do not like it when we fight back.

I am the youngest of four kids, each of us two years apart. But when you add the cousins on my dad's side, which you must because they spent a lot of time at our house, it was more like being the youngest of seven. There were three cousins, closely matching each of my siblings in age, almost as if it had been pre-planned. Our families lived two doors away from each other. The dads worked together at the electronics store, and the moms were busy having babies. Two girls and a boy in our house. Two boys and a girl in theirs.

Trish and Lance

Chicky and Jenna

Prince and Drew

Then came me. Solo. Rocking the onesie. I used to think maybe I was an accident. In a way, the experience of being othered as a Jew is familiar to me. It resonates with the way I felt in my family. There were six of them and one of me. If I wanted to play with them, it was on their terms. I can see myself as a little girl, striped T-shirt and shorts, long brown hair, unkempt, knocking on doors and asking if I could come in and play. Trish and Lance would flat-out say no. They were too old to play with me. Chicky and Jenna had to let me in because, technically, it was my room too, but they'd giggle and talk about me in their secret language. Prince often let me play with him and Drew, or any of his male friends, but first I had to pass the "initiation test." We were closest in age. I used to carry my stuffed bunny and blankie into his room for sleepovers on Saturday nights. I recall he had twin beds, cowboy sheets, and a pet snake. He was my big brother by two years and ten pounds, and I adored him. Now I remember those "tests" with a squeamish awareness of the uncomfortable power dynamic between us.

I remember all of it. Being teased and tricked, chased and choked, I can still see myself as a little girl bent over my sisters' desk with my pants pulled down, my cheek pressed against the surface of the desk. And I can sense the boy standing behind me, pencil in hand, close enough to touch me. Though I can't be sure who all the kids were in our bedroom that day, I can picture them as a group: sitting on beds, hands in their laps like good little students, watching. It doesn't matter who was holding the pencil, they were all participating. Even I was participating. As a child, I had no boundaries. All I wanted was to be included in the game. I would have done anything they told me to do, played any game they suggested. They were my family. I trusted them.

Years later, when I recounted these events to the therapist I was seeing because of anxiety and trust issues, I could hear her intake—the whooshing sound of sucking in breath. Regaining her composure, she said, There's a word for this. I said, Mean. She stared at me, her face impassive. So, I threw some more words at her: *Cruel. Mistreated. Unsupervised. Unparented. Unprotected.*

We were wild. They were not nice to me. I was dancing around the word she was trying to extract from my psyche as if my life depended on it, and in a way, it did. I couldn't bring myself to utter the "a" word about my girlhood, as if saying that word would crack my world in two. Finally, I said, "abusive." It's an adjective, not an accusation. Then she remarked that we were like those kids in the book *Lord of the Flies*—a story about a group of boys stranded on a deserted island after a plane crash. The dark side of human nature. *But that would make me Piggy!* I protested in my head. *He was fat and wore glasses and … they killed him. I was an athletic kid!* Anyway, I had to zip myself up and go back out into the real world, where I had a job, my own family to raise, and a husband I loved.

Some of my siblings still insist on the fantasy of our upbringing as something special, classy even, as if looking through a grease-smeared lens. I understand that nostalgia. There *was* something seductive about our family; terrible but also terribly entertaining.

Our mother was the supreme hostess; the rest of us were mere worker bees, following instructions.

You—put away the groceries!

You—wash the vegetables!

You—set the table!

Lois was in party mode, snapping her fingers, barking out orders. My dad had one responsibility: to pick up wine and spirits from the liquor store. Prince emptied the wastebaskets, or some similar task. The girls—Trish, Chicky, and I—were "on call" for the rest of it: set up, prep, and clean-up duty. Mom was a smart woman, possibly brilliant, better read and more educated than our father. She had a master's degree in social work, and when we were little, she worked downtown as a family therapist. But, for a feminist, a card-carrying member of NOW[4], Lois fostered some disturbingly sexist gender roles in our house. And she had an irritating habit of doling out tasks one at a time.

Napkins!

China!

Silverware!

She barked words as if each were a complete thought, which, in a way, they were. I had internalized the rest of the task: *fold the napkins in half and then again in thirds. Wipe the plates and the silver, every fork, knife, and spoon, individually, so there were no spots or crud.*

"They should sparkle," she'd add, handing me a damp cloth.

What about Prince? I thought. *Why doesn't he have to do this?* It felt as if in our house the three girls were all Cinderella. And the one boy was a prince.

Thanksgiving, Christmas, Passover. The only thing that changed was the menu: turkey, ham, or brisket. Mom always wore something flowy. Her sister, Aunt Sheryl, brought dessert. Her brothers ate, drank, *and* said bad words in Yiddish. Aunt Dusty drank too much.

The uncles were off-the-charts testosterone-filled men, old-school, like Dean Martin and Frank Sinatra, only Jewish. One was a blue-eyed pretty boy and the other a swarthy, rugged bachelor whose nickname was Balls. They both thought my dad was a bit of a loser and chided him for being an upright citizen. He had an average swing (we're talking golf) and a nuts-and-bolts kind of job—what it lacked in excitement, it made up for in reliability: We were upper middle-class. My dad led the

---

4 National Organization for Women

Passover Seder in Hebrew, the text as old as the hills, the cover of his prayer book made of inlaid ivory, a bar mitzvah present.

"This is who you married!" my mom's brothers taunted her. Because our father, Bert, was solid, which they found plodding, and they thought Lois could have done better. More athletic, perhaps, more successful, more charming. Athleticism was code for sexy. And by successful, their only measure would have been money.

And charming?

My uncles oozed a particular kind of charm that bordered on boorish. They laughed at Aunt Sheryl when she tried to stick up for our dad. She'd light a cigarette, smoke coming out of her nose like a dragon, and accuse them of being rude at the dinner table. They'd call her *meshugana*, which means "crazy," and chide her for not having a husband or a dinner table of her own big enough to host the family.

The uncles acted like it was all in good fun. Maybe for them it was, but I'd watch Aunt Sheryl grind that cigarette into her dinner plate, ash twisting into scraps of potatoes or kugel, her head shaking back and forth as if she were about to explode—and she was not laughing. Inevitably, she'd storm out of our house before dessert was served.

At the time, I thought my uncles were jokesters and my aunt was cranky. Now I see it differently: They talked over her, discounted her opinions, made fun of her, and called her names. Then, after she was gone in a huff, they devoured her homemade dessert. Reese Roll, dark chocolate and whipped cream. That was her specialty.

To the outside world we were one big happy family. At The Club, for example, we were Team Blumberg. There was a

25-meter pool, rectangular in shape, shimmering turquoise. Unlike the other country club kids, lying on lounge chairs, their hair blow-dried, Team Blumberg got wet. Prince channeled his aggression into speed, arms slashing at the water. Trish swam like a dolphin. Water was her natural habitat, butterfly was her stroke. She was in training for the Junior Olympics. Chicky was skinny. Not model-thin, she looked bony, easy to beat. But she had an elegant stroke and was a fierce competitor. I've always been an endurance swimmer. Not fast but possessing stamina. I didn't give up, I didn't give in, I just kept going.

Breathe. Kick. Pull. Repeat.

As a teenager, I wore a one-piece racer-back swimsuit, cut high on the thighs. I had the same exact suit in multiple colors: black, army green, and mulberry, and wore them until they disintegrated. Lying on hot concrete, the smell of chlorine baking into my skin, is one of my favorite sensory memories. On Sundays, I'd shower in the locker room and stay for barbecue. There was always a lot of golf talk.

Putt. Putt. Slice.

Birdies and Bogeys.

And, if we were eating dinner with the uncles, a lot of trash talk and cocktails.

"Can I work at one of your stores this summer?" I asked Uncle Balls, the summer between freshman and sophomore year at college.

"You don't want to work in the *schmatta* business," he replied.

But I did. I needed a summer job, and I liked clothes. Here's what I was wearing: jean miniskirt, black footless tights, high-top sneakers, and a shrunken T-shirt featuring ironic punk band.

"Give the girl a job, Balls!" Uncle Dick bellowed, slamming the table for emphasis. He was laughing at my outfit, challenging his brother, and flashing his trademark bad-boy smile all at once.

He could have been a golf pro, Mom always said about Dick, meaning he was *that good*. As if a professional handicap absolved him of everything else that he was: a con man, a grifter, a cheat. He lived with us for a while after his house burned down. Just him. I don't know where Aunt Dusty and the cousins went, but I do remember he always smelled clean, like he had just showered. And he wore pink V-neck golf sweaters that matched his complexion. Fortunately, no one was home when the fire started. Dick was working, Aunt Dusty was walking the dog, and the kids were in school. Even to my teenage mind, that struck me as convenient, to the point of being suspicious.

There's an episode of the FX TV show *The Bear* about an Italian family-owned restaurant where someone falls into a hole in the wall and the character Cousin Richie calls it failed Jewish Lightning. I had never heard that term, so I googled it. *Jewish Lightning* refers to a scheme that involves arson to collect insurance money. The hole in the wall was part of the preparation for some sort of man-made catastrophic fire.

My first thought was, *Oh! Like Uncle Dick!*

I worry that in writing about my uncle, I'm just confirming the worst tropes about Jewish men. After that episode of *The Bear* aired, the online conversation surrounding it was all about whether anyone should use the term *Jewish Lightning* anymore, but what interests me more is how a term like that even gets started. There's nothing particularly *Jewish* about Jewish Lightning, or, for that matter, financial fraud. There are plenty of high-profile Gentile men who have used ginned-up business statements to inflate their assets, secure hundreds of millions of dollars in loans, and thereby create wealth and power for themselves.

Such a man could even become president of the United States. Twice. Disturbingly, almost half the country seems to be okay with it. Yet there persists this complaint that Jews have a disproportionate amount of wealth and power, the subtext being, from ill-gotten gains. In *The Bear*, an Italian family was toying with the idea of insurance fraud. The brother who owned the restaurant was struggling with mental health issues, drug addiction, and a restaurant that could barely make ends meet. Financial struggles know no ethnic or religious boundaries. You're broke, you can't pay your bills, you're upside down on your mortgage, and sometimes it might seem like the only way out is to start a fire.

It's not about being Jewish at all: It's called being caught in an economic bind.

My uncle was financially unstable, but being financially unstable is not something people associate with the Jewish experience. It doesn't fit into the narrative of Jews as greedy, illicit power brokers. While this does not excuse my uncle's behavior, he was just a small-time crook, nowhere near the scale of some politicians. And Uncle Dick went to jail, something most politicians manage to avoid.

Sometimes it feels like my job in writing this book is to break down antisemitic tropes. One by one. As if, in providing a solid evidential rationale for why these stereotypes are false, they will somehow be diffused. Like when you have a knot in your shoulder muscle and massage it until it releases. Poof, it's gone.

As if antisemitism were rational to begin with.

Unlike his brother, Dick, Uncle Balls was a legitimate businessman. He owned several clothing stores in Detroit that sold knock-off classics for career women. My mother took me on shopping sprees at his stores as soon as I could fit into the clothes, which felt like punishment for growing up. Bags filled with polyester tops and slacks I didn't like and would rather die than wear. It was an embarrassment of excess. And most likely the reason I became a clothing snob. Organic fabrics. Pre-owned designer skirts. Ridiculously delicate tops that need to be washed by hand. It gives me immense joy to fold my clothes, T-shirts creased precisely in thirds, then in half, then in thirds again until they are as small as napkins.

Just like Mom taught me.

"No," Uncle Balls said, about the summer job. "It's a dirty business." But he had a twinkle in his eye, and I knew I could talk him into it before dinner was over. Uncle Balls's stores were scattered throughout working-class neighborhoods. Once or twice a year, my mother would drag me to every one of them. We'd stop for lunch, mostly so she could refuel with a cocktail before heading to the next Lehrman's.[5] That was the name of his clothing chain, as well as my mother's maiden name. It had been her father's business before my uncle inherited it. I think that's why Mom acted like she owned the place and took whatever she wanted. "Put it on the tab," she'd tell the store manager, eventually settling the bill with her brother, paying cost, not retail.

Lois's father gave the family business to his son, a man called Balls, who knew nothing about women's clothing. She settled for running the house and volunteer jobs because when she worked outside the home, she was still responsible for running the house and raising four kids. Bert was not about to pitch in. After a full day of shopping and a long drive back home, Mom would insist that I give my dad a fashion show.

---

5   Not the store or my mother's real maiden name

I'd give her this look that said: *He doesn't care and neither do I.*

She'd give me a look that said: *Do it anyway.*

So I modeled the slacks, along with the polyester print blouse that would no doubt smell like gym sweat an hour after I put it on, the stench so bad I'd have to perfume my pits between classes.

"Bert," she'd say to my dad, "look at your daughter." He had these weird cubist glasses for old people that allowed him to watch television while lying down in bed. "Nice," he'd say, without sitting up. As a kid, I always thought this was my mom's way of saying: Show your dad what he bought you today. An attempt to build a father-daughter bond that didn't exist. Now I understand it differently. It was all about Lois showing Bert what *her* brother, Uncle Balls, gave *his* daughter, meaning me, courtesy of *her* dad's business. It was more about provenance—the history of where the clothes came from—than the outfits themselves, or me, for that matter.

"Tell your daughter she looks cute."

"You look cute," he'd say, without looking at me.

My mother always insisted that my dad really loved me. *He just doesn't know how to show it* was her refrain. I knew that wasn't true. I'm pretty sure everyone in my family knew that wasn't true: That's why they got away with treating me like a stray cat, an adorable creature you want to catch and pet but also, sometimes, torture.

My uncles were wrong about my dad; he wasn't a putz or a schmuck. He was an honest, hard-working man and a decent husband. A good provider. But a lousy dad—disinterested to the point of neglect. As bad as my uncles were, and they were quintessential textbook bad boys, in some ways I loved them more than I loved my father. They at least saw me, if only as comic relief.

Prince reminds me of my uncles. They had the innate ability to land an insult like it was a joke and still get away with people thinking they were funny. Charming with a killer instinct. *You, out there in California, what do you know about the real world? Go back home already, have an avocado smoothie, call your therapist. Like you know anything about (fill in the blank: money, politics, family matters).* Of course, I'm paraphrasing, I didn't keep a journal at the time. I was too busy working and raising kids in Los Angeles.

Maybe because I'd done most of my adulting out of town, because they'd never visited me anyplace I'd ever lived, never been to my house, or attended an event I'd organized, our relationship was stunted. I'd see them when I flew in to visit my mom in Detroit. They didn't know my friends, my neighborhood, or my community. They didn't know my struggles or successes. It's easy to other someone you don't really know.

You, out there in California.

To invoke the L.A. cliché: La-La-Land. Flaky liberal hipsters and meditation centers. Just like it's easy to reduce Jewish people to a cartoonish image of a man with exaggerated facial features rubbing his hands together to suggest greed, to strip people of their humanity, especially people you don't know, but even a relative you don't really know or care about, to a stereotype.

I loved my family, but my survival instinct pushed me to put thousands of miles between us. I remember driving out West with Chicky the summer after high school graduation, everywhere we went, every restaurant we stopped at, I'd ask for a job application.

I was a flight risk.

Like me, my mother Lois was the baby of her family, the youngest of four kids. Having grown up with not one but two big brothers, our mother had a boys-will-be-boys attitude toward princes, and when you think about it, a laissez-faire attitude toward child-raising in general, which left me, the baby girl, unprotected. No one was talking about safe spaces back then. For my mom's generation, a generation of American Jews who fought in WWII or, like my mother, listened in horror to stories about the slaughter of millions of Jews in Europe, the world was a dangerous place, and survival skills were the biggest gift a mother could pass along to her children. Regarding her daughters, that meant a sense of humor, education, and financial independence, but mostly, acceptance.

Her mantra was: *It is what it is.*

Mine was: *It might be better somewhere else.*

Boy with the Elastic Smile

I DON'T REMEMBER HOW we met. Maybe he sat behind me in math class. Pulled my hair. No, that came later. We ran around like a pack of wolves shuffling from one basement to another, listening to music, hanging out. I remember his eyes. I remember his hair. I remember his smile. His Jagger lips. The way his skin stretched like Silly Putty, and I laughed when he twisted it into funny faces. How he used to stare at me across a smoky room as if to burn a hole. That I used to throw rocks at his bedroom window. Split-level suburban tract house. *Let me in.* The first time we kissed. He was wearing white jeans, a size too small, hair loose around bare shoulders. He smelled of Downy sheets. I smelled of Herbal Essence. No one home but us. Cranked up the stereo. Some sort of Latin hip swivel.

Hot Chili.

His mother warned him about me. Said, *That girl is playing for keeps.* My mother didn't even notice him—the hair, those lips, that smile—clomping down the stairs in a leather jacket and steel-toed shoes. His *not* being Jewish was like a superpower, an invisible cloak. The two of us in the basement, wrestling on the floor, unseen. He'd pin my arms overhead, the full weight of his body covering mine. As if to claim me. We were like brother and sister. It felt incestuous. I thought he was Indigenous. Thick brown hair, long and straight, parted in the middle. Strong arms, soft eyes, rumble in my thighs. I borrowed his sleeping bag and curled up in his boyish scent. Musky. Warm and sweet.

It was all a schoolgirl fantasy.

Once, after one of the middle-school mean girls pulled my bathing suit top off, he walked me home from the pool party like an emotional support buddy. We wound up rolling in the grass by the ravine behind my parents' house, him wiping away my tears with those lips that stretched time. Later I let him push the gas while I steered my mother's Pontiac Le Mans. It's amazing we didn't crash and burn right then. Later still (I can't remember when, my images of him aren't contained in a linear time frame) riding on the back of his motorcycle, my arms wrapped around his waist, wind whipping at my face. Me thinking, *If only he had two helmets. One for him and one for me. Life would be perfect. And we could go and go and keep on going and never turn back.*

Instead, I went to college.

He'd visit me at university. Draw a swastika on the note-pad hanging outside my dorm room like it was his signature. I understood it to be his calling card. *I'm here girl, let me in.* If anyone called him out, he'd laugh and say it was an Indian good-luck symbol. He could have been Indian, skin some-where between the colors of earth and sand. He was a Karl

Marx commie. A Trotskyite. Grabbing at political straws. My girlfriends were all textbook liberals, they didn't approve. I wasn't concerned with antisemitism back then, so I made a lot of excuses for the boy with the elastic smile. "He's just being provocative," I told my friends. He also spelled phonetically, surfing the line between anti-establishment and illiterate. He was a traveler, a singer in the band. Channeling Jim Morrison—the early years. Rebellious. Without facial hair.

A few years later, I was working in the music industry in Detroit when he dropped back into my life. Walked in the front door of my apartment as if he belonged there, climbed the stairs, took a shower, and fell into bed next to me. *Honey, I'm home.* And we became what I had always imagined since the moment I first laid on eyes on him, when I was still in a training bra, and he was barely a man. I felt a sense of connectedness to this guy. Easy, comfortable, intuitive. Protected. And by *protected*, I mean that feeling when someone wraps their arms around you like a safety net. I was not thinking *This is my future, let's get married and have kids.* I was thinking, *for right now, this feels good.*

The plus sign came as a surprise.

Pink or blue?

"A baby," he said, clutching his belly when I told him. As if he'd be the one carrying it. Standing there in my living room, barefoot in faded jeans and a shrunken T-shirt, a rock band plastered across his chest. I didn't even have a couch. He didn't take a step towards me; it was as if he were superglued to the floor. It was in that moment when he didn't move closer to me that I knew he was pulling away. And I experienced the distance between us grow from a few feet into a football field.

A week later he enlisted.

He would be in basic training before the baby was even born. And, bam, reality hit, that baby would be mine alone. The diapers, the fevers, the babysitters, all of it, mine. *This is not how it's supposed to be,* I thought, staring at the end of us. This is not how my life is supposed to turn out—a single mom at twenty-three. I drove to the women's health clinic alone. "There is no father," I told the intake counselor. When immaculate conception didn't work, I said the baby could have been anyone's. *That,* she believed. As if I were promiscuous, not pregnant with my teenage soulmate's child. He was the boy my broken-girl-self needed, not the man that I, as a grown-ass woman would choose.

I chose me, my life, in an instant, in the time it took to register that the baby's father couldn't commit and that he wouldn't be there for me or our hypothetical child. It was an entirely pragmatic decision—one that I was entitled to make. I did not agonize over this decision, did not cry, did not grapple with my convictions. No deep thoughts, religious or otherwise. Nor did I tell my parents or consult a rabbi. But if I had, they would have supported my decision because my parents would not have wanted me to ruin my life before it even started.

As for a rabbi, in Jewish law, the woman's life takes priority over that of a fetus. In Jewish law, a fetus only becomes human once it is born, not at conception. My support of reproductive rights has always been entirely based on agency: *my body, my choice.* However, knowing that abortion is legal according to Jewish law, I am that much more incensed by the invasiveness of the pro-life movement. It's become both a women's *and* a Jewish issue because, while I have nothing against Christian

values, as a Jew, I do not like having Christian ideology imposed on me. Likewise, I suspect, Christians would not want
Jewish ideology imposed on them.

It feels a bit disingenuous to cite Jewish law on abortion,
like it's a loophole.

When I became pregnant, *Roe v. Wade* was settled law. The
boy with the elastic smile paid for the procedure, dropped me
off at the clinic, and borrowed my car to get to work. He did
not stick around to hold my hand or pick me up and drive me
home. He wanted nothing to do with it, which mirrored my
feelings: I felt nothing. I was in self-preservation mode. *Girl,
take care of business.* I may have been sleepwalking through my
sexual awakening, but I was wide awake when I decided to ter-
minate that pregnancy. That's why, when the doctor asked if I
wanted to be sedated, I declined. Somewhere tucked inside me
was the need to *feel* this decision. I chose physical sensation;
the pain was excruciating—deep and sharp, the pull of something being sucked from my belly. My youth, maybe. An in-
fatuation I'd fantasized about since middle school. Afterwards,
they gave me crackers and juice. A girlfriend picked me up
from the clinic and took me out for burritos. It was the first
time I hadn't felt nauseated in weeks. I felt relieved. Giddy.
Hungry. Starving for grease. Sold my car to the boy with the
elastic smile and moved to Boston on a whim.

He got a uniform, a kid, and a wife. In that order. In the
picture he sent me she looked blonde, but when I met her, she
seemed bland. For a while I ruminated on what she had that I
did not. Aside from straight hair. Wasn't I pretty enough, soft
enough, sexy enough? Instantly, I went to what was wrong
with me, held a mirror to myself and found fault. My eyes are
small, my cheeks big.

Then I got over it.

I might have held on to that guy if I could have but no one could—not even her, the girl he married, she with the mousy hair, whisper-soft delicate features, and his baby. Every now and then he'd try to sneak back into my life like a pre-existing condition. He was not down for daddy duty. He was smokin' hot and spreading it around. Disappearing at will. Here's what it felt like to be with someone for so long, at such a young age, someone so wrong for you, someone who'd leave you in a heartbeat, who'd leave you with two heartbeats and not look back: It felt like I dodged a bullet. He may have joined the army, become an officer and an aviator, but I dodged the bullet.

I met his son once in the bar of an old-time Hollywood hotel. Red leather booths and ornate wallpaper. The midday sun was blazing outside, but inside, it was dark and cozy. I chose it because it was an iconic, touristy place, easy to find. His son had a summer job in Los Angeles. He drank beer while I nursed a glass of seltzer water. With lime.

"How do you know my dad?" he asked me.

How do I even begin to answer that question? I wondered. He was the brother I wished I'd had. A protector. We were Bonnie and Clyde minus the bank robberies. From different worlds, like Mork and Mindy. Dropped from space, on a carnal exploration. We were loosely connected, or attached at the hip, depending on whether we were in each other's presence or out of sight. I could have just said friends with benefits.

"We went to school together," I told her son.

I refer to him as "her son" because the same boy who left me to join the army left her alone with the baby to raise as a single mom. She seemed to have done a good job of it. The young man sitting across from me appeared to be responsible and educated. Nothing like his father.

"I'm worried about my dad," he told me.

"Why are you worried?" I asked the son of the boy with the elastic smile. One more sip and my seltzer would be gone. Part of me wanted to ditch this kid and duck out of the bar. I was not even sure why his father gave him my number. Instead, I asked him why he was worried. Because this child who could have been mine—I almost wrote *could so easily have been mine*, but there is nothing easy about having and raising children. I was a high-risk OB-GYN patient— two C-sections and a life-threatening ectopic pregnancy. I can't imagine going through that alone, without the love and support of a life partner. Nor can I understand forcing any girl or woman to have a child, especially one whose father isn't willing or capable of stepping up.

I wanted to finish my drink and get out of there, back to work, associate publisher for a luxury architecture and design magazine. But this boy needed to talk about his dad, who was teetering on the edge of being unhoused—living in a trailer, roaming the country working manual labor temp jobs. The kind of work that takes an intense toll on a person's body, with a time stamp on it in terms of how long you can keep it up. That's why this boy was worried about his father, and, for some reason, he wanted to talk about him *with me*.

I motioned to the waiter for another round of drinks.

The boy with the elastic smile became a disgruntled man, re-surfacing on social media a few years later. Talking about making America great again. Accusing Jews of owning the media. Moaning about elementary schools becoming ghost towns.

Oh, the unborn babies! How Hillary ran a prostitution ring out of a pizza parlor, and Michelle Obama is really a man. *You can tell,* he insisted, *just look at her hands, her index finger is longer than her middle finger.* Calling Black people *Negroes.* Poking fun at Jewish culture, joking about kosher salt—managing to use the words *kosher, slaughter, ceremony, incantations, Hebrew,* and *Yiddish* all in one succinct Facebook post, evoking blood libel, the age-old claim that Jews murder Christian babies in blood rituals, dating back centuries up through and including Pizzagate and QAnon. *Did you know that all the Jews who worked in the Twin Towers stayed home that day?* he emailed me. Blaming Israel for 9/11 *and* insinuating I had insider information, both in one fell swoop. I had become a representative for my people. JewGirl.

And a baby killer.

It's as if you (or maybe he said "we") set the baby down in the driveway, got in the car, shifted into reverse, and backed over her. Him ranting about abortion being a sin. Who knew he was even Catholic? A conquistador! I thought he was tribal like me. His skin may have been darker than mine, but he checked the box "White" like a Proud Boy.

He talked about libtards.

I called him racist and antisemitic.

Then, for a while, we just stopped communicating. I know this about myself: I tend to give people a lot of chances to redeem themselves; I cut friends and family slack, but sometimes, I need to press "pause." And if you push me far enough, "delete."

Somehow, he got left behind. The boy with the elastic smile fell from grace, from lead singer in the band to couch surfing. I tried not to think of him living alone, hooked up to the Deep Web. Unvaxxed. He got the virus so bad he was in the hospital hallucinating on oxygen, said he saw our baby all grown up. "She's beautiful," he told me, describing her as a cross between Lauren Bacall and Sophia Loren—two film legends, one a sultry (but also wisecracking) Jew and the other a smoldering Italian. He said she forgave me, too. He left out the part about him not wanting to take responsibility for this imaginary spirit. Now he wanted to make sure no woman could ever defuse seed again. His dreams of stardom a distant wound, reproductive rights in his sights; he recovered from COVID just in time for the insurrection. Praise the Lord.

I emailed him on January 7th, saying, *Please tell me you were not in DC yesterday.* I expected a long-winded, circuitous, right-wing rant that ended with *No, I was not in DC.* Then I would say, *Phew!* We had not seen each other in decades; our relationship had morphed into distant and infrequent political conversations via email. The way I looked at it, some people watched Fox News to keep a finger on the pulse of conservative talking points, but I had him, the (now gray-haired) boy with the elastic smile, to check in with. His answer was vague, something about having attended Trump rallies in the past, nothing about DC. True to form, hard to pin down. I figured the government probably had him on their radar anyway; he was ex-army with a right-wing social media feed.

It's tempting to dismiss men like him as crazy, but a better word might be disenfranchised, the result of life choices. He had a darkly brooding post-punk stage presence and he pursued his dream of rock stardom. That's a long shot, not a mental health crisis. And you can't really blame the government if you don't succeed or have a Plan B. The last time we were in the same ZIP code was at our high school reunion. When I saw him, I was reminded of the swastika that I had overlooked when my hormones were driving the car. It makes me cringe. So strong was my desire to be loved that I condoned his inappropriate behavior. He hugged me like the long-lost soulmate I used to imagine him being, ran his lips across my cheek, and apologized. It was a sweeping, non-specific apology meant to cover a multitude of things. And then he showed me pictures of his home. He was brimming with pride of ownership as he recounted how, after he recovered from COVID, he socked away enough money to buy a house.

He seemed grounded and conciliatory.

I was guarded but supportive.

He mentioned that, having served in the military, he was eligible for certain veterans benefits like prescription drugs. I did not mention that the money earmarked for VA benefits comes from a system he wanted to dismantle, or that the government spends approximately a hundred billion dollars more per year on veterans than women's health issues. That there is a direct correlation between ex-military and extremist white power groups. And that in today's political climate, with the legal questions and challenges surrounding women's reproductive health care, women with ectopic pregnancies are at greater risk of death. That food insecurity and child poverty are a growing crisis in this country, affecting around nine million children a year, and that making abortion illegal or inaccessible will only exacerbate those figures.

I had lost the desire to fight with him.

Reproductive rights were a choice my generation of women had. When I hear politicians try to straddle the abortion debate by mentioning "exceptions for rape, incest, and the health of the mother"—as if they're being generous, fair, and understanding, it makes me want to scream from their false concern. *What about a woman's life? What about her dreams and aspirations? What about her emotional well-being? What about the well-being of the potential child she may not be prepared to take care of?*

There are things I regret, like having unprotected sex, but abortion is not one of them. I don't even regret having had this relationship. We were young and attracted to each other. He made me feel safe at a time when my own family did not. To feel love is a gift and a growth experience, but sometimes it's meant to be fleeting. Having and raising a child, on the other hand, requires a lifelong commitment. The last thing I would have wanted at twenty-three years old would have been to be tethered to that holdover high school relationship for the rest of my life. It seems crazy to be writing about this issue. It was settled law. Then along came Christian nationalism and the triumph of conservative politics, and now "your body, *my* choice" is trending on TikTok along with other snappy misogynistic catchphrases like "get back to the kitchen" and "Repeal the 19th" (referring to the amendment that gives women the right to vote). Nick Fuentes, a white nationalist podcaster with access to the President appears to be one of the early influencers to jump on this bandwagon.[6] So here we are at the intersection of antisemitism and misogyny.

---

6   Nick Fuentes's post on X, "Your body, my choice. Forever.", has received 35 million views.

Jewish Geography

HERE'S A SCENE: MY best friend Maia's fiancé dropped her off at my parents' house. My mother stood at the door in a turquoise caftan and grilled him about his family. She fancied herself a cool mom—pizzazzy!

"What's your last name?" Lois asked him.

"Goldman," Harvey replied.

"I think I may know your father," she said. "Did he grow up in Sherwood Forest?" Harvey shook his head no. Undaunted, Lois continued her line of questioning, asking what his dad did for a living and where he had gone to school.

"Central," Harvey said.

"Oh! You must be Stuart's son!" Lois exclaimed, her face lighting up as if she had hit the jackpot in Vegas. "I dated your Uncle Sidney!"

"He's a nice boy," Mom decreed, after Sidney's nephew said goodbye, having never even set foot inside the house. Lois's opinion was based on some sort of tribal history, six degrees of Jewish connections and the halo effect.

It's called Jewish Geography, giving people you don't know the benefit of the doubt based on some whisper-thin triangulated sense of connection. It's a bit of a parlor game, and it only works in a tight community, non-transient, multigenerational, where Jews cluster together at temple, in specific neighborhoods, schools, summer camps, and clubs. (And, if you grew up in Detroit, Joe Cornell's pre-teen dance experience in preparation for the bar and bat mitzvah circuit.) Considering that we are a people who have spent thousands of years on the run, scattered across continents, it follows that we are also a people in search of community. Hence, the essence of Jewish Geography is connectivity. Being a minority, there's a small-world aspect to this parlor game. Or maybe because we've been othered, we seek to reinforce the ties that bind us together. Regardless, Jewish Geography provides a way of categorizing total strangers into a system of known vs. unknown, which extrapolates into safe vs. unsafe, particularly when dating. That's why my mom immediately liked Maia's boyfriend. Because of his Uncle Sidney, whom she used to date way back when.

Maia laughed. Yes, she agreed, he's a nice guy. That's also why my mom liked Maia, because she never rolled her eyes at her, like I did. It's kind of embarrassing to have your mom grill someone else's boyfriend, not to mention the flowy caftan and the way she threw in her own dating history. Sometimes it seemed as if she dated half of Detroit before marrying my dad. But, in fairness to my mom, in *her* day, dating was "dinner and a movie."

Not like my date with Jonathan, for example.

I met him at a Halloween party at a dance club in the suburbs. Maia and I were dressed up like S&M—fishnets and cat masks. She had the whip. We always coordinated costumes on Halloween. The older we got, the sexier the costumes. Halloween was a free pass for trashy getups and a dance party.

"What do you do?" Jonathan shouted over the music.

"Business school," I shouted back. Maia was working and I was finishing my degree. "You?"

"Law school," he said, his arm circling my waist.

"Where?" I asked, placing one hand on his shoulder.

"Detroit," he said, his mouth getting closer to my ear.

"Me too," I said. "Downtown."

When he went to the bar to get a drink, I asked Maia if she knew him. She gave me the lowdown on Jonathan. They went to elementary school together. "I think he lived in the Pink House," she said. That was the party house sophomore year in Ann Arbor where the cool Jewish boys lived. All those years wincing at my mother with her Jewish Geography and there I was, using the same ancient tribal yardstick: School. Community. Connectivity.

I gave him my number.

A few days later he called and asked me out. I offered to meet him at his house, since, as a rule, I liked to drive my own car on a first date, just in case I needed to make a quick exit. Also, I was hyperconscious of the black fishnets and kit-cat mask I had worn on Halloween. Not that it matters, but I wore a turtleneck and high-waisted jeans for the date. I looked good, not sexy. I don't remember much else, not what theater we went to, or what movie we saw, only that he badgered me into getting a "little" high and I handed him my drink when I went to the ladies' room. And that, halfway through the movie, I could barely keep my eyes open. I have a vague memory of practically passing out face down in a plate of pizza after the movie. I had never been that wasted in my life. By the time we got back to his house, it was clear that I couldn't drive home. I lay down on the couch, but he said I'd be more comfortable in his bed. Then he offered me a caftan, one he got in Israel. He said something about living on a kibbutz. Such a nice Jewish boy. This could be a Halloween article for some girls' magazine, like *Bitch* or *Teen Vogue*.

DO'S AND DON'TS FOR HALLOWEEN

COSTUMES: Create a buddy costume with your best friend. Ketchup & Mustard is cute. Do not let her talk you into something conceptual like she'll be Every Man's Fantasy and you'll be the Queen of Saran. Wrapping your body head to toe in Saran Wrap is not really a costume and after one dance you'll be poached, drenched in sweat. If you decide to dress up as S&M characters, which I do not recommend, don't agree to be the "M" part of the duo, even if your name starts with that letter, like mine does. She'll get the whip and, more importantly, because she's cute and petite, she can pull off kittenesque. You're all attitude, and in fishnets, you'll just look like Madame Kitty.

PARTIES: If you meet a cute guy, dance with him. Notice what a good fit you make, his broad shoulders and strong arms; tilt your head back and smile. Do not bother asking your girlfriend if she knows him; they may have gone to kindergarten together, but what does that tell you? If he's wearing jeans and a button-down shirt and says: "This is my costume," believe him. He could be a wolf in disguise. Of course, he's not a wolf, silly! He's a Nice Jewish Boy who goes to the same law school as one of your best friends from college. Do not assume that makes him trustworthy. Also, do not give him points for being Jewish; that only meant something when your mom was dating. Above all else, do not give out your telephone number while wearing a black garter belt.

CANDY: If he offers you candy at the movies, the kind of candy his buddy in med school scored, and you say "no" five times, don't break down and say "okay, just a half" the sixth time he asks. Do not let him hold your drink while you go to the loo. *Trick or Treat!* When you can't keep your eyes open, can't stand up, or walk straight, call your friend. Do not lean on the guy who put candy in your Coke.

AND MORE! When you realize that you shouldn't drive, don't ask to sleep on his couch. It may be safer to sleep it off in your car. Do not let him talk you into his bed because it will be more comfortable. Speaking of comfort, don't put on the caftan he got in Israel the summer after freshman year. It will be scratchy when he rubs his body on top of you, his head bobbing in and out of view. Although this wakes you up, since you can't move your arms or legs, can't speak, much less scream, because your tongue feels swollen and possibly paralyzed, it will feel like you've been buried alive in some ghoulish satanic ritual.

AND MORE! The next morning, when he stands in his kitchen wearing sweatpants and offers you coffee, stroking his furry chest and running his hands through his bushy hair, you have two choices: a) politely decline, or b) throw a cup of steaming hot coffee in his face. I opted for "a," but in retrospect, option "b" would have been the way to go. "This is not the kind of case you want to take to court," says Bob Fink, your friend from college. Even though you suspect he's right, it still feels like the boys are closing ranks.

What was I thinking anyway—that Bob would stand up for me? That he would walk into the dean's office, me at his side, and accuse one of his peers of sexual misconduct? That he would lay out the seamy details of my personal life in front of the dean of his law school—the Halloween costume, the drugs, the couch, the bed, the caftan, the litany of bad decisions I had made? Because I suspect that's how he saw it, a string of bad decisions made by a girl he used to date. *And now, hopefully, she'll learn her lesson.* Maybe if I had gone to him as a friend, he would have comforted me. But I didn't ask for comfort; I had girlfriends for that. I wanted justice. I wanted retribution. I wanted to destroy my attacker's future. That's why I asked Bob to use his connections to help make it happen, but he had his own future to consider. That included not just graduating law school but maintaining his reputation in the Jewish community. Sometimes I think he was more embarrassed by me than I was by having been raped, which makes sense because I wasn't embarrassed at all.

I was traumatized.

Can we talk about Jewish men for a minute? Roman Polanski, Harvey Weinstein, Jeffrey Epstein, Anthony Weiner. Monstrous men. Every time a high-profile sexual assault makes the news, I pray it isn't another Jewish guy. Not because Jewish men have a #MeToo problem; rape has no race, religious, or ethnic boundaries. But, rather, because *some* prominent Jewish men are giving Jewish people a bad rap. And that's a problem for all of us: moms, dads, daughters, *and* sons. So much for Jewish Geography as a social safety net. Being part of the Jewish community does not make anyone immune to the problems that exist in society. If society is broken, odds are the Jewish community will be similarly broken, too.

The term "monstrous men" was coined by the writer Claire Dederer in an article that ran in *The Paris Review* citing Roman Polanski and Woody Allen but expanding the list to include Bill

Cosby, Louis C.K., and a United States president—although she doesn't name-check the president, most likely because her article was published before a jury found Trump liable for sexual abuse.[7] Instead, she quotes Trump, "I moved on her like a bitch." Later, Dederer expanded on this term "monstrous men" in a book simply titled *Monsters*, casting the net wide enough to include men *and* women, not just sexual predators but also antisemites and other artists whose work she appreciates but whose lives she can't condone. Still, every time a high-profile complaint about sexual assault commandeers a news cycle, I google the man (because let's be real, it's almost always a man) fingers crossed, praying the monster isn't Jewish.

I thought I had gotten over this incident, that it was processed and filed in my memory bank under "experiences survived." I had done the work, gone to therapy, developed a yoga practice, let go of the past, and had learned, if not mastered, the art of being present through deep breathing. I imagined myself healed. Then came Kavanaugh. The Supreme Court confirmation hearing and Dr. Christine Blasey Ford's testimony. It was not easy to watch this prime-time duel of *he said, she said*. His arrogance, her emotions. Dr. Ford's accusation seemed to hinge on this one thing: her ability to corroborate her story. That's when it all came flooding back to me. That date gone sideways. I can't prove that he spiked my soft drink, or that I passed out in his bed just to sleep it off. That he proceeded to have sex with me while I was in a compromised state of consciousness, without consent. What if it were him up for nomination to the Supreme Court? Would I dare expose him—and myself—in the process? Would I be that brave? Most likely, in

---

7   New York City civil lawsuit brought by E. Jean Carroll

an act of reverse Jewish Geography, the entire Jewish community would crucify me for smearing the name of such a Nice Jewish Boy.

Who would corroborate my story?

There's Maia, but she'd be no help. She went out with that creep even after I told her what happened to me. I can imagine how a cross-examination of her would go. *So*, a prosecutor might ask, did she, Maia, really go out with a guy she believed to be a rapist? Or did she think her friend, *meaning me,* just got a little too high and, well, sex happens, making it sound like even my best friend didn't believe my story. Plus, she wouldn't be much help as a character witness. Maia might tell the story about how I once slept with a guy in college because it was raining outside and I didn't have an umbrella. Sheer laziness, I admit, but the decision to stay out of the rain was my choice.

Would anyone see choice as a distinction?

Then there's my friend Bob. I remember talking to him the very next day, or was it a few days later? Women need to keep better records. Would Kavanaugh be on the Supreme Court today, adjudicating the rights of women, if Dr. Ford had had the foresight to keep a high school journal?

Whenever it was that I saw Bob, I asked him to go with me to file a complaint. Instead, he outlined why I had no case. I try to give him the benefit of the doubt, not because he's an old friend, but because his counsel was based on conditions at the time, before "date rape" was even a concept. When he asked if I had gone to the police, I said: No, I went home and took a shower. Just like in the movies. Collapsed on the tile and let the water wash over me. He didn't say that was a dumb thing to do, that I washed away all the evidence, because he didn't think there was an actionable crime. There was only evidence of sex—a sticky substance between my legs in the morning—not necessarily *non-consensual* sex. There would have been trace elements of some sort of drug in my system. But there again, Bob, the lawyer-in-training, pointed out that I had admitted to taking half a Quaalude. What could I say? *Officer, I can handle half a 'lude, but I was so high he must have spiked my drink with something stronger.* It went on like that, no need to rehash the specifics.

Boys will be boys. That's my mom's generation talking. Years later, when I was pregnant with my son, I couldn't even say I was having a boy. Had to spell it out like a dirty word. I'm having a B-O-Y, I would tell people, carrying with me into parenting this rage, manifesting as hipster-edginess and an intolerance of any male aggression toward women.

It wasn't until the Kavanaugh nomination hearings that I revisited this incident with my friend Bob. I called him on the phone and asked if he remembered that I had told him about being raped by a guy he had gone to law school with. He said yes, he remembered the conversation. I mentioned that I was following the public evisceration of Dr. Christine Blasey Ford, making her out to be either lying or hysterical, that her raw emotional honesty was hard to watch, and it made me wonder if anyone would corroborate *my* story. I did not go into the whole "hysterical female" trope, about how back in the day women were institutionalized with some mysterious female condition for having anxiety or agitation, excessive emotions, because, well, powerlessness.

"What do you remember from our conversation?" I asked Bob.

"I only recall the conversation in the vaguest of terms, that it happened, but none of the details," he replied. His response

sounded more lawyerly than friendly. Then, in an uncharac-
teristic moment of self-reflection, he wondered out loud if he,
himself, had ever crossed the line and acted without consent.
It was an unexpected conversational detour; one I couldn't appreciate in the moment because I was so focused on *my* connection to the hearings. Now I see how, in bringing her story
forward, Dr. Ford was not just forcing women to relive their
trauma but also encouraging men to question *their* culpabil-
ity. Moments later, as if in conversation with himself, Bob
determined that "no," his record was clean. He was relieved.
Absolved. As for my story, he had forgotten the details.

I let it go.

I don't know what I was hoping to get anyway. A belated
apology for not taking my side? For giving cover to a sexual
predator? For supporting the buddy system over our friendship? A superficial *I'm sorry*, arriving decades too late? Instead,
I was smacked with how little he remembered (or was willing to admit remembering) about a traumatic incident that
had happened to me, a woman he'd known for decades. We
had gone to school together, our families were members of the
same club, and ever so briefly, we had dated in college.

I got to thinking, after I hung up the phone, that I don't
know how anyone could forget the kind of specifics I shared
with Bob about that date. I didn't fully comprehend at the
time that it was a brush with death. I saw it as "merely" a
sexual assault of my body. But, of course, I could have OD'd.
I was lying on my back, unable to speak or move my limbs.
All choice had been withdrawn from me, save the ability to
open or close my eyes. I decided to close my eyes and drift.
I remember thinking, *If I'm going to die, at least the high is
masking the panic.* If the situation had been reversed, I would

remember almost every detail of Bob's story, the way I remember all the experiences my girlfriends have shared with me over the years. Abortion. Date Rape. Near misses. Jumping out of moving cars. Cornered and fingered in a back alley by a stranger. Raped in a parking structure; in her dorm room, his hand over her mouth; on a camping trip during her semester abroad. Pot, secretly laced with PCP. All of it. It's not just overwhelming, it's indelible. Seared into memory.

My daughter, Sasha, said this to me recently, "It's interesting how every woman I know has either been raped or knows someone who has been raped, but no men know any rapists."

The math doesn't add up.

I have a photo of my daughter, Sasha, as a little girl at the Descanso Gardens with her two best friends from preschool. Her grandmother took the picture. Harry's mom was visiting Los Angeles and scooped up the girls for a visit to the botanical gardens. It was raining, but the trip had been planned for weeks, so they were not to be deterred. Chloe is wearing a pink rain slicker with a hood. Next to her, in a blue mermaid slicker with matching umbrella, is Lexi. The two girls are each holding rosebuds, not yet in bloom. Standing off to the side, on her own, in a yellow hooded slicker, holding a sprig of flowers in her hand, is Sasha. It's a snapshot. A moment in time, capturing girlhood innocence. What you don't see in the photograph, which I can't seem to forget when looking at it now, is that two of the three girls' mothers have been raped, one at knifepoint, and that two of the three girls will be raped in college. While I understand that these six girls/women do not represent a statistical sample, I also know that the statistics are not improving. It's like rape is status quo in America. Every

98 seconds someone in the U.S. is sexually assaulted. More than 1 in 3 women have experienced rape, physical violence, or stalking by an intimate partner in their lifetime. Ninety-one percent of victims of rape and sexual assault are female.

There's something I've left out. Not because it's embarrassing, but because it's more painful than the rape itself, which, as noted, I was barely conscious during. Out of sheer frustration, Maia and I egged Jonathan's house. We drove to his house, sat in her car (or maybe mine; I don't recall who drove), and threw eggs at his front porch. Howling with laughter. Sad clown laughter, that abyss between comedy and tragedy. We did a few other things, too, the kinds of things girls do when they're pissed off and powerless. We etched his name and telephone number on bathroom walls. We called the electric company to have his power turned off. We plastered flyers about him everywhere he might hang out as a warning to potential victims. We were so young. I was emotionally unprepared to process this thing that had happened to me, this amorphous event, which hung like a cloud over every first date I ever went on again.

A year or two after I was raped by the law student, we were reintroduced at the home of my mother's friend, Sylvie. My mom rang the doorbell. Sylvie opened the door and there he was, standing next to her daughter, Lily, like the cat who caught the bird.

"This is Lily's boyfriend, Jonathan," Sylvie said.

Jonathan stared right through me with this look that said: *I've never seen you before in my life.* Cool. Not a flicker of recognition. Sylvie's house was ultramodern, tons of glass. From the front door I could see all the way through to the backyard.

Just like I could see through Jonathan. *So, this is how it works,* I was thinking. *He graduates law school and marries a friend of the family, and now I'll have to smile when I see him at weddings and Sunday BBQ at The Club for the rest of my life.*

"Nice to meet you," he said, extending his hand to me the way you would any stranger.

"We've met," I replied, staring back at him, refusing his hand.

I was no longer that girl who collapsed in a heap in the shower, breaking down like wet tissue. Used. Paper-thin. His hand hung in midair. There was an awkward silence that I chose not to fill with social nicety. He was in my backyard now. Lily was at all my birthday parties when I was a little kid. Cake and ice cream, and paper party hats with elastic straps under the chin. It was bad enough what Jonathan did to me, what he got away with doing to me, but now he was attempting to erase not just the rape, but *me,* as if we'd never met or he didn't remember our date. I'm sure he thought he had the advantage because he was standing inside Sylvie's house and I was standing outside ringing the doorbell, because he was now a lawyer and I was just a girl he could pretend not to know. Perhaps he was counting on my shame to protect him.

I felt no shame.

I am often outspoken. Railing against the system. *Resist!* I marched at the Women's March on Washington and in Los Angeles on March 8th for International Women's Day. Screaming my truth. *Human rights are women's rights! She won!* But in this moment, it was my silence that transmitted defiance. My silence was a form of resistance. It stopped time. It spoke volumes. It said, NO, I will not shake your hand and pretend you did not rape me. I will not play that game. It forced everyone present—my mom, Sylvie, and her daughter—to catch up. I must have gone pale from the shock of seeing him standing there because Sylvie exclaimed, *Mars!* A nickname she'd given me as a little girl. Then she said, "You look like you're going to pass out." Taking me by the hand, she led me into her kitchen. Slick, shiny white and chrome surfaces, wiped clean. Not a spot, not a speck of dirt anywhere.

"Is this the boy who did that thing to you?" Sylvie asked, handing me a glass of water. She couldn't even name it. Sylvie was a no-nonsense woman. She wore slacks, not skirts, and she wasn't shy about language. *Cut the crap, Mars!* She'd laugh whenever I made up a story about why I did or didn't do something. Sneak a cigarette or research a paper that was about to be overdue. But this word "rape" she could not bring herself to use in reference to me. I was gripping the glass, careful not to spill water in Sylvie's pristine kitchen, wondering how she could know this story about me. I glanced from Sylvie to my mother, remembering that I had told my mom when it happened and putting two and two together, that she must have confided in Sylvie. They were friends, the kind that tell each other everything. Lois was hovering in the background like a bystander. She had discussed this incident with me only once, shortly after it happened. Also in a kitchen setting, although ours was more traditional, with a round wooden table and wicker chairs. It was never mentioned again. My mother called me her wild child; I was the strong one. Strength to my mom meant being stoic. It meant compartmentalizing bad stuff, tucking it into a box shoved in the back of a drawer where it's easier to forget. And getting on with life.

"Is this the boy?" Sylvie repeated.

"Yes," I said. The court of moms wrapped their arms around me, the arms of all women from all ages, like a patchwork quilt, woven together. Sometime afterward, I heard that Lily and Jonathan had broken up. I don't know if it had anything to do with me, but I'd like to think it did. I know he deserved worse, but this felt like a win to me. And, for Jewish Geography.

Warrior Princess

WARRIOR PRINCESS

Camo is my favorite color. Ever since college, when I bought a pair of used cargo pants from the army surplus store. They hung low on my non-existent hips, exposing a flat belly. And we marched across campus in protest. Now I wear camo everything. It complements my eyes, which are hazel. I even have a camo facemask from Etsy. I figure, if you must wear a mask, why not make it a fashion statement? Bonus: Camo never goes out of style. Wanna know why? Because we're always at war.

The war on drugs.

The war on terror.

The war against the virus.

The war on women and Jews is long and storied; entwined. It runs through the pages of my mind, on repeat. It slips into conversations and anchors the news. It's archival; it's here and now, front and center. It was, it is, it's always been. And someday ... what? We're supposed to believe it will be a footnote.

Like Vietnam. Not a daily reminder of our place in the scheme of things. And I will be able to stop wearing camo.

Technically speaking, camo's not a color. It's a combination of colors that integrate into a pattern. Swirling together. Similarly, my approach to writing this book is about patterns, like a patchwork quilt. This is how I process life, through stories, memories, and historical references.

And dreams.

I used to fly in my dreams. Above the treetops, across oceans, looking down on cityscapes. According to dream interpretations, this could mean anything from freedom and liberation to escapism, and everything in between—personal growth, resilience, and spirituality. To me, though, these dreams suggest the quest for a broader point of view, the desire to pull back the lens and reconsider experience from a distance. A reminder to let go of the root structure. I need that reminder because I am, by nature, grounded; when I walk, I stare at the earth in front of me. As a kid, I used to crawl through the dirt catching reptiles and toads at summer camp. If there were such a thing as heaven, mine would be dusty and filled with chameleons—those brownish-green lizards that change colors, depending on where they perch: earth or leaf.

Now that's a useful trick: the innate ability to blend in with your surroundings and avoid predators. Camo skin tone would be cool but impossible for a Jewish girl, it's easier to change your name. When I got married, I went from Blumberg to Maxfield. Poof! I could pass on paper. But only on paper. In person, there's something not quite "passing" about me—it may be this tendency of mine to crack a joke, to not defer or act demure. As soon as I open my mouth, there it is. The attitude. The impudence of my writing. Lifting the rug and mucking about in the comic brutality of life.

I'm a little too wry.

A little too rye.

As a young woman working in the music industry, a potential marketing partner branded me "rude and abrupt." My job was to secure free product in exchange for on-air promotional mention. We're talking airline tickets, donuts and coffee. Hot dogs and buns. Hot-dog guy called my boss to complain that I was rude and abrupt, because I didn't linger on the phone and make nice after he'd turned down my request. Because I didn't perceive that I had time to waste making *him* feel better about saying *no* to me. Because I wasn't sweet, didn't grovel, hadn't yet learned the importance of chit-chat. It wasn't until I perfected the art of giving great phone that I began to succeed.

And earned the nickname *Trade Queen.*

I've always thought of myself as a Warrior Princess. And others mistakenly ID'd me as a Jewish American Princess: lazy, spoiled, entitled. That's the trope about JAPs—that we're all daddy's girls. Adored. Adorned. Bejeweled. Pedestaled. A girl whose life's mission is first to be the apple of daddy's eye. And then, to snag a prince. But I was none of those things. I was a worker bee. Good at my job. Right away, the guy I shared an office with reframed my success as *masculine.* Giving me the nickname *Mr. Marcie.* As if success in and of itself were a masculine trait. He suggested I get a personalized license plate, slurring it together into one word: MrMarcie. Catchy, but I refused, on general principle: Personalized license plates are tacky. I didn't confront him on sexism. A girl has to pick her battles. Cutting him some slack, he may have been confused about my gender. The name *Marcie* does derive from the god (not the goddess) of war. Mars, not Athena. Which brings me back to camo: it's the uniform of war, also called battledress. I have a gray-green camo T-shirt dress with short sleeves that I wear over deep coal multicolored camo leggings, and I do feel tough when I'm wearing it. It sets a tone—fierce with a touch of sardonic.

I'm also a strong swimmer. I learned how to swim at The Club and developed stamina at summer camp where we had to swim out to the raft and tread water for 20 minutes, or the waterfront coach wouldn't let us canoe or sail or do any of the cool water sports. This was a Christian camp; they had vespers on Sunday nights. It was like church in the woods. The big girls wore whites, but the little ones, called Chips, wore our jammies. We sat on sticky wooden benches in a clearing, surrounded by birch trees, a giant cross looming skyward. Shorty, the camp owner/director, queen of all activities, decider of whether we got ice cream for dessert or an overnight in the woods, stood at the pulpit and led us in song. We had tree-sappy butts, Christmas in July, and Indian Council. We were Chippewa Braves learning the Sun Dance—all of us holding the ritual in the highest, most hallowed regard. Years later, my sisters and I asked our mom why she sent us to that camp. I mean, there were other options. Jew Camp, for example—they had showers in the cabins with an outlet for hair dryers and boy-girl dances on Friday nights.

"I wanted you girls to be able to fit in anywhere," Mom said.

Like chameleons, I thought. Only, she meant "assimilate."

That's not the problem, though, is it? The issue isn't whether *we* can get along in a non-Jewish world. The problem isn't really on our end at all. The question is whether *they* are willing to let us co-exist. As I write this chapter, antisemitism is not just on the rise; it's being mainstreamed. The president[8] dined with a Holocaust-denying white nationalist. A Republican congresswoman[9] posted on Facebook about a secret Jewish space laser responsible for California wildfires. A Kennedy suggested that the COVID virus was engineered to target Caucasians and Black people, while sparing Jews and Chinese people.[10] The social media platform X has become a hub for antisemitic rhetoric.[11] To ignore or discount these things is to engage in normalcy bias, like, *hey, these people are just crazy outliers.* That mindset reflects a cognitive deficiency that enables people to disbelieve or minimize threat warnings. I don't ascribe to the theory, meant to be comforting, that these are isolated or "fringe" events. Social media is the modern town hall. These people have won elections, been appointed to government positions and/or have access to the president.

We're the outliers.

My mother knew this, of course. Her social life had been limited to the Jewish community. Temple and The Club. She wanted more for her daughters, so she sent us to a Christian summer camp for girls, where we learned about Indigenous culture. To this day I remember the Christian prayers and the Native American dance steps. I can still do a mean stomp-hop-toe-heel.

THE CLUB

Summer break, between freshman and sophomore year of college, I was having Sunday dinner at The Club. Standing next to me was a friend of my parents. We were both scanning the

8   Donald J. Trump, elected President twice, 2016 and 2024
9   Marjorie Taylor Greene
10   Robert F. Kennedy Jr. United States Secretary of Health and Human Services
11   Elon Musk, Chairman and Chief Technology Officer of X denies this accusation, saying that antisemitism violates X's stated policies

room for our people. I was looking for my mom and dad and siblings; he was looking for his wife and kids—the sweater-set girls. I remember them in cashmere sweaters, even in the summer. In case of a chill, a pastel sweater draped over each of their delicate shoulders. Their hair neatly brushed, pulled back with barrettes or a headband color-coordinated to match their outfits. When he saw his daughters, his face lit up as if they had shot the moon in hearts. No one had ever looked at me like that. Especially not my father. To him, I was just another kid to dress. Plus, the way I dressed really pissed him off.

"I wish I could be one of your girls," I said to the sweater-set girls' dad. It just slipped out of my mouth without giving it much thought. He turned toward me with a sly smile, his gaze scanning the whole of me, top to bottom. I was wearing low-slung faded jeans, a tank top, no bra, and flip-flops. The din of silver and china rustled in the background, cocktails flowing. "Maybe something could be arranged," he said. In that moment, I became aware of my body, its waif-like sexiness and power to seduce. I just pocketed the information for a later date.

"Ugh!" Chicky exclaimed when I told her what he had said. "That is gross. What a slime bag. He's old and bald. I am so creeped out."

"You're such a priss," I said, mocking Chicky. "Plus," I teased her, "you gotta admit, he is kind of cute for a dad. Also, he's not bald; he's shaved."

And he was nice. *Our* dad was always complaining about how we kids were costing him a fortune. Meaning *me,* as Trish was the favorite, Chicky was the good student, and Prince was the son—*I* was costing him a fortune. I was the fourth kid, the unnecessary drain on expenses. I could read it in his eyes. Flatlined. Like it was a bother to look at me.

The Club was a huge part of our lives growing up. Birthdays and barbecues. It looked like a sprawling English manor, stone floors and musty rooms, old-world charm. Cobblestones, a golf course, and a pool. To this day I love the smell of chlorine better than an ocean breeze. It's the kind of place where David Beckham and Posh Spice would live. Only it wasn't a single-family home. It was a private Jewish country club; menus with no prices, bills that require nothing more than a signature; you must be invited to join *and* make a sizable donation to a Jewish charity. Or be a legacy member, like us. We didn't have a lot of money. My dad was always walking around the house turning off lights, mumbling about the electric bill. The first time I smoked was in the ladies' card room with the twins Alice and Eve, after we rifled through open lockers in search of three cigarettes. If I close my eyes, I can still hear the crunch of cleats on pebbles, can retrace my steps from the pool, past the putting green, to the caddy shack where I would buy a bag of cheese popcorn and flirt with caddies. Because my birthday is at the end of June, I had a pool party every summer to which my mother invited the children of her friends, who were also members of The Club.

It sounds clannish. Like Jews only hang out with other Jews. A recent survey by the Anti-Defamation League indicates that seventy percent of Americans think Jews stick together more than other Americans. But do Jewish people stick together out of choice or necessity? Certainly, when The Club was built in the early 1900s it was out of necessity. Jews were not welcome as guests, much less allowed to join Gentile clubs in Detroit. Like communities of color, they were often restricted from swimming in public pools. That's why my grandfather and his buddies built The Club in the first place: no one else would have them. Chicky always says we were "trespassing in the land of privilege" because if it weren't for Grandpa Joe being a founding member, our family might not have been able to join The Club. In some ways, that explains why Lois insisted her daughters find a career, not a man. We were raised to be *from* this community, to carry with us into the world this sense of a privileged upbringing—back when the word "privilege" was more aligned with class than skin color. And to move *away from* this insular existence and become full-fledged members of the greater American society. So, although The Club evokes sensory memories of my childhood, I always had the understanding that I was just passing through, on my way to a different, bigger, more expansive, and purposeful life.

COMBAT ZONE

My dad was sure I was a loser, reckless and wild. A child who would not just *never amount to anything* but one who *refused to grow up*. In my dad's worldview, growing up meant taking a soul-sucking job selling ink and paper to businesses that used ink and paper. Which was a *heck of a lot of companies,* he said. This was before cell phones and the internet. I ignored him and held out for a position in the music industry and then, a few years later, got laid off from my dream job at a record company on Black Friday, along with hundreds of people across the country. He listened to my sob story, shaking his head, and when I was done talking, my father reframed the situation in three words.

"You got fired."

As if it were my fault, not the fault of an economic downturn. "I knew they were overpaying you," he added. It was just too much cash to be on the up-and-up. Okay, there may have been some truth to that—there was that $12,000/year expense account, no receipts required, which, in hindsight, seems to smack of payola. My job was to secure display space in retail store windows, promote in-store airplay, and schmooze the people who reported weekly sales figures to the trades. Product, concert tickets, T-shirts, lunches, licit or not, whatever it took to break a record or boost the sales numbers was implied both in my unwritten job description and my untracked expense account. In hindsight, the schmoozing might not have been kosher.

When my boss called me into his office to tell me that my position had been eliminated, I started to cry. Sat there on his stylish mid-century couch, next to the coffee table stacked with music magazines, under the framed gold records, blubbering. "You mean I can't come to work tomorrow? But yu-yu-you're like family. I love you guys." Then *he* started to tear up. That's when I offered to work for free, just until they could afford to pay me a salary again. I should point out that this was a mega entertainment company, not an indie label. They weren't going out of business; it was a corporate downsizing, and I was being let go.

"It's not your fault," my boss said, launching into a prolonged explanation along the lines of: *My hands were tied ... the suits in New York... fucking bean counters ... out of my control.* The next day he stopped by my duplex and took me for a slow spin in his Lincoln Continental with the tinted glass and custom leather upholstery. He was driving like an old man, which wasn't his style at all. I saw him as a player, at the top of his game, running the Detroit branch of a major record label, but there he was driving like my dad, inching his way around the block, creeping up to stop signs, laying on the brakes long enough to deliver a eulogy. "Don't worry," he reassured me. "You'll be okay. It was between you and Jim. I wanted to keep you, but they said Jim had a wife and kids to support." Then, realizing he had overshared, he told me if I repeated this conversation to anyone, he'd deny it ever happened. After a while, he circled back to my duplex, coming to a full stop. "You can use me as a reference," he offered, as consolation. I opened the passenger door, placed one foot on the pavement, about to step out, and then I turned around, facing my now ex-boss, and asked him why he came here to tell me this. "I wanted you to know how great you are," he said. Then he said something like *Stay in touch* or *Don't be a stranger.*

We never spoke again.

A few months later, I moved to Boston. Turns out you can collect unemployment anywhere in the country; all you need to do is prove you're looking for work. "Boston!" My dad practically spit the city out of his mouth when I told him my plan. "How will you get a job? You don't know anyone there. Connections are everything." When my dad talked connections, he meant temple, the Jewish community, and The Club—the one with a formal dining room that overlooked the golf course.

Not Club 66.

It was the kind of place where girls with no experience got jobs. Next door was the Naked i. The women who worked there were pros: They had a pole. Both existed on this one-block strip called the Combat Zone, where you could get pizza by the slice or a peep show. All I knew was that I needed to make money. Fast. Or I'd have to go home. And I wouldn't give my father the satisfaction. So there I was at Club 66 talking to a tough-looking woman named Crystal. Tatted arm sleeves and heroin-chic thin. I handed her my résumé. That piece of paper held it all: my dignity, education, work experience. I told her that I'd been laid off from my dream job in the music industry on Black Friday. I didn't tell her about the abortion, or that one particular bad date that ended up with me on the floor of a shower in a puddle of tears, or getting evicted from my apartment back home on account of my cat. She could probably sense all that because I was sitting across from her in a dark booth in a skanky "cabaret" asking to be hired as a dancer.

"That's a nice jacket," she said, fingering the sleeve of my gray wool suit from Saks Fifth Avenue, the one I had charged to my mom's account before I left town. I was wearing it because I had just come from an interview for a job that I didn't want and probably wouldn't get anyway. I was running out of funds. And feeling desperate.

"Are you sure you know what kind of club this is?" Crystal asked. There was a stage lit up like a runway, a bar and mirrored walls. Onstage a girl was bent over in a wide-legged forward fold, only she wasn't wearing yoga pants. The scent of whiskey and wet dreams permeated the place.

"I think I get the idea," I told her.

"Well," Crystal said. "You can try out. Do you have a stage name?"

I shook my head no.

"You look like Snow White. What kind of music do you like, Snow?"

"Oh!" I exclaimed. "My taste in music is eclectic—R&B, punk, rock. Reggae. Also, I like gospel." Then, feeling the need for clarification, I said Black gospel—The Staple Singers. The

Mighty Clouds of Joy. Not Southern gospel. Or Country. I'm from The D. I grew up on Motown.

She squinted her eyes, staring at me like I might be crazy. *Girl,* I thought to myself, *you are not in Detroit anymore, and this is not an interview for a music industry gig.*

"Soul," I said. "I like soul music. And rock and roll."

Crystal told me to go backstage and ask to borrow something to wear from one of the girls. She offered to hold my purse. It was a slim leather portfolio. All it had in it was my ID, lunch money, and copies of my résumé. One of the girls gave me a pink negligee, and someone handed me her stripper shoes, but I opted to go barefoot. That became my signature move, dancing barefoot. For a moment I just stood on the stage, completely still, staring at my reflection in the mirror, my back to the customers.

If life seeks to knock me down, I thought, *fuck that, I'll take a swan dive to rock-bottom.* We were all swans diving, every one of the girls dancing in that club was either broke or broken; we were in survival mode. The pale-pink lace teddy was kittenish, at best. Possibly ironic. The DJ was playing Funkadelic, the lights dim, the air stale with smoke. It was 1 p.m. in the real world, outside the door, but inside it was always after-hours. And I was a princess. Not a Disney princess, a warrior princess. And warrior princesses do not wear lace. I slipped the lingerie straps off my shoulders, let the pink teddy fall to the stage, cupped my breasts with my hands, and turned toward the bar. Then I strutted that stage like a supermodel, haughty; like a whore, naked; like a prima ballerina, graceful; occasionally popping a hip and nailing a turn.

"Where'd you get those moves?" Crystal asked afterwards.

"Trena and Vanessa," I responded, a nod to my classmates growing up in Detroit.

"Whatever," Crystal said with a shrug. "When can you start?"

It was a temporary snag in the dream sort of job. Some of us were just rock chicks scraping by. Venus was putting herself through art school. She had a dress with layers and layers of shimmering beads that rustled when she walked and a matching headdress, like a tiara on steroids. She was so mesmerizing, she didn't even have to dance. Cleo had a custom-made fuzzy pussycat costume that looked like footie pajamas but with Velcro seams, orange and black tiger-striped ears, and a tail. I wore a black tutu, going for a sort of dead ballerina vibe, under a black satin tour jacket from my job at the record company. It didn't bother me to take my clothes off. I liked that there were strict rules. Men could look but not touch, and they had to buy me a drink just to talk to me. It was all out in the open: transactional. It felt empowering.

THANKSGIVING

Gopika was wrapped in muted tones of shimmering sandstone and clay. Right from the start I was on the fence about our relationship. *How is this woman in a sari going to understand me?* I would have preferred a Jewish therapist who, I assumed, would intuitively understand where I was coming from. We'd have this immediate shorthand, and she'd fix me up fast. But this was a sliding scale, state-funded mental health clinic, which says so much more about *my* economic status than Gopika's abilities, and I was in no position to be picky.

"I'm smart, educated, and have a decent, although not well-paid, entry-level job in advertising sales," I told Gopika, by way of introduction. Not super attractive, but not without a certain appeal. Plus, I looked good on paper. By then, I was only dancing on Sundays, just to make enough money to make ends meet. "The problem is," I told Gopika, "I've never had a real boyfriend. That's why I'm here, because there may be something wrong with me that I need to figure out."

Being in sales and marketing, I was confident with the art of the pitch. I approached that first session like a job interview, only in reverse. First you identify your skillset. Then, instead of saying how you will help solve a prospective client's problems, it's the exact opposite—you've got to identify your problems and tell the therapist what you want them to fix. I made it clear that I didn't want to be in therapy for years, I just wanted to address this one issue: that I'd never had a proper boyfriend, one who takes you on dates and remembers your birthday and maybe wants to marry you. I was in my mid-twenties and tired of going out with losers who treated me like shit.

"Tell me about your childhood," Gopika said.

"My childhood was normal," I told her.

"Describe normal," she responded.

See, this is why I wanted a Jewish therapist. She'd intuitively understand what my upbringing was like. She'd be able to picture the house, the holidays. Sundays with bagels and lox for breakfast and Chinese takeout for dinner. The brother who was treated like a prince; two older sisters, one a drama queen and the other an overachiever; the mother who only wanted more opportunity for her daughters than she had, not understanding that by raising us to follow our hearts, we were destined for downward mobility.

"You know," I said. "Normal. Parents. Siblings. A dog."

I wasn't lying. And I wasn't in denial, either. I thought my upbringing was typical. But I knew that I had to give her something to go on and was happy to lay all my emotional baggage at Prince's feet. So I piled it on thick, told her about the teasing and taunting and tormenting. The name-calling. He called me Mouth. Maybe it was because I talked a lot. Most likely it was because I tattled on him. Now, I think he was trying to shut me up.

Gopika was listening, nodding her head, but I could tell she wasn't buying it. She wasn't even taking notes.

"Once, he choked me in the laundry room," I told her. "My sister Chicky was screaming, 'Stop! You're killing her!' She had to pry his hands off my neck. I almost passed out."

"It's not your brother," she replied. "Tell me about your father," Gopika insisted.

I thought: *Predictable.*

It's always the father. Or is it the mother? I'd never been in therapy before. My mother was a social worker in downtown Detroit, but she had a NIMBY attitude toward therapy—Not In My Backyard—which really meant not in her house, not her children, not us. As if her clients, people from underserved communities, had problems that Jewish families did not share. It's the same lens, in reverse, through which some People of Color view Jews—as if Jews cannot be subject to systemic prejudice because we have white skin. But I digress. I change the subject. I do that when people ask me about my father. There's nothing to say, other than that we weren't close.

"My father was like any other father," I told Gopika. He was there, in the background, he paid the bills; I went to the dentist every year. He loved me, he just didn't know how to show it. That's what my mother always said. And that's how I ended up dating Leo the lawyer for two years. We went out every Thursday and Sunday, like clockwork. On Thursdays he took me out to dinner at nice restaurants. On Sunday nights, we sat on the couch in his apartment, ordered Chinese food, watched TV, and had sex. Afterwards he would ask me to grade the sex. Was that an A or B? he'd want to know. In *his* head he was still in school. In *my* head we were about to be engaged. On Monday mornings, I'd turn my underwear inside out and go to work.

Looking back, I see that Leo was not all that into me, but at the time, I thought he loved me because, in my worldview, Sundays were reserved for family. That meant Leo and I were like family. This is how I rationalized Leo's schedule: Fridays were for grabbing a drink after work with the gang, Saturdays were for running errands, going to the gym, and catching up on work and sleep. And Sundays were reserved for me and Leo.

"He's dating someone else, dummy," my roommate said.

"No, he isn't," I insisted. "He's busy." For some reason I was comfortable with a level of neglect that most girls would not accept. I didn't see it as neglect. I saw Leo as family; he loved me like my dad: in small doses, for dinner on Thursdays and Chinese food on Sundays. I'd call my mom from Leo's apartment every Sunday night.

"Is your father alive?" Leo asked me once, after I said, *Love you, Mom.* And hung up the phone.

"Of course, he is. He answered the phone."

"Oh," Leo said. The kind of "oh" that hangs in the air and is more like *aha.* Because if my dad ever answered the phone, all I said was, *Can I talk to Mom?* Or *Is Mom home?* Not even *Hi, Dad. How are ya?* And if my mother answered the phone, it never occurred to me to say, *How's Dad?* Or, *Let me say "hi" to Dad.* We didn't have that kind of relationship.

In hindsight, that may have been a red flag for Leo.

After things went south with Leo, I started therapy with Gopika. But I laid down some ground rules. One—we needed to set goals, like a job. What are we trying to accomplish and how do we get there? Two—I'm willing to do the work, I said. Leo and I both had the same tendency to apply real-world strategy (mine work, his school) to relationships that required more of an emotional component.

"Oh, so you want therapeutic tasks?" Gopika asked.

"Yes," I responded, feeling like I had handled this first session well.

Sometime later, Gopika gave me an assignment: Go home for Thanksgiving and ask your parents if anything happened to you as a child. Anything out of the ordinary. Already I could tell she thought it was out of the ordinary that I had no memories before the age of four. Typically, first memories form between two and four years old, but my earliest memory is of dangling over the banister. So, either I was missing some early childhood memories or Gopika was overreacting. Still, I was happy to go home for Thanksgiving.

I'm so tired of replaying this scene, I could write it in my sleep. After Thanksgiving dinner, the guests had left, Mom was in a caftan, barefoot in the kitchen, and we were doing the dishes together. She asked me if I was dating anyone. I said, "Funny you should ask, because my therapist wants me to ask you if anything happened to me as a baby that I don't know about. Anything that might, you know, have something to do with me and ... men." I don't think "intimacy issues" was in my lexicon at the time. I was sure she'd say no anyway; it was all so stupid.

Instead, she said, "I knew this day would come."

Of all the responses I imagined hearing from my mother, this was not one of them. Not by a long shot. *Therapy! Sweetie, there's nothing wrong with you that a new dress wouldn't fix.* That, I could hear her saying. Or *Have you thought about growing your hair? It looks so much prettier long.* Even the suggestion of a nose job wouldn't have surprised me. *It's not too late ...*

She may have known this day was coming, but I was not prepared.

Lois put down the dish towel and stepped into the hall. Albert, she yelled, using my dad's full name, your daughter has something to discuss with you. He was already in bed. When he didn't respond, she walked down the hall and into their bedroom to wake him up. I went into the den and sat cross-legged, yoga-style, on the couch. It felt surreal. Like when the main character in an art film is in freeze-frame as the world swirls around her. My mom came into the den first; a few minutes later, my dad shuffled in wearing slippers and a robe. They each pulled up a chair to sit across from me. Even the seating arrangement indicated a seismic shift in position. I was on the cream couch, and they were in the uncomfortable chairs facing me.

"Your daughter is in therapy," Lois began, "and she wants to know what happened when she was a baby." Albert nodded his head, staring at the floor. His robe was brown and black striped, very masculine. But his exposed calves were bare and pasty. He seemed shrunken without the accoutrements of manhood—the suit, the jacket and tie, the buttons and cuff links. The wallet and keys.

Tell her, she insisted.

He said nothing. He looked tired, his boom gone.

So she spoon-fed him the words and that's how the story came out. In dribs and drabs. Her accusing him, his head hung low, like a dog who got caught chewing his owner's Italian leather boots. I'd seen my mother angry before, detected a nasty tone in her voice, heard raised voices and slammed doors, but this was different. Her tone was measured. Lois was in therapy mode, but there was no therapeutic neutrality. Her entire presence was that of a scold, finger wagging in his face.

"Go ahead," she insisted, pressuring him. "Tell her that you never wanted her."

And that's how I heard my origin story—she egging him on, he acknowledging her story as the truth. In court this would be called *leading the witness* and someone would object. But there was no one here to object. I felt like a bystander watching a tennis match, my head whipping back and forth, first to her for the accusation and then to him for his non-verbal response.

"Tell her about the day she was born. How you made the nurse take her out of my hospital room." He nodded "yes" obsequiously. "Tell her what you said," she insisted. Then, when he said nothing, she said it for him: *It's either me or the baby*. Making him nod his head to confirm the words. My bull of a dad had transformed into a sheep right before my eyes. It went on like that for I don't know how long. I began to understand that I was a pawn in their relationship. It wasn't even about me. I was a fight that began before I was born and lasted my whole life.

I thought, *Fucking Gopika*.

Because it might have been easier to carry on with the joke about me being an accident. The whole thing about my siblings and cousins being born in pairs, two by two by two. Two boys and a girl in their house, two girls and a boy in our house, our houses on the same street, two doors apart. Then came me.

Rocking the onesie. I was comfortable with this story, though it only hinted at the truth—that I was unwanted by my father and an act of defiance by my mother. An argument in the making. When my mother chose to have a fourth child, I became the third rail in their marriage. The deal they struck was that he would cover my expenses, but I would be *her* child. My existence was not to disrupt his life or their marriage.

Not to be heard or seen.

No wonder she didn't protect me—she couldn't. The politics of my position in the family were complicated; her power only went so far. My father would not get involved. It had nothing to do with me: the way I dressed, my big mouth or dirty room, that I talked back or broke the rules, my politics or religion, that he believed in God and I was a humanist, that I was progressive and he was conservative, that I moved to Boston and he valued community, that he believed "my country right or wrong" and my allegiance was more conditional, that he was a veteran and I was a peacenik, that I was a communist or democratic socialist. Neither of us was. Nor were we Zionists. There were no settlements or land to fight over. There was no right or wrong, they were both right and wrong. In having me, an intractable decision had been made.

It was an ancient argument that I had absolutely nothing to do with yet had everything to do with me. In that way, my entire life coincides, symbolically, with Israel. Before I even opened my mouth or took my first step, it was my very existence that incited the conflict between my parents. And, although I looked like my sisters, had my mom's peachy complexion and Bert's big ears, still ... I didn't really belong in this family. I did not have a shared childhood experience with my siblings in the same way that I don't have a shared life experience with white Christian

America. In that moment of clarity, I disliked both of my parents equally—the one who loved me perhaps more than her marriage itself and the one who viewed me as an unnecessary expense, and, subconsciously, a threat to his power.

The next day I flew back to Boston, took a cab to my apartment, stripped off my clothes, and crawled into bed just in time for the dam to break. Alone in my dinky 4th-floor walkup in the North End with the stove that doubled as a heater and the empty fridge, curled up in a ball, my knees tucked into my chest, hands covering my face, I lay sobbing. Memories flooding back to me. My eyes closed, I could see myself as a child, in shorts and a T-shirt, my hair long and tousled, riding a bike, holding a frog, petting the dog, smiling. Always smiling. I was happy. Not just happy but cute. I was a cute little kid. Curled up in a ball, immersed in a stream of images of my childhood self, repeating to myself, as if a mantra, this new discovery: I was cute. *I was cute. I was cute. I was cute.* I was neither bad nor angry; I was a cute little girl.

When I told Gopika what happened, she nodded her head, explaining that in therapeutic terms, this was called a cathartic experience. We're just getting started, she said. I know she wanted to help me process this information. Peel back the onion, layer by layer. But I was terrified of Gopika: someone who wasn't seduced by my sense of humor and false bravado, someone capable of seeing through the defense mechanisms that took years to develop, someone with the power to reach into my past and slice me open. Mostly, I was afraid of what else there was to discover, so I never went back to Gopika. And I never went home for the holidays again. Gopika may have seen this as a psychological breakthrough, but I experienced it as a rupture. It was too much information.

My mother was strong-minded and a gambler—casinos and the stock market. I'm sure she thought Albert would come around once I was born. *Who doesn't love a baby?* But Albert was a man of his word, and when he told his wife that the baby would be her responsibility, he meant it. Her saying, "Your dad really loves you," was wishful thinking, a cover-up, a white lie meant to make me feel better, to feel like I belonged. But the unintended outcome was that she reframed the word "love" to encompass neglect. She meant well, but her lies contradicted my lived experience. When someone makes you question your perception of reality, it's called gaslighting.

Here's where I connect my lived experience of being the unwanted child to being Jewish. What's the big deal, society insists: *You're white, you have privilege.* The big deal is that throughout history white Christians have murdered Jewish people. From the Spanish Inquisition to the pogroms to the Holocaust to the Tree of Life Synagogue in Pittsburgh. Jews are seen as a group of people existing outside the dominant culture who can be identified and targeted. When someone tells me I'm white because of the color of my skin, but I know in my bones, from history and personal experience, that when push comes to slaughter, or the economy falters, I am not *really* white, and the *not really* factor is being Jewish, that, too, is a form of gaslighting. Having grown up in a family where I was othered, I know how it feels to be tolerated, officially part of the family—smile, click, you're in the group photo—but when there are no cameras around, gone, too, is the family vibe. I understand that as the United States leans further into becoming a White Christian Fundamentalist nation, my welcome here may be over. And I may have to join my people in a long, storied history of diaspora.

Passing

ON MY WEDDING DAY I joked that I wasn't sure if the marriage would last, but that no matter what happened, I was never giving up the name Marcie Maxfield. I liked the alliteration. It sounds like a stage name. Scrubbed clean of ethnicity. My family name is Blumberg. The two 'B's stumble over each other on the way out of the mouth, landing with a harsh thud. It's softer in German—*Blumenberg*—which means "flower mountain."

In the United States, the name Blumberg just means Jewish.

Names are important in the Jewish community. They signify being a member of the tribe. The first thing out of my mother's mouth when I told her I had met my husband, the guy I was going to marry, was: *What's his name?*

"Harry," I said. "You'll like him, he's polite."

"That's nice," she replied. "What's his last name?"

"I don't know."

"You don't know his last name?" she hollered through the phone wires from Detroit to Boston. That scream said it all.

What do you even know about this boy? Who are his people? Have I not raised you properly? The last name is everything!

In a way, names are an identity clue—Jewish or not? Although, one can't rely on this system because you could be Betty Smith and belong to The Club. Betty was a friend of my mother's. There's this myth that Jewish last names were Americanized at Ellis Island because the immigration people couldn't spell Polish, Lithuanian, Hungarian, et al. surnames. Like it was a clerical course correction. *Oh, your name is Churelutszky; we'll change it to Cohen.* Simple. Only, not accurate. Many Jewish immigrants petitioned to change their own names *after* they were already living in America. In part, for simplification. Also, to assimilate and increase their chances of success by being less easily identified as Jews.

Anyway, at the time, I had more pressing concerns, like whether I would ever see this boy again. Not only did I not know his last name—I didn't have his phone number, either. We had met on the ferry from Boston to P-Town. I don't recall what he was wearing. All I remember is the hair: this outrageous punk-rock mohawk with bleach-blonde wings shaved into his scalp. Even his eyebrows were bleached white. That's why, when he tried to strike up a conversation with me, my first instinct was to ignore him. His hair was a red flag that signaled serious commitment to a questionable style trend, and I was thinking, *Why do guys who look like this hit on me?*

I was with a group of East Coast preppy girls I had met through work. Pearls and Ponytails. They were talking to some stockbrokers in khakis and boat shoes. I didn't think I looked different from them, but it's all in the details. The other girls were wearing blouses and Bermuda shorts, and I was in cut-offs and a T-shirt. Harry describes meeting me like this: "Something about her looked out of place. Actually, everything about her looked out of place: Her hair was a mess, her T-shirt was too tight, her shorts were really short, and she looked bored as hell. I felt like I was rescuing her."

In a way, he was. It was cold on that boat. I was not properly dressed for being on the water, no sweater draped over my shoulders, so when he offered to buy me hot coffee in a Styrofoam cup, I said yes. We talked non-stop the entire ferry ride—mostly about sea stuff: boats, the tide, fishing. And lobsters. Lobsters mate forever, he told me. He also told me how some lobsters crawl out of their shells to grow bigger ones. In between the old shell and the new one, they're vulnerable to all kinds of prey; they literally risk dying in order to grow.

"They're called shedders," he said.

"Shedders," I repeated. "I know the feeling."

I had been living in Boston for less than a year. It felt a bit like drifting at sea—bewildered, clueless—and a lot like being between shells. When I left Detroit, I had shed pretty much everything I knew to be life: family, friends, a sense of home and career. "Rudderless" would have been a good word to describe my life at the time. I could barely afford the rent, and I was dancing for my supper on Sundays to supplement a full-time job in advertising sales that did not cover my living expenses.

When we docked in P-Town, he shook my hand, hoisted his backpack onto his shoulders, and said, *See ya around.* We didn't exchange last names or phone numbers, but I kept thinking about him all day, and by the time I got back to Boston, I knew I wanted to see the guy with the mohawk again. That's when I called my mom and I told her, in jest, that I'd met "my husband." It wasn't like fireworks, pow, love at first sight. It was more like a slow fuse, an hour-long conversation with a stranger that felt more comfortable than any first date I'd ever been on. Plus, he was on his way to help his grandmother with household chores. Guys don't come much nicer than that.

"You know nothing about him," my mother said. "Call me when you find out his last name."

I figured I'd run into him. Boston is a small town. And then, as if the universe was conspiring to make it happen, the day after I met the boy with the mohawk, *The Boston Phoenix* came out with an article on the music scene in Kenmore Square and there he was, on the cover of the Entertainment section, standing outside an iconic punk club called The Rat. Wearing cutoffs and a ripped sweatshirt. "That's him!" I screamed, jumping up and down, waving the paper around like the apartment was on fire.

"Him, who?" my roommate, Cleo, asked.

"The guy I met on the boat. The one with the hair. It must be a sign!" I declared with optimistic certainty.

Cleo grabbed the paper from me, ripped out his picture, and stuffed it into her purse. That girl carried a purse the size of a suitcase. God knows what she lugged around with her, probably tiger ears and a change of clothes. I didn't ask. I swear I do not know what possessed me to let her move in, but she paid half the rent most of the time.

"I'm going to The Rat tonight," she said. "I'll look for him. Wanna come?"

I declined because I had to get up early for work the next day, but I owe her a huge debt because she found my husband for me. Well, sort of. She brought home two guys from The Rat that night, a guy for her and his friend who was tagging along. He and I ended up talking about relationships, fate, and the boy I met on a ferry. It was that guy, the one Cleo brought home as an extra, who gave Harry my number—which I had written on a scrap of paper, in eyeliner, with instructions to give it to the guy with the mohawk if he ever ran into him at a club.

Two days later, he did.

Within a week Harry and I were at the movies together, the lights down low, his face in silhouette. All I could see were the clean strong lines of his profile. I could tell that underneath the ridiculous hair, he was a good guy. Plus, I liked how trustworthy he looked in the dark. I knew he was solid, that he was the kind of guy who would be there forever, from the moment I caught a glimpse of his profile in the dim light of the Essex movie theater.

Sometime later, after I'd met Harry's father, his mother, his aunts, his sister who lived in New York, and two cousins (one in boarding school and another with red hair), his best friend Chip, and the guys in the band he was a roadie for, which is to say, after we were way more than a minor fling—I met his grandmother, Roz. He introduced me as his girlfriend, Marcie. Sounding a lot like my mother, the first thing out of her mouth was, "What's your last name?"

"You're Jewish!" she exclaimed when I told her my name was Blumberg. She said it with warmth, as if I were a long-lost relative, like she might clasp me to her bosom, fold me into her floppy arms in an awkward embrace. Then she told me she was Jewish, too. I looked at Harry. We weren't married, but we'd known each other long enough for me to meet most everyone in his family, and yet, somehow, I didn't know they were Jewish.

No one had mentioned it.

I didn't have to tell people I was Jewish; My last name telegraphed my identity. But Roz's last name was

Mortimer-Maddox. Very WASPy sounding. Hyphenated. I assumed she was a Mortimer and Harry's grandfather was a Maddox. Also, I thought, *That's so cool: she's super ahead-of-her-time feminist.* It didn't occur to me that both her last names belonged to her husband, the minister, and that Roz might be passing as not Jewish. She asked me where my family was from.

"Russia on my dad's side and Hungary on my mom's," I told her.

"I'm Hungarian, too," she exclaimed. She wanted to know where in Hungary. I said Budapest because that's what my grandma liked people to think—that she was from the big city. It sounds ritzier than Beregszász, which was a peasant town that's now called Berehove and is in Ukraine. It's hard to keep up with European geography; the borders keep shifting.

I liked Roz instantly. She reminded me of my Grandma Molly, short and round-faced, with a cheeky smile. They both had that Old World off-the-boat-in-a-babushka look. She made us tea, we chatted about gardening, and then Harry said we had to get going.

"So, you're Jewish," I said to Harry as soon as we got in the car, laying on a heavy Yiddish inflection so it sounded more like a question that ended with an exclamation point than a statement. He kind of, sort of, did look like he could be Jewish. Whatever that means. He's got blue-green eyes, and his nose is long and has a slight bump, although not as pronounced as my dad's, who had blue-gray eyes. Or my sisters, who both had nose jobs. Which is, let's face it, another kind of passing.

My mom called me at work once, all remiss, apologizing for never having offered me a nose job when I was a teenager. "We gave Trish and Chicky nose jobs," she said. The implication being: *and they are both married.* There was this not-so-subtle subtext to the conversation, as if my nose might be the reason that I was still single. I hung up the phone and ran to the ladies' room to check out my profile in the mirror, from all angles, as if seeing it for the first time, wondering, *Do I need a nose job?* I'd never really considered it before, never once mentioned wanting one, whereas Trish and Chicky couldn't wait to have their noses done. Trish's nose job was perfection, but Chicky's a little less so, and as a young girl observing the results of my big sisters' cosmetic surgeries, even if I *had* wanted one, I didn't trust the downward-trending success rate.

It's dangerous to pick apart one's facial features as if they were an accident of genetic arrangement. Anyway, I was not unhappy with the sum of the parts of my face. I was, however, tired of being alone. And Harry seemed like a nice guy. A nice Jewish boy. Even if he didn't know it.

"No," Harry said with absolute certainty. "I'm not Jewish. My grandmother is, or technically speaking, she was, then she married an American minister from England and became Episcopalian."

"It doesn't work that way," I said. "You know that, don't you?"

I didn't go into the whole Jewish law thing about how Judaism is matrilineal, and if your mother is Jewish, then you're Jewish, too. How it's an ethnic/genealogical-based religion, and the mother's womb is the connective tissue of Jewish identity. It's the baby momma who defines bloodline because, back in the day, before paternity tests, you couldn't be sure who the father was. Also, on a more practical level, when the menfolk went off to war, they left the women at home with the kids and in charge of their religious upbringing. Or, that a child born to a Jewish mother will forever be a member of the tribe, no matter what his or her religious beliefs or practices are. Or, how the Nazis used a familial matrix to identify, target, and kill Jews.

His grandma being Jewish makes Harry's mother half Jewish by Christian standards and full-on yid by Jewish law, so that makes my husband either one-quarter Jewish or one hundred percent Jewish, depending on how you calculate ethnicity—bloodline or upbringing.

"It's not a big thing in my family," Harry insisted. "No one ever talks about it."

That's what makes it a big thing, though. The *not* talking about it, the sweeping it under the rug, the hiding of this one detail surrounding his grandmother's immigration to the United States from Hungary. It may have been a life-or-death family decision, a form of escape. The Mortimer-Maddox-Maxfields weren't just raised Christian; they did not even mention the Jewish side of their family. To me, it seemed like their silence was an act of whitewashing their family history.

Roz had three daughters: Harry's mom, her twin sister, and their baby sister, Mara. All daddy's girls. The twins looked like their dad, thin and angular. But Mara looked like Roz—round-faced and cheeky. One night, over way too many sips of Port, Mara told me that, growing up, the twins didn't even know their mother was Jewish. Why would they? They were raised in the church as the minister's daughters. Then, when they were preparing for cotillion, they found out they were Jewish the hard way. The twins were not allowed to have, or even be invited to, those parties. It was all about white gloves and white Christian girls coming out in society.

It didn't occur to me to ask how anyone found out, but I doubt the minister would have outed his wife and kids.

Perhaps birth certificates were required, which would have documented Roz's maiden name, Holtz. More likely, some confidant knew and exposed the family secret, which was really a foundational lie.

This may sound like an archaic tradition, so what, boo-hoo; poor minister's daughters couldn't put on fancy dresses and go to, much less *have*, a coming-out party. But I know how important it is to be accepted by your classmates and invited to their parties. Harry's mom and aunt were about the same age as I had been when I was paired up with Ira, a Jewish boy in middle school; the message being: *Stick to your own kind and don't mingle with the good Christian boys.* On top of this, *they* had no Jewish community to fall back on. So I can imagine how devastating this would have been for the twins—to be outed and othered as Jews—and why they locked themselves in their room, crying, for weeks. I doubt they ever forgave their mother for ruining their teenage lives by being exposed as a Hungarian Jew. This may explain why the twin who was to become my mother-in-law seemed less than thrilled about her son marrying a girl whose last name was Blumberg.

There's a town named Blumberg near the Black Forest. I drove through it when I was backpacking in Germany during college. Suddenly my name had roots—a village with trees and rolling hills, a museum, six churches, and two castle ruins. It got me so excited that I asked the guy driving to stop the car, just so I could take a picture of the sign that read: Willkommen in Blumberg. Later I called my father with "news" of my discovery.

"Dad!" I yelled into the phone. "There's a town in Germany with our last name. Is that where your family was from?"

"I'm Russian," he said, before passing the phone to my mom.

Oh, yeah, I realized, feeling stupid. How did I not know that? But, honestly, how would I have known? We didn't have any Russian relatives that I knew of. My grandparents on my dad's side died before I was born, and before them it's like a black hole in the family tree. Sure, now and then, my mother would tease my dad and call him a Russki, which I thought was slang but is, in fact, derogatory. But no one ever explained why someone with a German last name would be from Russia.

Anyway, I didn't go to Europe seeking heritage. I went to eat baguettes in Paris, art-gawk in Italy, and castle-hop in Germany. Superficially, I understood that we were Jewish. Humanistic, not Reform. Ashkenazi, as opposed to Sephardic. But those were just labels. All that *Ashkenazi* meant to me as a young girl was that I had peachier skin, a rounder face, and frizzier hair than my friend, Maia, who I assumed was Sephardic, meaning from somewhere like Spain or Morocco, maybe even Turkey. Somewhere warm, that would explain her olive complexion, which looked like a year-round tan, and feathery black hair. All the boys thought she was cute. It would be decades before I learned that Maia was Ashkenazi like me. That you can't necessarily look at a Jewish person and tell if they are Ashkenazi or Sephardic, or even if they are Jewish. Because if it weren't for her last name, Stein, you might think she was Mexican.

Then again, just to confuse the issue, there are a lot of Mexican Jews, many from Spain and Portugal, who had escaped the Inquisition. During the Spanish and Portuguese Inquisitions in the 15th and 16th centuries, Jews were imprisoned, tortured, killed, forced to leave the country, or convert to Catholicism. Others, called "Crypto-Jews" or "conversos," practiced Judaism in secrecy. Closeted Jews. They hid in the closet so their neighbors wouldn't see them when they lit candles and said prayers. That is the furthest thing from what I can imagine myself doing. I wouldn't bother to light candles in secret. My attachment to being Jewish is cultural, not religious. That's why I am such a firm believer in the separation of Church and State, and watch in horror as Christian nationalism takes hold in the U.S. Not because I don't want to be forced to practice Judaism in secret, but because I don't want to be forced to adhere to Christian practices in public.

None of this shed any light on the issue of my German last name. To be honest, I didn't give it much thought. Somewhere along the line, call it Tribal Knowledge, someone told me that German Jews were conscripted by Russia as slaves, and I thought, *Oh, so that's how it happened.* Adding to that my own reductive spin on Jewish history: *Then they got hit with the pogroms and scattered throughout Europe just in time for the concentration camps, the lucky ones emigrating to America or Israel.* This, of course, is an oversimplification of the Ashkenazi story. Like my father, I didn't want to delve into all that doom and gloom. What I wanted was a simple answer to why my dad's last name was German, and yet he was a Russian Jew.

I'm not sure there is a short answer to the thousands of years Jews moved around Europe, avoiding persecution. A more on-point explanation about Jewish names is that in the 18th century the Austro-Hungarian Empire required that Jewish people take German last names. It was an attempt to build a nation-state, collect taxes, etc. And possibly, on some level, to force Jews to assimilate. Ironically, with all the European Jews floating about the United States, it has had the exact opposite effect: Our German names identify us as Jews.

While it is true that some Ashkenazi Jews with German last names migrated to Russia, got hit with the pogroms, and then scattered throughout Europe just in time for the concentration camps, there were other ways out of Russia. One was through China. From Siberia to Manchuria, in blistering wind chill, Russian Jews migrated to the city of Harbin when Russia built the railway connecting the two countries. Opting to freeze their butts off in exchange for better social status, the Jewish population in Harbin grew from hundreds to between ten and fifteen thousand residents. In some ways, China was a get-out-of-jail-free card. That's how Russian Jews ended up settling Harbin, bringing with them skills as shopkeepers and contractors along with their families, pianos, and ballet. In the early 1900s Jewish entrepreneurs, having escaped the pogroms in Russia, built Harbin's first hotels, banks, department stores, and synagogues.

I know this because when Harry got a job in Shanghai and we moved to China, I went to the Harbin Ice Festival with an acquaintance named Beth. We were only there for two nights; Beth organized the driver and hotel. I was most interested in visiting the Shangri-La Ice Palace Bar and Restaurant that looked like an igloo in pictures, the steam rising from bowls of spicy hot pot soup, consumed while wearing mittens and scarves, and then, after dinner, downing a shot of vodka at the ice bar. There was also a Museum of Jewish History and Culture in Harbin that I wanted to see.

"We might not have time to do everything we want to do in Harbin," Beth replied, when I suggested visiting the Jewish Museum. So much to do, so little time. Ice sculptures, a tiger feeding zoo, and arctic swimmers. She also wanted to visit the St. Sophia Cathedral, the largest Russian Orthodox church in the Far East, more than a century old. I acquiesced on the spot. It was automatic, this fallback position, to concede to the dominant culture.

Today, when I consider that I traveled to Harbin, which is practically in Siberia, and missed this Jewish Museum, it saddens me. At the time, it was nothing more than a reflex, another way of passing. *Do not make your Jewishness a big thing.* That said, I had an unexpected and revelatory experience at St. Sophia's, now a museum of art, history, and architecture. On exhibit was a photo display of the town's first settlers, and there, in black and white, were grainy images of Jewish families with curly dark hair, some combination of eyes and noses that looked very much like we could be related on my dad's side. Seeing these pictures made it real, and for the first time in my entire life, I felt connected to the Russian side of my family's heritage.

Bear with me, for a little more historical detour.

Eventually, things soured for Jews in Harbin, and they either moved on or suffered tragic fates. It's likely that some of those Russian Jews exchanged the harsh weather of Harbin for the economic promise of Shanghai, where there already existed a prominent Sephardic Jewish population from Baghdad. Shanghai was a safe harbor for international people without papers, so in the lead-up to WWII, with a new wave of Jewish Diaspora, paperless European Jews landed in Shanghai. Then, when Japan invaded Shanghai and allied with Nazi Germany, the Japanese military interned all Jewish people in the Shanghai Ghetto for the duration of the war.

Today, the Shanghai Jewish Refugees Museum is the only historical site in China that reflects Jewish life during the 1930s and 1940s. It includes a wall on which the names of more than thirteen thousand Jewish refugees are engraved, like the Vietnam War Memorial in Washington, DC—except these Jews survived. They had been displaced, squeezed into a ghetto less than a square mile in size, yet allowed to live. Among the names listed on the wall is Blumberg. Sandwiched between Jonny Blum and Ernst Blumenberg are Frieda Blumberg, Leib Blumberg, Martin Blumberg, Philipp Blumberg, and Ursula Blumberg. It's quite amazing to find your name on a ghetto wall in China. It has the impact of making history very concrete. I touched the wall, running my fingers over the names as if reading my family name in braille, gut-punched by how little I knew about the history of my people: my family and the Jewish people in a broader sense. I learned that if it weren't for the lack of resolve of the Japanese, these Jews would all have been murdered. But for some reason, although the Japanese viciously invaded China, they defied Hitler and allowed Shanghai's Jewish community to survive. After the war, most chose to leave China. Many went to Israel.

Here's what I imagine happened in my family: My dad's ancestors started out in Lithuania, part of the Russian Empire, where they bought the name Blumberg. They must have been rich because "beautiful" last names like *Flower Mountain* were the most expensive. Then some members of the family got sent to Siberia for bad behavior, meaning *just for being Jewish*. Eager to escape the pogroms, they fled Russia to settle Harbin. From there, they moved to Shanghai in search of the good life, only to wind up in the ghetto.

It could be true. Who knows?

My father never once talked about his parents to me, let alone his grandparents. Other than to correct me when I called from Germany to say I'd driven through his homeland. And

I never asked, because any such story would be born of flight and starvation, guns and salvation, and is best kept in the dark days of the past.

Who's gonna dredge that stuff up over dinner at The Club? No one. That's who.

Me? I'm from Detroit. Motown and the Tigers. There isn't an ounce of the Old Country in my persona. As a young woman I lacked any sort of attachment to a Jewish identity that should be held sacred, proudly on display like Black is Beautiful. Our features, our noses, and hair, required fixing and styling. They were never *in style* in their natural state. So, yeah. At first, I appreciated the lack of ethnicity the name Maxfield offered, at least on paper. I could send off a résumé without being typecast. But it hasn't stopped strangers from saying I remind them of a particular Jewish actress. Jewish and funny. A little bit bawdy. Or asking if I'm from New York. When what they are really asking is, *Are you Jewish?* So much for whitewashing my ethnicity. Even with the name Maxfield, I'm easily identifiable as Jewish. These days I embrace my identity. I would never light the candles in a closet. When Passover rolls around, we fling open the doors and invite our friends, Jewish or not, to join us in celebration.

Wasp's Nest

HARRY INVITED ME TO his parents' summer home in Maine. It sounded cozy and romantic, snuggling under a big puffy down comforter. We were in that can't get enough of each other phase, *every waking moment, on the phone, in a cab, on the metro, en route to a bar or show or club to hear some music.* Wherever we went, it was an all-out non-stop display of can't keep my hands off you.

"Sure," I said. "Sounds fun."

I was a little nervous about staying with his family, but I'd never met a family who didn't like me. I was personable. Chatty. I told great stories. I laughed a lot. Cleared the table and helped with the dishes. I was clean. Polite. A good guest. Smart, college-educated, from a respectable family in the Midwest. Gone to all the finest schools. University of Michigan, summer abroad in Spain.

His mother, Nan, greeted us at the door. "You must be exhausted," she exclaimed, exaggerating the ordeal of driving from Boston to Maine, making it sound like we had crossed the desert on foot. *How long did it take? Are you hungry? I made some divine "sammies" with cucumbers and mayo. Or do you prefer tomato aspic? It's Harry's favorite. Would you like some water, dear? Fizzy or flat? We're having lobs for dinner. From Waterman's.*

It was a verbal onslaught of hostess jabber. Not to mention a lot of insider lingo. *Lobs. Sammies. Waterman's.* I was barely inside the screen door and already feeling super uncomfortable. *This is not going to be chill,* I realized. Also, it was not a summer home—it was more like a cabin. Wooden planks nailed together to create the floor, walls, and roof. Hats, purses, sweaters hanging on rusty nails like a tetanus landmine. It reminded me of summer camp, which I loved but hadn't been to since I was a kid. My tastes had evolved. I had become a person who enjoyed some modicum of creature comfort. *Drywall would be nice.*

There was stuff everywhere, stacks of magazines—*The New Yorker* and *The New York Times*—piled on the floor behind the couch, which Harry's dad, an artist, designed and built. There was a mattress on top, covered in a quaint bedsheet, floral. Wooden ships and ducks, dozens of white porcelain pitchers and blue-glazed decorative dishes were displayed on horizontal pieces of wood that held the studs, i.e., the framing, in place. Tin plates and bowls and chipped china on open shelves in the kitchen, catching dust and bugs. It was rustic and charming, and obsessive-compulsive, all at once.

"Why don't you take her to the shed, dear?" Nan suggested to Harry.

The shed? I thought, conjuring horror movies in the woods. Strangers with paper bags over their heads lurking about in the dark. But it was pretty much what you'd imagine a shed to look like—bunk beds, lumpy mattresses, ratty electric blankets. No ax in the corner. I looked at the electrical outlet, exposed and unprotected, attached to a wooden plank next to the bed and cringed. This had to be intentional, the unfinished decor, as if a new mattress would be *too too too bourgeois, darling*. At least there was a toilet in the shed. I stared into the tarnished mirror above the sink, black clouds forming at the edges, my hair starting to frizz from the salty ocean breeze. *Already, this weekend was waaaaaay too long.*

"What's tomato aspic?" I teased Harry.

"You won't like it," he said, squeezing me in a hug. Then, letting go of my waist, he suggested we mosey over to the house.

Mosey? Did my punk rock boyfriend just use the word "mosey?" I declined his invitation, saying it had been a long drive. "I'm gonna rest a minute," I demurred, lying. I had no intention of lying down. Instead, I sat on the bottom bunk, sinking into the mattress sag, and gave myself a pep talk. *It's not like we're stuck here*, I thought. *Tomorrow we'll drive into town. Find a pub, have a beer. There must be a pier somewhere.* But the next day came and went, and we did not leave the property. We slept in the shed at night and hung out on the deck during the day, ate dinner early, and when the sun went down, we huddled by the fire in the cabin. Okay, the view was amazing, the air pristine, the water sparkled through beech trees in the distance. Maine was growing on me.

Harry's dad was a cross between a lobster fisherman and an artist. He had a seaman's beard and weathered skin. He'd built this cabin by hand, every plank and nail hammered by him and his son. It was a labor of love. He was also a sculptor, and his pieces were scattered all over the place, next to the ducks and wooden ships. Delicate marble buttocks, brass penises, vulva molded in plaster that teetered on stems and undulated. Also a labor of love, one that I've come to appreciate. But back then I had no idea what to say, where to look, what to touch, or how to comment. No frame of reference for this beyond shabby chic cabin or its overflowing contents. The "eclectic" mix of refined erotic art and bric-a-brac from Goodwill.

Meanwhile, my hair was getting frizzier by the hour. I could almost feel it crimping and coiling. Forget the dust, the dirt, the damp, my biggest concern was my hair. Should I wet it, try to tame it with product and blow it dry? Or wrap a scarf around my head? Maybe a baseball cap? It was too short to pull back in a ponytail. All I could think was, *if I could just get my hair to look like theirs, stick-straight, then maybe I could relax and fit in.*

At night it was so cold I curled up in a ball and jammed my hands in my armpits to get warm. I always think of Anne Frank when I'm cold, sort of a reality check—like, *Girl, you have nothing to complain about.* She was sent to the camps in the fall and didn't die until March. It breaks my heart, not just her dying, but that bone-chilling winter-in-Europe for months with nothing to protect her from the bitter reality. The prolonged suffering. And here are these people who could well afford to slap up some insulation and drywall to provide a bit of creature comfort but, for some reason, chose to suffer.

During the day, though, the warmth of the sun made it bearable. Conversations centered around highbrow snooty stuff like art, food, and literature. Harry's aunt was a fact-checker at *The New Yorker,* and I was sure his mom read *The New York Times* book reviews as CliffsNotes for dinner conversation. I was reading *Interview with a Vampire*, which I kept hidden in the shed like a guilty pleasure. No one talked about the background soundtrack of jazz and classical music because it's not meant to be commented on; it was used as ambiance to imply a cultural aesthetic. Call me Neanderthal but, growing up in Detroit and having worked in the music industry, I had an almost encyclopedic knowledge of Motown, soul, and rock music. Music with lyrics and a beat, music that makes you wanna get up and move. That's why I didn't mind dancing at the club; it was all about the music for me. I spent hours making the perfect playlist. As far as I was concerned, playlists were an art form.

"Doesn't it bother you to know men are looking at you?" Harry's sister, Kay, asked.

Oh great, I thought, *so Harry told his sister I was a dancer! And now they all know!* We were sitting on the deck watching the waves, the sun bouncing off the water. I was wearing a Pretenders T-shirt and ripped jeans. Kay was wearing a shapeless pullover and sweats, her thin blonde hair cropped short, her pale skin bluish from veins, her tone of voice more bored than curious. Kay was a daddy's girl. She reminded me of my sister Trish, calling our dad "Pop." They had their dads wrapped around their little pinkies, so I knew she wouldn't understand my refusal to ask my father for financial help. Also, although Harry's family was by no means wealthy, these were people for whom even the appearance of striving was déclassé. And dancing at Club 66 was the definition of striving. I was struggling, clawing, hip-popping my way to independence. In any event, I suspected she wasn't interested in my response; she just wanted to ask the question about men watching me dance.

"Truth is," I told her, "I don't even notice them."

When I danced, I was in my head. I wasn't ashamed of my body. I was ashamed of my hair frizzing uncontrollably, my last name, my ethnicity. My country club upbringing. Being Jewish, from the Midwest, hopelessly out of place in this WASPy East Coast environment where plastic vaginas were displayed as art, but real women's bodies were considered taboo.

Somehow, by the end of that weekend, it felt as if I had won over Harry's mom. Maybe it was because I'm a good kitchen helper, although his aunt did admonish me to use more soap and hotter water. And then, boom, six weeks later Harry moved to California. To find himself. It was one of those meet-cute, fall fast, and say goodbye too soon relationships. I've always been tempted to write a rom-com, like *When Harry Met Sally*, only in reverse, but this *JewGirl* idea is a scab I can't stop picking at.

After Harry moved, Nan adopted me. She invited me to her champagne and oyster birthday brunch in Boston and Christmas with the red plaid tablecloths and roast beef. I even house-sat for my future in-laws when they went to Los Angeles to visit their son. He was dating someone else by then. They all went to Mexico for the weekend—Harry, his parents, and the new girlfriend. When she returned, Nan invited me for drinks and a gab.

"Bring Dani," she insisted.

Dani was my new roommate, short for Daniella, sometimes referred to as Crazy Dani. We worshipped together at the cosmetics counter; we prayed for the phone to ring; we survived on popcorn and wine and shared everything. Clothes, lipstick—there was almost no line where I ended and she began. Even our list of New Year's resolutions was the same: lose weight, talk less, more pie, get a raise, learn to cook, practice being soft.

Nan showed us pictures from her trip to California, her arm draped around the new girlfriend's shoulders, beaming.

"She looks sweet," Dani said, jabbing her elbow into my ribs, hardly able to contain herself. *Oh my god,* she whispered under her breath, *you are never getting him back!* Harry's mom held court at the kitchen island, shredding cheese, slicing veggies, crushing garlic for homemade gourmet pizza. We regaled her with tales of the single life. Dani told the story about her ex-boyfriend who started dating another girl who lived in our neighborhood.

"He didn't!" Nan said, chopping onions. She chopped like a chef; careful, efficient, fast, producing uniform slices of onion. No tears. She was wearing a Boston Ballet T-shirt, her hair long and natural, no makeup. Earthy but cool.

"Now I see his car parked on my street every time he spends the night at her place!" Dani moaned.

"The nerve!" Nan exclaimed, sliding the onions off to the side of the cutting board with the knife's edge before refilling our wineglasses. It was as if she were one of the girls. Then Dani told her about the time we had egged his car. It was a funny story, only *we* didn't egg his car. Crazy Dani slashed his tires. And I egged Leo's car. Leo was the nice Jewish boy who only took me out on Thursdays and Sundays. The one Dani insisted, but I refused to believe, was dating other women. One Saturday night we hid in the bushes across the street from Leo's apartment and watched as he pulled up in his fancy sports car, walked around to the passenger side like a proper gentleman, and opened the door for a girl who was not me. Not at all like me, even. She was wearing a dress with lots of cleavage. Here I was starving myself, as if he'd love me more if I weighed less, and there he was dating this woman who was poured into—and spilling out of—a tacky white halter dress with ruffles. Dani was practically bouncing up and down trying to get me to tell Nan about Leo. *Tell her about Sunday nights! Chinese takeout! The stakeout at the Ritz!* The Ritz was Dani's story; I was just her wingman. Dani's and my stories got mashed up for maximum impact.

We were like stand-up comedians. Funny. Colorful. A bit outrageous. And Nan loved us. She invited us to all her soirées.

At the time, I thought she liked us because Dani and I were fun—an entertaining but slightly deranged duo. Now I think what made us okay to have around is that I was Harry's *ex*-paramour. Emphasis on "ex." As in, a wild and crazy but short-lived phase. What Nan didn't perceive was that I was only hanging out with her to keep tabs on him via his family. I missed Harry and was holding on to the possibility of us. I liked to keep him (and his family by proxy) in my sights—a person of interest. *Sorry, Nan,* I thought, *don't get your hopes up. Harry is not going to marry the nice schoolteacher/librarian you took to Mexico.*

Years later, when Harry and I got engaged, everything changed. Overnight I became *that woman.* As in, my son will not marry *that woman.* I used to think it was because of those nights Dani and I spent drinking and oversharing at Nan's kitchen island. Or because I was, unfortunately, *when she met me,* an exotic dancer. It must have shocked her. To me, at the time, it seemed like a cool temporary gig for a rock-and-roll girl with rent issues. Still, despite Nan's super-chill, lefty-leaning, arty lifestyle, I worried that she couldn't get past the fact that I had been, for a very brief period, the *wrong kind* of dancer.

Now, when I think about it, all of it, everything that followed—the insults and slights and digs and false greetings and backhanded compliments—it all makes sense. The entire

Jewish side of her family, living in California, that she failed to introduce me to and declined to see when she came to visit. The way she pretended not to know how to pronounce the word *bar mitzvah* and called it a "bah mah whatzi. And then there was the infamous JAP joke.

It was never about me and Dani or the Combat Zone.

It was about me being Jewish.

It started with the wedding plans. Harry's mom wanted her father, the minister, to officiate, and I said no. I wanted Rabbi Wine. I'm going to be honest here, because there's nothing left to protect. I didn't even consider the idea of a minister at our wedding. Dismissed it out of hand. For one thing, the wedding is the bride's domain. It would be held in my parents' condo in Detroit, and the same rabbi who married my siblings would marry us. Nothing to discuss. But Nan asked a second time, this time circumventing me and going directly to Harry, asking if his grandfather could co-officiate at our wedding in my parents' condo. It wasn't just that I didn't know the minister and had never met him. I didn't want to be married by a minister. Being a Humanistic Jew, I didn't want any mention of God in our ceremony. Harry was in the middle of us, passing messages back and forth.

"My mom wants to know if my grandfather can marry us," Harry said. At the time, we were living in a cockroach-infested apartment in Los Angeles. I'd seen one of the neighbors take a piss on the side of our building. Just the fact that people were invested in the details of our wedding when our lives were so precarious made me want to laugh.

"I know," I replied. "She already asked me, and I said no."

Here's the thing about me and Harry. We had never had a serious conversation about the future. We both liked music.

He was more of a punk rocker, and I was more into soul. We wore the same style pants—Levi's 501 jeans with the buttons, no zipper. Different sizes. We shared T-shirts. Drank beer. Went to clubs and baseball games. He liked cartoons; I didn't understand them. And, most importantly, I have always felt comfortable being my authentic self in his presence. That was huge. We never talked about kids. I just assumed we'd have them someday.

Religion? We never discussed it. It had never once come up since the time I met his grandmother, and she told me she was a Hungarian Jew. That is, until we got engaged and my mom pointed out that my soon-to-be in-laws might be antisemitic, and I shrugged it off, attributing my mom's concerns to her outdated worldview that all Gentiles were somewhat antisemitic until proven otherwise.

"Harry," I said. "This is a deal-breaker. I'm Jewish and our kids will be Jewish."

"Whatever," he replied. "I'm an atheist."

"Thank God!" I laughed. Relief passed over me, flashing him my *we're getting married* smile. "You'll love Rabbi Wine. He is, too. An atheist, I mean."

But the damage was done. Harry's grandfather, presumably unhappy at being rejected, didn't attend our wedding. Roz, his grandmother, the Hungarian Jew who hid her Jewish identity from her daughters, *she* came. And my relationship with his mom shifted. In a way, we both came out of the closet. Me as a Jew, she as an antisemite.

We became adversaries.

Something else shifted. My relationship to Judaism became more real. This was the first time I had stood up for myself as a Jew and acknowledged, out loud, that my children would be raised Jewish. Non-negotiable. So, even though I joked about never giving up my married name—Maxfield—it was a complex choice. I didn't want to lead with my religious identity, or carry my father's name, stamp my religion on my résumé, but I didn't want to compromise it either. And I was most certainly, unequivocally, not trading Judaism for Christianity. There would be no mention of God at our wedding. Or in our children's upbringing.

But there would be Christmas and Santa Claus.

A few years later, Harry's family visited us in California. Nan walked in the door of our house carrying an apron and a jar of sun-dried tomatoes. When I tried to take them from her, she held on tight. These were not gifts; they were the tools of her trade. Behind her was my father-in-law, bearded and jolly, and behind them both was Harry with their luggage. It was two days before Christmas. This was the first time the in-laws had come to stay with us, and I wanted everything to be perfect. I was serving Honey Baked Ham, just like my mother did. Store-bought, always delicious. Glazed to perfection.

My mother-in-law had other ideas. The next day, she sent Harry to the market for the makings of a traditional Christmas dinner. And because I wanted his family to like me, was still struggling to feel like *his* family was *my* family, I was willing to forget about the ham and let Nan commandeer our kitchen. That's how my Honey Baked Ham got relegated to the lanai. Sounds Hawaiian, but we lived in a bungalow in Glassell Park, northwest of downtown Los Angeles. In place of a garage, we had a lanai—a porch with a roof, concrete floors, and criss-crossed open plank walls that were covered in bougainvillea, bright red, pretty to look at but dangerously prickly. That's where I hid the Honey Baked Ham when Harry's family came for Christmas.

"Don't forget the suet!" Nan reminded my husband as he headed out the door, on his way to the market to buy ingredients for the new menu: roast beef and Yorkshire pudding. She was standing at our kitchen sink wearing an apron she had brought with her. Then she turned to me and said, "You need your rest, dear. Scoot!" Out of the kitchen she pushed me, taking control.

The "rest" I needed was because I was pregnant with our second child. I curled up on the couch in the lanai with my daughter and the banished Honey Baked Ham, reading and napping, ignoring the bustle in the kitchen. The smell from the neighbor's garbage bins wafted through the open walls—yesterday's Mexican food—and I worried it would ruin the ham, which I wanted to eat right then because I was pregnant and hungry and didn't want to wait for Nan's roast beef dinner.

What the fuck is suet? I wondered.

I wanted *my* mother, and her store-bought Honey Baked Ham, mustard-glazed, sliced so thick you could eat it with your fingers. She hosted an annual Xmas Eve party for wandering Jews with nowhere to go, wore a bejeweled caftan, and played jazzy Christmas music. Frank Sinatra. Ella Fitzgerald. It was an intergenerational affair—kids smoking pot in the bedroom, adults drinking cocktails in the "lower level" (aka basement). My best friend, Maia, sneaking vodka into her virgin punch. Lois, always the center of attention, cigarette in one hand, cocktail in the other. It was a full-on holiday celebration. Not a stuffy sit-down dinner, the table set with a red tablecloth I didn't own that must have been packed in Nan's luggage and would probably be left behind, as a hint.

More laundry, I thought.

It was strange to be treated like a guest in my own home. On the surface it was meant to give me a break, but Nan is a woman best understood by reading between the lines. She was stealing *my* holiday like she thought I stole *her* son. We were engaged in a tug-of-war. I imagined pulling her hair, which she styled in a long braid like a schoolgirl, only it was gray. At some point, Harry's aunt and sister arrived. They swooped in, swathed in Christmas colors, all red and green, plaid and velvet. I was in this ultra-utilitarian black stretchy maternity outfit that I wore pretty much every day. Out of respect, I brushed my hair and put on some makeup. My father-in-law sat at one end of our table, my mother-in-law at the other. I'd spent Christmas with Harry's family before we got married; they were warm and cozy and crèche-filled. Nan clinked her glass with a spoon. Everyone turned toward her, the smock apron gone, replaced by a green silk blouse with a burgundy velvet ribbon in her hair. Her pale skin rouged, lips lacquered red like war paint. I expected a prayer. Grace. Something uncomfortably biblical. Instead, she launched into a JAP joke.

"How many JAPs does it take to change a lightbulb?"

For a moment, no one said anything. Not a word. Not even a gasp. The roast beef sat in the middle of the table, bleeding; the smell of charred animal flesh filled the room. There was a lone pea next to my knife that must have fallen from a serving dish. I picked it up and smashed it between my fingers. This is the exact moment when I understood that I would never belong in this family. Time froze. I looked at each of them, one by one, my sister-in-law with her dad's blonde hair, my mother-in-law cloaked in WASPy affect, velvet and ribbons, acting like she was a Daughter of the American Revolution, as if she could trace her lineage back to the Christian pilgrims—and not, as I knew her secretly to be, the daughter of a Hungarian Jewish immigrant.

Obscure fact: Only the female wasp stings. They are described as brightly colored stingers with narrow waists. I felt my pregnant belly protectively. My Jewish babies. No one stopped her, so Nan continued with the joke.

"It takes three," she said. Three JAPs to change a lightbulb. "One to whine. One to file her nails. And one to call Daddy."

Never mind that I was pregnant *and* working full-time at a music magazine while my husband was in-between jobs, picking up extra cash as a driver. They saw me as a JAP. A spoiled Jewish American Princess pushing their son to do better. The essence of this joke is the insinuation that Jewish girls are like hothouse flowers or heirloom tomatoes: cultivated, sheltered, precious. Fragile. That we couldn't survive in the real world without Daddy's help. I'd worked in bars and nightclubs, in a Chinese restaurant and a Greek coffee shop. I worked the candy counter at a movie theater in high school and cleaned a sorority house one semester in college. They had a pinball machine upon which my boss laid out lines of coke for me and some other girl. We turned up the stereo system and scrubbed the bathrooms with frenzied focus. And I was a dancer. The kind who got paid for drinking with the customers. I would take just about any job I could get rather than ask my father for a handout.

For a three-letter word, JAP packs a whole litany of antisemitic punch. It conjures an archetype of the Jewish girl as lazy, complaining, dependent, relying first and foremost on Daddy, and subsequently on her husband. She is comically aspirational, drawn to brand-name bags and baubles. Materialistic and shallow. And, yes, some Jewish girls are like this, but these attributes can be found in many cultures, from the Kardashians to that quintessential Daddy's Girl, Ivanka Trump. Still, the word persists as a specific slur against Jewish women.

Like the N-word, the J-word should only be uttered by someone Jewish. As in, *OMG, I feel like such a JAP today. I got a mani-pedi and then went shopping on Ventura Boulevard.* On my mother-in-law's tongue, the word was unacceptable. Not just because she was a self-hating Jew who didn't acknowledge her Jewish roots, but because she must have known better and said it anyway. My immediate reaction was shock.

Did she just tell a JAP joke? In my house? At my table? On Christmas?

Had she been there, *my* mother would have told me to laugh it off. Or she might have reminded me that she had warned me, before we got married, that my future mother-in-law was antisemitic. Which she did. But my mother thought everyone who wasn't Jewish was antisemitic. I chalked it up to generational bias, as if antisemitism were an ancient phenomenon. "It's not like that anymore," I responded, with all the naïveté of a girl head over heels in love. *Mom, don't ruin this for me, please!*

At the time of this Christmas dinner, Harry and I had been married for close to five years. I was no longer naïve or floating on a love cloud. When I think of that meal, I think of the silence surrounding that joke. As a Jew, I've been inculcated with the historical and synergistic relationship between silence and complicity. It's just as bad to say nothing, to look the other way, as it is to pull the trigger or tell the joke. Maybe worse. To tell the joke is ignorant and inappropriate, but to remain silent is not just a sign of tacit approval. Silence is what enables the trigger to be pulled, again and again, without getting your hands dirty. When you think, for instance, of the everyday citizens who looked the other way as millions of Jews were gassed and burned, the smell of human flesh wafting into their villages impossible to ignore. The sheer enormity of communities complicit in silence. Then and now. In today's political landscape, it's the people who vote for extremist politicians, cozy up to white Christian nationalists and neo-Nazis, who look the other way when immigrants are snatched off the streets in the U.S. and sent to prison in El Salvador and still, somehow, maintain that they are not racist or antisemitic, that it's about crime, economics, or family values.

That joke made me feel not just othered but targeted. I *had* been sort of lazy, holed up in the lanai while they were busy making Christmas dinner *their way*—roast beef and Yorkshire pudding. They came into our house as guests and took over, changing the entire menu. Was I supposed to offer to help and set the table?

I was infuriated with all of them, but mostly Harry, for not saying anything. Of course, I *can* stand up for myself, and that's what I did. Stood up and grabbed a carving knife from the kitchen counter on my way to the lanai for a slice of Honey Baked Ham. It felt like a bold move at the time but in retrospect, it was walking away from the problem. When Harry finally came out to see if I was okay, I told him his parents were not welcome in my home. "But it's Christmas Day," he protested. And, because I'm not a heartless bitch, I said, "Okay, they can spend the night. But tomorrow—they're gone."

A few months after that Christmas fiasco when my mother in-law told a "joke" instead of saying grace (and I kicked her out of our house), we got an invitation to a Holtz family reunion in Santa Monica. Harry was out of town, but I was intrigued. *Who were the Holtzes?*

I called my mom in Detroit to confirm, *Is Holtz a Jewish name?*

"Most likely," she said. "Why do you ask?"

Well, I told her, "It seems my husband has a secret stash of Jewish relatives living in Los Angeles and they're having a party."

Harry and I had been alone in Los Angeles. Without relatives. At least *I thought* we were without relatives. Now, it turns out, we had the Holtzes, and my curiosity was piqued. Harry was working on a cruise ship en route to Alaska, so I went in cold—no background information, no clue who they were or how we were related.

It's funny how you don't know you're in a life-changing moment when it's happening. This was L.A. I worked in the music industry, went to lots of parties, chatted up strangers, and never saw them again. My expectations were low, especially where my in-laws were concerned. There were about twenty people seated at a long table, banquet-style. I recognized one woman from Boston, a redhead named Nell, as Harry's cousin ("second cousin," she clarified). She had been at our wedding. She waved and pointed to the seat next to her like she was holding a place for me. So I sat next to Nell and across from a Parisian woman with the most fabulous head of bushy blonde curly hair. She was wearing jeans and a striped boatneck T-shirt. Effortless chic. Next to her was a French woman from Morocco, dark hair and olive skin, with a thick accent. They were married to the Holtz brothers, whom I immediately nicknamed The Men with French Wives. There were artists, writers, filmmakers, and a lawyer from San Francisco.

Sephardic Jews. Ashkenazi Jews. French, North African, and Hungarian Jews. And Nell, the redhead, who was not a Holtz, but I think her mother might have been. Plus, the host, Josh, and his family—Jewy-Jews. A nicer way to say that would be *observant*. Or Modern Orthodox. And Lilith, the matriarch, from Ohio. Conversations layered and crisscrossed the table. I was immediately welcomed as one of the tribe.

The Holtzes gave me a crash course on their family tree. I remember straining to make sense of it all. What surprised everyone was that I didn't know a thing about them. An entire branch of my husband's family had been kept a secret. They filled me in on Harry's grandmother Roz's side of the family, the side of the family the Maxfields don't talk about: Jewish Hungarian immigrants. How the family moved to the United States from Hungary in the early 1900s. There were five kids in all. Two of the brothers settled in Cincinnati, and Roz married the minister and moved to New England. These people at the table, Nell and The Men with French Wives, were the next generation, Harry's contemporaries.

"You know, Roz," Nell said to me. I nodded my head yes. I knew she was Jewish but had forgotten her maiden name was Holtz. There I was at the reunion brunch with these amazing relatives who were trying to fill in the gaps and explain the Holtz family tree—generations of a family my mother-in-law had kept quiet about in a mad attempt to hide this one little detail from the world: She was Jewish.

My mother always said she was lucky my dad's parents died young. It was a blessing, she joked, meaning she didn't have in-laws to contend with. Tread lightly, she cautioned me on that phone call about the Holtz family reunion. But the first thing I did when I got home from brunch was call Nan, guns loaded. Sometimes I can be impulsive.

"Did you know we had relatives in Los Angeles?" I asked her. I said "we" because Harry and I are married, and, theoretically, his family is mine. But, of course, these were *my* people, not *hers*.

"Yes," Nan replied.

"Why didn't you tell me?" I asked. "I've been living here for almost five years, desperate for family, and all along you knew we had relatives out here? That there were homes where I would have been welcome for Thanksgiving and Christmas, Hanukkah and Passover, cousins for my kids to grow up with, and you didn't think to tell me?"

There was a long silence. And that was it; nothing more was said. One door shut, and a window blew open.

B-O-Y

I KNEW I WAS having a boy (call it mother's intuition). I didn't need amniocentesis to tell me the sex of my baby, but the doctor insisted. "Just to rule out the really bad stuff," he said. As if having a boy wasn't bad enough. Even though I did not want a boy, I did want a healthy baby. So, if it's possible to be relieved and anxious, both at the same time, that's how I felt when the test results arrived.

"We're having a b-o-y," I told my husband, spelling it out the way some people whisper bad words; things one shouldn't say in polite company. Harry is not a super-macho guy: He likes to cook *and* he does the dishes. He also loves baseball. I sensed that he would have been happy either way, pink or blue. But let's face it, of all the sports, like football, basketball, hockey and soccer, baseball is the girliest. Afternoon games are slow, the sun is shining, and the San Gabriel Mountains dot the horizon beyond Dodger Stadium. Baseball has the ambience of a family outing. It's all about hot dogs and peanuts. Bring the kids—daughters and sons.

The b-o-y.

"It will be all right," Harry tried to reassure me.

I wasn't so sure. My experience with boys was iffy, at best. There's the sexual assault, for one. My father was a gaping hole in my life, and my brother and I are more like frenemies. Siblinemies. In terms of male-female relationships, Harry is the shining star in my life, and he even hit me once. Only once, though, because I made it clear that shit would not be tolerated. We were driving home from the beach, listening to music. Harry was trying to control the radio. He wanted to leave it on KROQ, but I was channel surfing. He'd punch KROQ, I'd punch KCRW. He'd put it back on KROQ and I'd punch JACK FM. This went on for a few minutes, the battle of the car radio. I thought we were goofing around, and then Harry punched me in the arm.

And I went ballistic.

Practically crawling out of my skin, I undid my seat belt and opened the window, as if maybe I could fly away. "Stop the car!" I demanded. But he kept on driving, full of apology, saying he was sorry, that it was wrong, assuring me that it would never happen again. I was not hearing it; my system was on high alert, *Danger!* I was in fight-or-flight mode. I needed to get out of the car. *Right There and Then!* After I opened the door, threatening to jump out of a moving vehicle if he didn't slow the fucking car down, he pulled over and I escaped while he was rolling to a full stop. "Where are you going?" he asked as I slammed the door shut. We weren't married yet; I had only just moved to California to live with Harry. I had no girl-friends to call, but I knew my way around L.A. well enough to catch a bus on Beverly Boulevard to Western Avenue, walking distance from our apartment.

I needed space, headspace. A crowded bus would be fine.

My reaction had been visceral. I remember thinking, *Oh, no, you don't. No one hits me ever again.* Harry slugging me in the arm triggered a sense memory of being hit as a kid, and not by my dad. Sure, our dad spanked Prince and me on Sunday mornings, but that was a ritual spanking. No one got hurt or even took it seriously. It probably had very little to do with anything Prince or I did. Even as a child, my understanding of those spankings was spot-on: that my dad was bigger and older than me, and nobody was going to stop him because he was the man of the house. I don't know what Prince's takeaway was. Maybe something similar? Something about age, strength, and gender. Other than those Sunday morning spankings, my father never hit me, but there were fights in our house. We were a scrappy bunch of kids, and when Harry punched me, he struck a familial nerve. I had an immediate gut reaction*: never again.* Which is, of course, the Jewish mantra: #NeverAgain. Never again will Jews be the victim.

It never happened again. Harry and I got married. It was bliss. We had a little girl. More bliss. Then, a few years later, I became pregnant with our son, and my maternal instincts went haywire. I was at war with my own internalized trauma. It felt as if I were carrying the enemy in my belly. Boys will be boys, my mother always said, but if that means choking their sisters until they turn white and almost pass out, no thank you. Not in my house. My daughter and I played tea party and dress-up. She'd hang out with me on deadline when I worked at a music magazine, enchanting my coworkers by flashing her magic smile and waving a peace sign. I taught her to write "Girl Power" on Post-it notes and let her wander through the office sticking them on everyone's desk or computer. We were content.

I thought all my babies would be girls.

The stork had other ideas.

"Is that him?" I asked. That was the first thing out of my mouth when Harry handed me our newborn son. It doesn't sound so bad until you compare it with my first words when Sasha was born. "She's perfect." See the difference? And it got worse before it got better. The maternity ward nurses left Sammy in a bassinet next to my bed. I pressed the buzzer and asked them to please return the baby to the nursery. When they didn't come get him fast enough, I limped into the hall, blood dripping down my legs from the C-section, and screamed, "Someone please take the baby." Not a pretty "new mother" moment. I was exhausted, uncomfortable, overwhelmed … and I just didn't love him.

Yet.

It took a day or two, maybe a week, before I fell for the b-o-y. Within a month I had nicknamed him my "Buddha Baby." He was sweet, fat, and innocent. The early years were dreamy as he transformed from Buddha Baby into Cuddle Bear. He was my son, my sun and my moon. My mother took to waving her pinky in my face when I bragged about him, how cute he was, and sensitive, too. It was Lois's way of pointing out that Sammy had me wrapped around his little finger.

So what, I thought, beaming. He was special. They were both special, Sasha and Sammy, but he was an unexpected source of joy. He was smart, funny, and ambidextrous—he wrote with his left hand and threw with his right. He loved to read and play with LEGOs. It was my son, not my daughter, who learned how to sew. In first grade, he made a sock monkey and took it to school for show-and-tell.

That's why it came as a shock when, in second grade, the boy-shit kicked in. It started in the Frontierland Store at

Disneyland. Sammy asked for a toy cap gun with a holster, just like Indiana Jones, and I said no. "YOU NEVER BUY ME GUNS!" Sammy screamed. All the other mothers stared at me: *Bad mommy, get control of your kid.* Rarely did I say no to this boy—ice cream, another half hour of TV, "five more minutes, please." It was always, "Okay, Okay, Okay." But there in the cowboy aisle on Main Street, I drew a line in the sand. No Guns. And he erupted like a two-year-old. Kicking and screaming.

A meltdown over toy guns is one thing: It's embarrassing. Then he started hitting girls. I treated it like an isolated incident the first time it happened. No biggie. The second time, when he elbowed a Japanese girl on the school steps, giving her a black eye, I was mortified. Not to mention that it was perceived as an international event with racial undertones, requiring an official meeting in the principal's office with the girl's father. He was in a suit and tie, no smile. I was outdressed, sheepishly trying to defuse the tension. "It's just a temporary imbalance between his emotional and intellectual developmental skills," I said, repeating verbatim what Sammy's kindergarten teacher had told me a few years earlier. Modern mom-speak for "boys will be boys." He doesn't have the words to express complex feelings, she had said, so sometimes he lashes out in frustration. He'll grow out of it, she assured me.

Sammy was now in second grade. He had all the words he needed to tell someone to move, bug off, or get out of the way. He just wasn't using them. When he slapped a girl across the face with his parent-teacher communication notebook, the situation could no longer be ignored. It was my *Houston, we have a problem* moment. Three strikes and suddenly I was wide awake.

Second grade was the year my son and I slogged through the mire of my childhood—the legacy of growing up unprotected. As a mom, my first instinct was to be on Sammy's side, to be my son's strongest advocate. But as a woman who was once a little girl, I knew better than to give cover to male aggression. I tried talking to him, reasoning with him, limiting his television time. I sent him to his room for a time-out. That was pointless: Sammy's room was his sanctuary. He'd rather be alone in his room than just about anywhere else in the world. I thought about how my father had disciplined Prince and me but ruled out spanking. It sends a mixed message because, technically, spanking involves hitting. It seemed counterintuitive for the punishment to involve some form of the crime itself. Plus, in my experience, it didn't work. I mean, if it worked, my father would only have had to spank us once, not once a week on Sundays. Likewise, grounding Sammy wouldn't have had the same impact as grounding Sasha. Sasha was a social butterfly. For her, missing a party or a playdate was devastating. *The end of the world!* But Sammy didn't particularly like playdates; Sammy's playdates were more for me than him, so I could hang with the other moms, swap parenting stories, and drink wine.

I had read the usual books on raising sensitive boys. Books about being a boy mom and decoding boy behavior. Nothing helped. Then I did something the experts did not advise. I took away unconditional love. "No," I told my seven-year-old son, the light of my life. "Mommy will not love you if you hit girls."

He might tell you that I sat him on a chair in his bedroom, taped his wrists together, bound his ankles, and left him there until dinner. "This is what prison feels like," I warned him. Not that I knew what prison felt like, but he was a little boy;

he got the message: *If you can't control your hands, someone else will have to control them for you.*

"Doesn't he get a trial?" his big sister asked from the sidelines, clearly relishing the drama as much as sticking up for her brother. I wasn't thinking clearly. My head was exploding. Blood racing, heart pounding, I was seething Code Red. *No bully in my house, baby!* There was this overwhelming urge to shake some sense into my son, as if he needed to be broken like a horse. But, also, I knew that I couldn't use corporal punishment to get my point across. So, instead, I used psychological warfare. The threat of going to jail, or worse, losing Mommy's love.

It was a rough year. I don't know who it was tougher on, him or me, but that was the year Sammy learned the meaning of zero tolerance, and I confronted my childhood demons: my anger toward my mother for not establishing boundaries in our home. "Mommy!" I would whine when she came home from work, grabbing her skirt to tell her what happened—I'd been teased or chased or hurt somehow—but she'd put two fingers to my mouth to shush me, saying, "Nobody likes a tattletale." If she didn't see it, she did not want to hear about it, especially not when she walked in the door in her dress-up clothes with her purse and important papers after a long day of work. Even if she'd just been out with the girls, she still didn't want to hear it. Those were the house rules.

As a kid, the youngest in my family, I was labeled the instigator, as if it were my own fault if I got hurt. I saw that dynamic at play with my son. He blamed the girl he hit for embarrassing him in the first place. It's true, she *had* embarrassed him. She took his notebook, the one that was meant to be passed back and forth between his teacher and his parents—a notebook that contained private and personal messages documenting his behavior, and she read it out loud in front of all his classmates. That's when, or rather, why, he grabbed the notebook out of her hands and slapped her across the face with it. I saw his point. I understood his frustration, but I could not support his behavior. Yes, this girl had invaded his privacy and shamed him in public, but no, it wasn't okay to respond with aggression.

We laugh about it now. Sort of. He and his sister like to tease me and watch me squirm. They still hold the "jail" incident over my head as the worst example of parenting ever. And I let them have it, my worst Mommy moment. Secretly, I'm smug about the whole thing. I didn't spank or hit my son, nor did I give him a meaningless punishment that had nothing to do with his actions. *You hit a girl? Now you're grounded.* Instead, I scared the c-r-a-p out of him. I showed him what happens to boys who hit girls when they grow up to be men who hit women. They get handcuffed and sent to jail. It's not always true, of course; sometimes men get away with mistreating women, but my son, Sam, won't be one of those men. He never hit a girl again, and Disneyland no longer sells toy guns. I know that sounds like a small win. We live in a moment in history when men who abuse women can fail upwards, all the way to the White House. Maybe it's no small thing, though. Maybe raising strong, kind, thoughtful, decent, totally amazing boys is the most radical thing a mother can do.

Macro/Micro

THE PLAYGROUND WAS CHAOTIC, bursting with energy. Kids swinging on ropes, climbing the jungle gym, playing in the sandbox. Sammy let go of my hand and ran off to find his friend Diego. Sasha's friend Lexi announced she wasn't ready to speak to their friend Chloe. Chloe glommed onto Sasha. Sasha tugged at my sleeve and reminded me that it was her turn to take Bunny home for the weekend.

"Don't forget!" she said, bobbing up and down in her *OhOhOlive* dress for emphasis. Olive's mom made dresses out of repurposed overalls and bright-colored swaths of cotton, using end bolts from the Fashion District. It was that type of preschool—environmentally concerned, filled with upcycling stay-at-home moms working side gigs.

"I won't forget, sweetie," I replied, planting a kiss on top of Sasha's head and fluffing the spot where I'd had to cut a piece of chewing gum out of her hair earlier that morning. Then I reassured my daughter that I was on my way to talk to Rodney.

Rodney was the kindergarten teacher. He was soft-spoken and wore African print shirts with drawstring pants. The kids loved him. The parents thought of Rodney as a child whisperer, like a magician, turning toddlers into little people. Rodney handed me the bunny-care instructions. I checked my watch to see if I had time to linger in the classroom and study the instructions in detail, maybe score some points with Rodney, not that he had a bad side. But, as a working mother, I was often in a rush. This was not a "drop and run" set-up; it was a community whose parents were engaged. And I was cognizant of being the mom who dropped off early, picked up late, and brought store-bought pastries to class parties.

"How is Sasha doing?" I asked Rodney. He had begun moving around the room, setting up the paint and clay and story areas. "I mean, in general," I stammered.

Rodney stared at me for a long beat, taking in my trendy L.A. professional attire: skinny black jeans, cropped; graphic T-shirt featuring an alligator in camouflage print, and leopard flats. I worked in the marketing and PR department for a nonprofit wildlife organization. Then he said something about how he was giving the kids a safe space to be themselves, that they had all the time in the world to be pressured by school and society.

"Of course," I replied, embarrassed for having even asked how Sasha was doing. She was fine; why wouldn't she be? She was cocooned in Rodney's world.

Before leaving, I glanced at the happy-colored walls, sunshine and tangerine, upon which the kids' art projects were displayed. They were working on life-size self-portraits, the individual outlines of each child traced in pencil on paper, looking oddly like those chalk drawings one sees at a crime scene. Later, with Rodney's guidance, the kids would personalize their identity collage with hair made from dyed straw or cotton balls, button eyes, and fabric swatches. All the parents loved Rodney, but Rodney only had love for the kids. The kids and his animals—lizards, guinea pigs, and Bunny. Bunny was the only pet that went on weekend sleepovers.

On Saturday Sasha's friends, Chloe and Lexi, came to our house to play with Bunny. They dressed her in doll clothes, took her outside to see if she would eat grass, protected her from the cat, squealed when she pooped on the floor, and took turns cuddling with her on the couch while watching movies.

"Let's put her on a leash and walk her with the dog!" Chloe suggested.

"Can we give her a bath?" Lexi wanted to know.

"Can I sleep with her tonight, Mommy, please?" Sasha begged.

By Sunday, Sasha had tired of Bunny. "You can play with the rabbit," she told her little brother.

"I'm going to bring Bunny home when I get big and go to Rodney's class," Sammy announced to his dad. Harry was working on his computer. "What do rabbits eat?" Sammy asked, cradling Bunny who was tucked securely inside his T-shirt with its ears sticking out of the neckline just under his chin. "Ooh, that tickles," Sammy said, squirming.

"Let's find out," Harry said, closing his laptop. He googled what to feed rabbits, then the two of them scoured the kitchen for lettuce and broccoli and fruit to serve Bunny, but first, they weighed Bunny on the food scale.

"It's a science experiment," Sammy announced. "Bunny: before and after food."

"I'm not sure you'll see much change," I laughed, tousling Sammy's hair.

On Monday morning, I dropped Bunny and the kids at school. *Scratch that off the list,* I thought, while driving to work. Mentally going over everything that was on my to-do list for the week and sighing from the weight of it all: *media proposal, dentist appointment, my mom's birthday, Harry leaving on an extended business trip, the Halloween costumes still to figure out.*

Halloween came and went; the kids trick-or-treated. Sasha was a turquoise princess, Chloe was a lavender princess, Lexi was a ninja, and Sammy was a scary brown tree that was so scary he was afraid to put on his costume.

"It's just brown tights and a brown shirt," Sasha teased him. "Don't be such a baby." Sammy stared at his feet, refusing to put on his costume.

"What if we add green leaves?" I suggested. Sammy nodded yes. Crisis averted.

The following Monday morning, Chloe's mom called to say the JCC preschool was closed. "Why?" I asked in a panic. I had back-to-back meetings all morning. Chloe's mom said she had no idea, only that Lexi's mom had called her and told her to call me. The phone tree was up and running. *There's been an incident* was all anyone knew. Soon, the word "incident" was elevated to "act of vandalism."

"Vandalism" could be nothing more than a teenage prank, I thought, relaying the information to my husband. Mischief, like "teepeeing" houses on Halloween. Egging cars and smashing pumpkins. Graffiti on the sides of buildings. Things I'd done myself as a kid. Well, maybe not graffiti or smashing pumpkins, but I knew boys who did.

"Can you go into the office late this morning?" I asked Harry, offering to come home for lunch and cover the afternoon.

"Sure," Harry replied.

On Tuesday, when the preschool was still closed, the parents began to discuss whether it was more serious than pranksters. Babysitters were hired; stay-at-home moms and dads were leaned on; families juggled schedules to make it work.

JCC stands for Jewish Community Center. This location served the Hollywood/Los Feliz neighborhoods in Los Angeles.[12] While the school program was informed by Jewish roots, its students and staff reflected a diverse, inclusive community. Black. White. Brown. Asian. Latino. Gay. Straight. Single parents. Working moms. Stay-at-home dads. Everyone was welcome, Jewish or not. The preschool's mission was to facilitate connectivity and to support families in raising joyful children.

The first thing I noticed when the JCC reopened was that the bones of the school had been physically altered. The entrance to the facility, which had enjoyed an open-door policy, was now bolted down and replaced by a steel fortress, with bars and a new state-of-the-art surveillance system. Walking into the eerie stillness of Rodney's classroom was heartbreaking. The walls were bare, having been stripped of kids' art and painted white. The magic gone. Gone, too, was the kindergarten zoo.

"The animals were slaughtered," Chloe's mom whispered to me.

"I heard there was blood splattered on the walls," Lexi's mom added.

"I hear we're going to be assessed for that new security system," one of the dads said.

---

12   Now called SIJCC

I stared at the blank wall in horror, picturing Bunny's blood on my daughter's life-size self-portrait/collage. "We need to craft a story to tell the kids so that all the kids hear the same message," I said, putting on my PR and marketing hat. *That's what they do at work when an animal gets sick or dies, although I had no idea what they would do if the animals were massacred. We had no protocol for that.*

"Have you seen Rodney?" someone asked. "He has the look of a woman who has been raped. Dead eyes."

"He looks like he's gonna pass out," another parent observed.

No one bothered to question who would do such a thing. Because, as Jews, we are familiar with crimes against our community. At the time, the police attributed it to "hazing," likely related to gang activity. While this could have had nothing to do with antisemitism, the first thing that crossed my mind was that it might have been a hate crime.

"Mommy," Sasha asked, after school, dunking a vegan chocolate chip cookie into organic milk. "Did you hear what happened to the animals?"

"No, sweetie, what happened?"

"Rodney said they all got 'dopted and Lexi cried because she was s'pose to take Bunny home for Thanksgiving. What's for dinner?"

"Mom's burritos," I told her. That was my *it's-been-a-long-day* specialty: a build-your-own spread of tortillas, chopped veggies, and fixings—guacamole, salsa, cheese, rice, and beans. Store-bought, pre-cooked grilled chicken.

I ended up putting Sammy in kindergarten at the public school along with Sasha, who was in second grade by then—even though it was a logistical nightmare, being only half days, and it meant we had to hire a nanny for after-school care. If anyone asked why, I said it was more convenient to have both kids in the same school. But the truth was that I just didn't like having to be buzzed into the playground when I picked up and dropped off Sammy. It felt too much like a detention center; every time they made me identify myself just to get inside, I remembered the incident. It was a "before and after" that I preferred not to think about.

This isn't just my story to tell, it's bigger than me and my family. This story belongs to an entire community of teachers, administrators, and families. I was merely a bit player in an event that hit too close to home. At the time, I regarded the incident as an inconvenience. I had so much on my plate: juggling a career, parenting, financial stress, and a husband who traveled for work. I didn't have the bandwidth to contemplate the possibility of antisemitism on top of my day-to-day struggle to survive.

Even though it was present in my daily life at work.

Earlier that year, in September, I had taken a personal day for the Jewish holidays. I was in the kitchen making dinner for the family, including my husband's cousins, The Men with French Wives, and their kids. Apples and honey, roast chicken, potatoes, salad, and challah: a round bread that represents the circle of life; the continuity of time passing. When the phone rang, I picked it up without screening. It was my supervisor calling under the pretense of a work emergency, something about a billboard advertising campaign that couldn't wait until the following day.

Funding for my position came from the City. Nothing was urgent, nothing couldn't wait; it was a behemoth organization that moved like a tortoise crawling through a mountain of ape shit. Coming from the private sector, where things *had* to happen fast, where my job depended on rapid reaction time, this made me crazy. While it was a great position for my skill set, personally, it was not a good fit. I blame one of those stupid magazines targeting working women for getting that job in the first place. I had read an article that said if you want to get hired, you should stake out the campus before your interview and show up looking like you already work there. So, I arrived for my interview with the management team, my hair blown straight, wearing a dress I had worn after Sammy was born and before I'd lost the baby fat. A midnight-blue boxy jumper that was too big and fell way below my knees. Usually, I wore it with boots, but I wore black flats to the interview. Then I soft-talked my way through the meeting and got the job. The problem was that I showed up as "me" on the first day of work. Short skirt, big hair, clunky boots. I think they felt duped. It *was* sort of a bait and switch. "You don't even look like the person we hired," my supervisor said to me a few weeks later. She was right, because if I'd shown up as myself for the interview, they probably wouldn't have hired me. Every time she pissed me off, I'd go into the ladies' bathroom, bend at the waist, flip my hair over my head, and ruffle my feathers. As the days stretched on, my hair grew wilder. I thought of it as statement hair.

"Sorry to bother you," she apologized over the telephone, launching into the questionable advertising emergency that required a phone call to me at home on a Jewish holiday. Then, as if an afterthought, as if she were interested in my personal life, she asked if I had gone to temple, which was none of her business. She wasn't my mother.

As kids, our mother insisted that we go to school if we didn't want to go to temple. Meaning, we couldn't just hang around the house doing nothing or go shopping with friends. Our options were clear: temple or school. Lois, on the other hand, stayed home preparing dinner. Like my mom, I stayed home to prepare the holiday meal. Up to my elbows in brisket. We were hosting dinner for twelve people, which required cleaning the house on top of grocery shopping and cooking the meal. Harry, who was not raised in a Jewish household, had gone to work. We didn't belong to a temple. I figured the JCC preschool provided, if not exactly a religious education, some semblance of belonging to a Jewish community for the kids. Also, like I said, it was none of my supervisor's business.

"Just got back from temple," I lied. "Now I'm making dinner, and I don't have time to talk."

Fucking bitch, I whispered under my breath when I hung up the phone. Rattled. I slammed a few pots around before pouring myself a glass of wine. A few hours after that phone call, when Harry came home, I let loose a tirade. Calling me at home on a Jewish holiday is like me calling her on Christmas morning, I complained to my husband as soon as he walked in the door. "It's like she's checking up on me."

"You need to tell her that," he said.

"She already knows it," I replied. "That's why she called me in the first place—to ruin my day. Because she doesn't think it's fair that I get to take my holidays and hers, too. Like I'm gaming the system. It's not *my* fault Christmas is treated like a national holiday in this country."

"You need to talk to her," Harry said, pouring himself a drink.

"Yeah, right. People don't like being told they're being antisemitic. It doesn't go over well, and it certainly won't make things better between us, since the *intention* of her phone call was to ruin my holiday. Anyway, I wouldn't give her the satisfaction."

"So, don't," Harry said, hugging me longer than usual, his body like a weighted blanket, trying to ground me in the moment. It was Rosh Hashanah. The Men with French Wives were coming for dinner. The Jewish New Year is a time to celebrate.

A few months later, I was having lunch with my supervisor when she started complaining about Jewish kids being spoiled brats and the moms who indulged their whiny demands. She told me that she had been at the supermarket after work the day before, and there was a Jewish family holding up the line. The kids were begging for candy, making a big fuss, totally out of control.

"Why are Jewish kids so spoiled?" she asked me.

"How do you know they were Jewish?" It was hardly the point, but I thought I'd stick with her story.

"I could tell," she replied.

"I'm Jewish," I reminded her.

"Yes," she acknowledged, "but you're not like them." I glared at her. Then she said, "It's not like I'm saying anything about *you*. I'm sure you're not like that at all. I've seen you with your kids."

Here's what I was thinking: *You've never been to the market with me and the kids after a full day of work for me and a full day of school for them, not to mention afterschool programming, because I can't pick them up until 6:30, after I get off work, exhausted, frazzled, pissed off, hungry, unable to hold the parenting line while standing in line at the grocery store, willing to give my children any little sweet they want just for a moment of peace.*

"It's got nothing to do with being Jewish," I said.

At some point I went to Human Resources and filed a complaint. "Are you sure you want to do this?" the HR guy asked me. I said yes, and the complaint was filed. To my knowledge, nothing came of it. Because, as he implied, it might just sound like a pissing match between two women. It didn't have the gravitas of, say, dead animals. No one died. It was just another microaggression.

A year or so later, we moved to Paris for Harry's job and our kids transferred to an international elementary school in the 16th arrondissement, which is a fancy-schmancy neighborhood. We ended up renting an old, charming, affordable flat in the Marais, and although it was nowhere near the kids' school, it was a straight shot on Metro Line 9. Our metro stop was Place de la République, which, as it turns out, is a central gathering point for protest marches. So, I was aware of the anti-Israel sentiments in Paris, but only inasmuch as they couldn't be avoided while weaving through a sea of pro-Palestine public demonstrations to or from the metro. *Palestine Libre. End Zionism. Israel Etat Raciste. Israel Stop Killing Children.* And the universal sign language: *Jewish star = swastika.* This was during the second intifada, which means "uprising" or "shaking off," in 2000. Anti-Israel marches are not new; they're on repeat.

Although I didn't know this until I moved there, the Marais was once known as the Jewish Quarter, home to Jewish residents since the 13th century. Being Jewish in Paris seemed to me to be a clandestine affair. The temples were not big architectural monuments, they were housed in unmarked nondescript buildings—beautiful, of course, because it's Paris, but they didn't stand out. Identified only by a small plaque at the entrance. Closed to the public. We were invited to join a friend and her family at services, probably Yom Kippur or

Rosh Hashanah. Pretty much, we're the kind of Jews who only go to temple on the High Holidays, if at all. My children and I arrived early, in "good" clothes, meaning not sneakers and jeans. We had taken our seats. I was futzing with Sasha's hair, which is lovely, golden brown, thick like mine but straight like Harry's, when Sammy pointed to a man in dark clothes walking up and down the aisles, holding something that appeared to be a metal detector. Like those guys at the beach in Santa Monica searching for coins or jewelry in the sand, only he wasn't mining for gold or silver. It was a bomb sweep. *Was there an actual bomb threat,* I wondered, *or was this standard operating procedure in Paris?* Which is worse? A credible threat or SOP? Either way, it was enough to discourage me from joining the synagogue. It wasn't that I was afraid; I figured they'd clear the temple if there was anything suspicious. It was that the potential for danger was too *in my face* for comfort, and I didn't want my kids, who were still in elementary school, to be exposed to fear surrounding Judaism at such a young age. I'd never even told them how the guinea pigs died.

The International School, on the other hand, was a big inclusive lovefest. Kids from over fifty nations, merging and cooperating, oblivious to the politics that existed in their home countries. At the beginning of every school year, they held an annual event called "International Day" to celebrate the diversity of the student population. Imagine a giant bake sale, with sweets and gastro delights from around the world, staged in classrooms arranged loosely by continent and geography. Neighbor states clustered together in rooms decorated with cultural pride, flags, and maps. I stumbled into the Middle East, having eaten my way through the Americas: Rice Krispies Treats, chocolate chip cookies, burritos, and churros.

On the wall was a map of the Middle East. When I stopped to look at it more closely, where Israel ought to have been on the banks of the Mediterranean Sea bordering Syria, Jordan, Lebanon, and Egypt was a blank state, an outline of what was and wasn't Israel—amplifying the space between what exists and what will never be accepted. Twenty-two Arab countries, each identified by name, and an outline of one state, its name omitted. I glanced at the women in headscarves at their food tables. These were the mothers of the kids with whom my children learned and played.

One of their sons had a crush on my daughter. He told me as much at the bakery where the kids hung out after school. What he said was that I needed to be more mindful about how Sasha dressed—cropped T-shirts and skorts (a cross between shorts and a skirt). Because it gave him uncomfortable feelings. I liked this kid. He was skinny, his pants a little too short, sprouting into a hormonal surge, and I laughed, saying maybe he should talk about those feelings with his own mother. I thought it was cute; he seemed so innocent. Looking at the moms, I felt a hopelessness about all of it: Israel and this kid who probably would not dare talk to his mother about those kinds of feelings because theirs was a traditional culture that covered things up (or erased them) rather than discussing touchy subjects.

"Where's Israel?" I asked the moms. Meaning, *why isn't it on the map?*

"Across the hall," they answered.

Israel had been given a table in Europe next to Switzerland, a country that has long enjoyed a reputation for being internationally neutral. I grabbed a glass of Israeli wine and some cheese fondue and tried not to let the Middle East ruin my day. I knew *why* Israel wasn't identified on the map. What I didn't understand was why Israel wasn't included on a map hung in a classroom at the international school that fostered a welcoming and peaceful environment for all nations. I could have complained to the headmistress, who was from England and would therefore have known all about the United Nations resolution adopting a plan to partition the former British territory into two states—one Arab and the other Jewish.

On the eve of the day Israel declared its independence in 1948, it was attacked by five neighboring Arab nations. Here's a bit of tribal knowledge, from my mother: She said the Brits didn't think Israel had a "snowball's chance in Hell" of surviving. Not that the land itself is Hell, but that a snowball would melt in that heat. That creating a Jewish "home" as reparations after WWII was a hollow gesture made by global players who expected the Arab nations to conquer the Jewish settlers and accomplish what the Germans did not—total annihilation of the Jewish people. In effect, a final solution to the "Jewish problem."

Against all odds, Israel survived.

I'm not a scholar, but while my story is momentarily set in France, let's take a deeper dive into the history of Jews in Paris—a saga filled with breakups and makeups. Jewish people settled in France as early as the Middle Ages. Restricted from owning land and most professions, they became moneylenders. The practice of charging interest (that we have all come to expect as the cost associated with taking out a loan) was known as "usury" and regarded as unsavory by the Christian population. Unsavory or not, it was the only way Jews could make a living—ground zero for the stereotype about Jews as greedy money-grubbers, morally suspect, willing to provide business services that "decent" Christian people would never deign to engage in. Then, surprise, the moneylenders prospered! For some reason this was an unexpected outcome. No one put two and two together: Money equals wealth. Because historically, land equaled wealth, and Jews were not allowed to own land in France. Once Jews became rich, the royals expelled them, confiscating all their money and possessions, which sounds more like an ugly divorce than a bad breakup. Over the next few hundred years, Jews were kicked out of France, invited back, and kicked out again. By the early 17th century, Jews had returned to France and things went back to normal, which is to say, *not so great, but not so terrible, either.* It was Napoleon who, in the early 1800s, emancipated French Jews, abolishing laws that forced them to live in ghettos like the Marais (loose translation: swamp), where our family rented an apartment during the four years Harry worked in Paris. Equality was granted to French Jews in 1831, a mere thirty years before the American Civil War and subsequent emancipation of slaves in America. At last, Jews were permitted to enter previously forbidden careers in the arts, commerce, trade, and government. Then came the 20th-century nightmare—WWII, the German occupation of France, the Vichy government, and roundups of French Jews sent to German death camps. An estimated 75,000 French Jews were sent to Nazi extermination camps, 11,400 of whom were children. Only 2,500 French Jews survived the camps, including 300 children. I mention the children because it makes people uncomfortable when bad things happen to kids. Jewish adults, not so much.

Antisemitism is once again on the rise in France, fueled by extreme right-wing politics and a growing population of disaffected, radicalized Islamists. In 2015, seventeen people were killed in coordinated attacks, including a massacre at the satirical magazine *Charlie Hebdo* (which had published cartoons of the Prophet Muhammad) and the related shooting at a kosher supermarket in Paris, which resulted in the killing of four Jewish hostages. In 2020, the *Charlie Hebdo* trial kicked off another series of jihadist events, including the beheading of a schoolteacher who dared to show the infamous cartoons to his class while teaching about the concept of free speech. Since the *Charlie Hebdo* attacks, assaults against Jews in France have been on the uptick. The net result of this surge in antisemitism was that many French Jews, feeling unsafe, began immigrating to Israel. You know a situation is dire when Israel seems like a good place to hide out from jihadist attacks. Am I even allowed to use sarcasm when speaking of such tragedy? Ah, WTF. *Charlie Hebdo* would approve.

Circling back to my kids' preschool, I'm not sure if killing animals counts as a micro or macro aggression, let alone a hate crime, but while we were living in Paris, a few miles from our home in Los Angeles, at another Jewish Community Center, the stakes were raised. There was an armed attack on the North Valley Jewish Community Center in Granada Hills. The shooter, a self-avowed "white supremacist," injured five people and murdered a Filipino postal service worker. The North Valley JCC is about the same distance from the Hollywood JCC that my kids attended, as the shooting at a Pittsburgh temple was from where my grandma Molly was raised. Too close for comfort. I am at an age, with a certain vantage point in life, where I can connect the dots between my family history, my childhood experiences, and those of my children. Between my experience of being singled out as a Jew, the "horns and a tail" story, and my boss's insinuation that all Jewish kids are brats. From the slaughter of animals in my daughter's kindergarten class to the subsequent shooting at the North Valley JCC. When people tell me that my experiences are from another generation, that it isn't like that anymore, I nod my head in agreement. It isn't. It's worse now.

(I've Never Been to) Israel

EVERY YEAR ON PASSOVER, at the end of the Seder, bellies full, we raise a glass of wine and say, *Next Year in Jerusalem.* A calling to the homeland. Years come and go, lots of wine has been consumed, but still—I've never been to Israel. Not for Passover or a pilgrimage.

I've backpacked through Europe, studied in Spain, sailed across the Straits of Gibraltar from Tarifa to Tangier. I've ridden elephants in Thailand and camels in Morocco, crossed the desert from Marrakesh to Essaouira, but I've never been to the Negev, floated in the Dead Sea, or shopped at the shuk. I've been to Mexico so many times, you need two hands to count the trips: I've been boozy in Baja, I've been bougie in Cabo, and I've been beachy in Mazatlán. I've been drunk on tequila, dropped out in Yelapa, and kicked out of Señor Frog's. I've been to San Blas, where I met the most beautiful boy; he was singing and playing acoustic guitar, we made love on a grass mat on the floor. I wanted to stay forever, but I had to get back home—to the United States.

Israel is the Jewish state, and I am Jewish, but I was born in the state of Michigan, and I live in Southern California, which seems, from the pictures I've seen, to share a similar climate to Tel Aviv. Warm and breezy. Not enough rain. But I'm not a hundred percent sure, because I've never actually been to Israel. Though I think I'd like the food there, they say the falafel is delicious. And I love Israeli couscous. As a young girl, I saved up my allowance to plant a tree there. It's a thing Jews do to promote the greening of Israel. My tree was planted in memory of my dog, a German shepherd named Eric. This was around the time of Golda Meir—the first and only female head of state in the Middle East. Back in the day, Israel was a beacon of democracy and feminism. Of hope and possibility. To that end, Israel *has* transformed into one of the most developed and advanced countries in the Middle East. Leaders in tech and manufacturing. Though, sadly, Israel is, and has always been, plagued by conflict, and *that* has something to do with why, despite all the places I've been, I've never been to Israel.

But, also, Israel just wasn't a convenient travel destination.

More than anything else, our travels reflect my husband's career path. He worked on themed-entertainment projects in a "gig" economy, which means you go where the work is. Harry's jobs took us to Europe and Asia, not the Middle East. It's largely because he has been employed overseas that we've become so well-traveled. When my husband and I weren't on location, we lived in a three-bedroom bungalow in the San Fernando Valley. Our kids went to public school. Our son is burdened by college debt. Our daughter shares an apartment with roommates. I feel the need to dispel the idea, seeded by disinformation, that Jews are an elite group of power brokers with an undesirable sense of globalism versus nationalism, the politics at the root of being called cosmopolitan. The crazy stuff that breeds in the dark corners of the internet, gets chanted at rallies, picked up and broadcast on media, creating a feedback loop of alternative facts.

Cosmopolitan no longer refers to a well-traveled person or a sexy drink city girls order while wearing fabulous shoes. The word has been co-opted by the far right and used interchangeably with the term *coastal elites* to imply over-educated, latte-drinking, international jetsetters or tech investors. Words do not exist in a vacuum; they contain history, and the etymology of "cosmopolitan" as a political epithet originated during the Russian purge of dissidents under Stalin. Specifically targeted were Soviet Jews because they were thought to be more connected to their Jewish identity than to Russian nationality. So, when someone in *our* government[13] uses that word, it's noteworthy. Today, in the U.S., *cosmopolitan* is a dog whistle, a secret verbal handshake, a right-wing smear against intellectuals and internationalists. It's also code for *Jew*. The word is meant to imply that Jewish people are rootless elites. Diaspora. Dislodged. Might as well throw in the Devil. That we have all the money and divided loyalties, that we aren't *really* American, that our allegiance is and always will be, first and foremost, to Israel—a country I've never even visited.

I went to Vietnam, though. Twice. Toured Hanoi with a guide who was old enough not just to remember the war but to have been a soldier on the Vietcong side. I asked him how it felt to take American tourists down into bomb shelters.

---

13   Stephen Miller

He told me this: People don't make wars; governments do. It was a bit of a hall pass on the horrors of war. But also, this fundamental belief in the goodness of humanity—everyday citizens—is what enables people to forgive and forget and to begin the process of building bridges. Forgiveness is what allows U.S. citizens to be welcomed by the Vietnamese. I wound up falling in love with their country, floating down the Mekong Delta, biking through the jungle, stopping to watch local artisans turn rice into pasta. I visited the War Remnants Museum in Ho Chi Minh City, formerly known as Saigon. Stood in a sculpture garden filled with downed American helicopters and tanks, each with a plaque citing statistics—the number deployed and the number of human lives destroyed. Wandering through that museum, humiliated, I was forced to contemplate the lingering effects of Agent Orange, to look at pictures of children born without limbs, twins physically attached. We exited the War Remnants Museum through a photo exhibit highlighting international resistance to the Vietnam War: marches and protests around the world. It made me feel somewhat absolved, as I'm old enough to have demonstrated against that war, as a girl choosing to march rather than go to the mall. I'm Jewish. And American. And shamed by the senseless wars *my own country* has waged, but I am not (remotely) responsible for the war between Israel and Hamas just because I'm Jewish. Because even though I support the existence of Israel and planted that tree, I don't vote there.

It's because I don't vote there and have never been there that I tend to be cautious and circumspect when weighing in on the political situation in the Middle East. This much I *can* say, unequivocally: I want the state of Israel to survive. A place where Jews live and thrive, free from antisemitism. *If dogs run free, then why not we?* Those are the opening bars of a song by Bob Dylan, and I think fitting as Dylan, née Zimmerman, is a modern-day Jewish prophet in the form of a poet/singing minstrel (even if he was, for a time, a born-again Christian). But dogs don't run free anymore; there are leash laws. And Israel is no longer a beacon of democracy. The center couldn't hold. Golda Meir was blamed for Israel's military unpreparedness when another surprise attack against Israel—the Yom Kippur War of October 1973—threatened its survival. Followed by two Palestinian intifadas.[14] Now, Israel operates as a State in perpetual existential fear. The October 7th Hamas attack on Israeli citizens is only the most recent conflict.

I'm beginning to have a deeper understanding of the phrase "beside myself." I sit with that feeling a lot now. There's me and my day-to-day. I take my French bulldog, Rue Bader Girl, to the dog park, walk the nature preserve, go to the gym, shop for groceries, etc. Then beside myself, sits me as a Jew, in absolute horror as events unfold. Members of the Boulder, Colorado Jewish community were firebombed for peacefully marching in support of the return of hostages still in Gaza. It no longer feels possible, politically correct, or let's face it, *safe* to support the existence of Israel, call for the return of hostages, *and* oppose the destruction of Palestine, as if you must choose sides, and once again, the center cannot hold. As I edit this book, I realize it can't just be me ranting into the wind. It feels like the writing needs to be weightier because the stakes are higher, and there's pressure to get it right. Publishers have told me to tone down the humor; fellow writers have told me that publishers are no longer accepting work from Jewish writers; friends have told me to put this project away, on a thumb

---

14 Translation: uprising

drive in the safe, hidden like a diary, and yet, that's even more reason to continue. Because to silence my voice is a form of erasure and I won't back down.

I've condensed and oversimplified the Israeli–Palestinian conflict because it's complex and I'm not a historian. I tend to uncover story as it relates to personal experience. That's why I was so keen on the Birthright tour—Taglit—for my kids after they graduated high school. If you have one Jewish parent, Israel will send you on a 10-day, all-expenses-paid trip to the homeland, departing from New York.

I thought this would give Sasha and Sammy a greater sense of their Jewish identity, especially since they had been raised all over the world and in a "culturally" Jewish household, which is to say, kind of lax on religious studies. In a way, their upbringing was the opposite of mine. Whereas I was raised in a Jewish community that functioned as extended family—temple and the country club, confirmation parties, bar mitzvahs and BBQs—surrounded by so much Jewish culture that our mother felt the need to send us to Christian camp to ensure we would be comfortable assimilating with non-Jews, *my* kids were raised as expats, cultural nomads in a diverse world. I sent them to Jewish summer camp, just so they'd have some sense of belonging to a Jewish community. I saw Taglit as an extension of summer camp with the added bonus of international travel.

"Go!" I told my young adult daughter. It'll be a blast. Just get your butt to New York and wake up in Tel Aviv. She said she couldn't afford it. "What!" I exclaimed. "You live rent-free in our house, work part-time at the mall, and you can't afford a round-trip ticket to New York?" She glared at me as if to say, *If you want me to go so badly, why don't you buy the ticket?* A mother hates to deny her daughter anything, even something she doesn't seem to want in the first place, at least not enough to work for it. Still, I offered to pay half the cost of the plane ticket to New York, and she said she would save the rest. Instead, she went to the movies; she bought tickets to Beyoncé; she stopped at Starbucks every day, and in the end, she didn't have the money for a plane ticket. I'd never been to Israel, and I wanted my daughter to have this experience, but more importantly, I wanted her to *earn* it. We were in a stalemate. It was like Israel and Palestine were in the house; we just couldn't agree on terms.

Sasha didn't end up on Taglit, but our son did. After college, Sammy moved back home, got a job at a movie theater, saved his money, bought himself a ticket to New York, and from there, he went on Taglit, which is the Hebrew word for "discovery." After the official tour, he hooked up with some kids from the Birthright bus and went *WWOOFing* through Israel. It's a thing young people do—**W**orld**W**ide **O**pportunities on **O**rganic **F**arms. Free food and lodging in exchange for day labor.

I feel compelled to share my parenting philosophy because I don't want to reinforce the stereotype about Jewish kids being spoiled. More than that, I feel the need to share financial and family dynamics: the hard work and part-time jobs. I can't just write about travel but must also contextualize it by describing my husband's overseas career posts. I need to get in the weeds, to get personal, not to plead poverty but to defend our lifestyle—lest you dismiss me as a privileged narrator, which, admittedly, I am, because privilege in America has been redefined to mean not only "white" but also to describe not just rich but *solidly okay.* Head above water. Owning a home.

All this travel history simply because I wanted to highlight the many places I've been, in contrast to the one place I've not been—Israel. People think Jews and Israel go together like sneakers and gym shoes, as if the words *Israel* and *Jews* are interchangeable. Related. Conflated. But my relationship with Israel is complicated. I support the existence of Israel, but I don't support all of Israel's policies. It's no different than being American and disagreeing with my own country's politics, except that Israel isn't my country; it's the Jewish homeland. My relationship to Israel is symbolic.

Blaming American Jews for what happens in Israel is an insidious form of antisemitism that happens all the time. I can't count how many times I've been in a discussion about antisemitism in the United States and someone says, *But what about the Zionists?* Spitting the word "Zionist" out of their mouth like an incantation summoning the Jewish Devil. In its most simplified definition, Zionism means supporting the right of Jewish people to self-determination in the land that is now called Israel. But the term has been rebranded as a dirty word and used as such in discourse, specifically on college campuses, to exclude Jewish students from participating in left-leaning organizations that support marginalized peoples in a connect-the-dots thought process that goes something like this: Jews are Zionists, Zionists are racist; therefore, Israel is an apartheid regime. In this paradigm, Israelis are depicted as white colonial settlers and Palestinians are viewed as a displaced People of Color. But this is putting a Western spin on Middle Eastern politics. Jews and Palestinians are both Indigenous peoples.

The conflict in Israel is complex. It's not just about land, religion, or ethnicity; it's about whether the surrounding Arab countries are willing to recognize the legitimacy of Israel. A country I've yet to visit because there always seems to be a war or bombings, or the uncomfortable issue of settlements, a travel destination closer or more convenient to where we're living, or a vacation spot where violence is in remission. That said, I want there to be a Jewish homeland—a place where Jews belong. It doesn't seem too much to hope for amidst all the Arab nations, the existence of that one state (the size of a postage stamp, relatively speaking) where Jews are safe to live their lives. Even though I've never been to Israel, still, every year at Passover, I say *Next Year in Jerusalem*, tossing a symbolic wish into the universe, a prayer, in the hopes that Israel will still exist a year from now, and for years to come, in case I ever *need* to go there. In case we don't have a safe space *here* in the United States anymore.

Complicit

THE PLAN WAS TO slip into town to visit my mom, *just my mom*. I told her as much. Mom, I said, please try to understand.

Whenever I went home, we'd have dinner with Prince, and sometimes it was fine. But when it wasn't, when it felt as if the two of them were ganging up on me, teasing me about anything, all of it, my clothes, my ideas, *my life*, it was unbearable. They'd push my buttons, I'd get all crazy, and by the time dessert came, I was ready to scream or cry. Then I'd get on the plane, fly back to Los Angeles, and vow never to go back home again.

"I'm just trying to avoid reliving my childhood," I told her. It was a solid plan. I could sense her nodding her head "yes" through the phone.

"Whatever you want, baby," she said.

No matter how old I get, she still thinks of me as a child. They all do: Trish, Chicky, and Prince. Up until a month ago, Trish's ringtone for me was a crying baby. Like I'm still that kid who broke Mom's lipstick tracing flowers on the wallpaper, then lied about it, despite telltale pinky-orange smudges on my fingers.

Only, now I'm the person who can't ever get a story straight, or who has spent too much time in therapy, and lived in California too long. Unreliable and unstable, even though I have a career, a husband, and two great kids. More to the point, if they could poke holes in my words or lifestyle, then *anything* I may remember, believe, or say about our childhood is therefore suspect.

But I loved my mother, so I flew into town on the red-eye Friday night, taxied to the burbs, and immediately made myself useful running errands. Returning clothes, buying her new sheets. I spent a few hours cleaning up her computer, deleting all the junk mail and unsubscribing her from mailing lists. The next morning, we went to church.

Pentecostal church.

Her part-time caregiver, Davina, was an ordained minister and my mom liked to hear her preach. "Church" is perhaps too ornate a word to describe this house of worship. Davina's congregation met in a storefront, somewhere deep in The D. No stained-glass windows, just ceiling tiles and folding chairs. Everyone there was singing their hearts out, dressed to impress. In their "Sunday best," as Lois liked to say. After singing, came the testifying—to the pain of existence and the power of God, people in wheelchairs praising the Lord, the unemployed begging Him to deliver their next meal. Someone hoping to pass an exam, get a new job, or give birth to a healthy baby. My mom, Jewish to the bone, hair professionally colored and styled, fingernails painted in OPI *Best Day Ever* pink, stood up and testified. She had to use my shoulder as leverage to get up from her chair, but she managed, and once she was on her feet, she thanked Davina, *her* caregiver and *their* preacher. I stood up, too. Held my mom's hand and thanked Davina for taking care of our mother while her daughters lived their lives spread out across the country.

As soon as we left church, as soon as we got in the car, Mom, on a spiritual high, called Prince to tell him that I was in town and confirm dinner plans. "Won't that be nice?" she said to me as she hung up on him. My hands were squeezing the steering wheel so tight, I could barely see. Lois's eyesight was impaired, but she could tell I was pissed. That much I was transmitting, jumping on the brakes the way I used to slam my bedroom door. It was like being transported back to my-self at thirteen. *You're not the boss of me!*

"Don't cause problems," she said. And there it was—this idea of me causing problems. My setting boundaries translated into me being difficult.

The girl with an attitude problem.

I remember as a teenager, trudging through the snow with my neighbor on our way to catch the school bus, freezing our butts off as Prince drove right past us, honking and waving; him in the chartreuse coupe our parents bought for the kids to share—a blinding lime-like shade of green now called Brat and trending on TikTok. I'd give him the finger and yell "asshole" as he passed us on his way to the same high school the three of us attended, him driving the car, she and I taking the bus.

When he went to college, he took that car with him.

"You can borrow mine," Lois offered, missing the point. Our entire mother-daughter relationship could be summed up by that concept: missing the point. That car was supposed to be *ours,* not *his.*

Something shifted for me as an adult. His "joking around" became intolerable. I had hoped our relationship would morph into something that reflected mutual respect. When that didn't happen, I tried to set boundaries, like coming to town just to visit my mother. Although if I'm being honest, my therapist didn't approve of this plan. She thought setting boundaries meant saying something along the lines of *I don't like it when you tease me. Please stop.* Imagine how that strategy would work with a man like Trump, for example. It would be like throwing a Molotov cocktail on a bonfire.

Here's how it played out: I dropped Lois off at her condo and went to a yoga class while she napped. When I returned, feeling calm and peaceful—namaste, baby—all hell broke loose. First, she called Prince to cancel the dinner plans, then she called him back and said *she* was coming to dinner, but not me. Then she collapsed on the kitchen floor, all melodrama-mama. I had to pick her up off the vinyl tile. Panicked. For a moment I thought she'd had a stroke. I was in the bathroom when she knocked once and, without waiting, barged in and threw money on the countertop while I was washing my hands.

"There," she said. "I'm paying for your flight from L.A. Now will you come to dinner?"

I started to shake—every cell of my body vibrating, reduced to a five-year-old about to have a full-body temper tantrum, but I didn't have the energy to fight about it anymore, so I took the money, even though I didn't ask for it. Even though I hadn't complained about the airfare. Stuffed it into my wallet, showered, dried my hair, and put on my armor: knee-length black dress, sleeveless; black tights; black hiking boots. A killer jacket with a camo scarf wrapped around my neck. And drove Mom to dinner at The Club.

Prince arrived late. He greeted each person at the table one by one. His kids, their partners and children. Patting his son on the back and kissing Lois on the cheek. No wife. Then he sat down in the empty seat next to me and didn't acknowledge my being there. All the back-and-forth about my showing up and now he was acting like I didn't exist. His son-in-law, who seemed oblivious in the kindest way possible, asked me what Harry did for a living, followed by a barrage of questions about where we lived, if I was working, what the kids were up to.

"I haven't seen them since they were babies," he said.

"They're good," I responded, but they were no longer babies. Sasha and Sam were young adults, trying to figure out what to do with their lives. We barely knew these people, nor they us. My father once said, *Family is everything, everyone else is shit.* He meant *this*, these people I barely knew. This family that didn't know me at all.

Earlier that day, Lois had accused me of causing the rift with Prince, citing a social media fight we'd had. "He told me you broke up with him on Facebook," she said. "He said he just wanted to say Happy Birthday and you deleted his message," she continued, adding that his feelings were hurt.

"I cannot believe he told you I hurt his feelings on Facebook!" I laughed. We were standing in the kitchen, she was wearing something flowy, more like a housedress than a caftan. And she was dead serious. I had to explain to her that he had posted a Happy Birthday message on my Facebook page, adding a decade to my age, and that I didn't "break up" with him; I unfriended him.

Lois burst out laughing. In her mind, her kids were fighting, but it was a silly fight, and squabbling was a form of sibling connection. The sound of us fighting was like the pitter-patter of little feet to our mother. She was in her happy place.

"It's not funny," I reprimanded her. When I deleted his message, he reposted it. I remember feeling a sense of panic that he was aging me on Facebook. That's why I deleted his post the instant it appeared. Both times. The third time he posted it, I deleted the message and unfriended him. At least that's what I recall—that I had deleted his message three times, but it may only have been twice. Memory is subjective. In earlier drafts of this book, the brother character was named Dev, which could be short for Devyn or Devil. I liked the ambiguity. Plus, when we were kids, Prince had dressed up as a Devil on Halloween. Then, because I couldn't remember what *my* costume had been, I went scouring through a box of old photos until I found a picture of the two of us, surprised to discover myself clothed in red, head-to-toe, with a tail and pitchfork. Prince was a gangster, wearing a trench coat, with a fake mustache. *Even better,* I thought. Memories are not photographs; they're recollections infused with emotional truth.

It should be said that although Prince is smart and successful, it's possible he's not social-media savvy. Maybe he thought there was a glitch in the system, that his message had disappeared by mistake, and that's why he reposted it. More likely, he thought the whole thing was funny. I can picture his impish grin. Chicky says *that's just his sense of humor,* and I'm sure she thinks I overreacted. She doesn't work. To her, social media is a nostalgic link to friends and family. For me, a woman in publishing working in the design industry in West Hollywood, social media was an image platform. My connections were way more than friends and family. They were clients and business associates in Los Angeles, a brutally age-conscious community for women. It wasn't just the joke about my age that upset me; it was that in reposting a message I had deleted it felt as if my boundaries were being ignored. That triggered uncomfortable feelings of being a powerless little girl.

I mention boundaries a lot when writing about my family. It's because I was never taught to set them as a girl; now, when I try to establish healthy boundaries, my family is re-sistant. But Mom was not to be denied a glimpse of her kids together, even if it was a charade. So, there we were, having dinner at The Club. I remember her smiling—the grande dame. Eyebrows tattooed on; lips and cheeks both pinky-or-ange; wearing a glow of satisfaction. Her kids were together; that was all that mattered. It was a family affair. I got up and walked outside to the patio, from where I could see the pool and golf course. The smell of freshly cut grass. Sand traps and white flags dotted the horizon. Taking it all in to preserve the moment, my childhood stomping grounds. *This is the last time I will come here*, I promised myself. Wiped my eyes, went to the dessert table, and piled onto my plate all the things my adult self won't allow me to eat. Cheesecake and pecan pie. With whipped cream.

Near the end of her life, my mother made me promise that, after she passed away, I'd be there for Chicky, on the phone, as needed. "Sure," I had said, "we talk all the time anyway." Chicky lived in the Southwest, and I was in Los Angeles. We could spend hours burning up the phone lines, dissecting our childhood.

Here's how a typical phone call might play out:

"When you think about it," Chicky says, "the four of us grew up in the same house, but it was like each of us had com-pletely different childhoods. Prince was the boy. You were the baby. And Trish was the eldest, but she abdicated the role of eldest child and shirked it off on me, the middle child."

Chicky's big on birth order, I think, rolling my eyes. My view of our family dynamic is different. In my mind, she's like Switzerland. Chicky doesn't like it when I say that, because it means she only *appears* to be neutral. Switzerland claimed to be neutral during WWII, but Swiss companies profited from the Nazi war machine. They bought gold looted from European Jews (some of it in the form of dental fillings extracted from corpses), provided bank accounts, and held valuables in safe-deposit boxes, which were later tangled up in bureaucracy when survivors tried to claim their family assets. Worse than all the financial misdealing, they refused Jewish refugees at their borders.

Switzerland was more complicit than neutral.

Ever since we were kids, Chicky has played the role of mediator, emcee, and to some degree, boss. Never taking sides, acting as if she were above the fray. Now she prides herself on getting along with all her siblings.

"Prince is my little brother," Chicky says, "and he's always been nice to me. He used to sit on my bed, put a warm washcloth on my forehead, and rub my shoulders when I had a headache."

"He used to tease Trish and me," I remind her. He called me *Mouth* and Trish *Big Nose*, or *Nose* for short. Although this shames me to admit, sometimes I chimed in. I didn't even know what I was saying, but as a little girl, I understood that the safe play was to be on Prince's good side. That was my survival strategy: *go along with the game.* Now I can see how these childhood experiences contributed to my development. I was called "Mouth," and they used a pencil against me, but those things—my voice and writing—have become my power tools, the source of my strength. And, though I have no memory of Prince massaging Chicky's forehead, I don't doubt that it happened, just that it was neither Trish's nor my experience of our brother. When pressed, Chicky admits it only happened once. *That is so like Chicky,* I think, *to take something that happened*

*once and turn it into a character trait. But hold up. I don't re-
member Chicky getting headaches.*

"Did you really have migraines as a kid?" I ask Chicky.

"Yep," she says, her exhale loud enough to hear through the
phone, and she reminds me, Prince was always good to her.

I remind her of the time Prince slugged her hard enough
to trigger an inflammatory reaction that lasted for months,
swelling and fevers that landed her in the hospital. The doctors
thought they might have to amputate her arm. *But that wasn't
Prince's fault,* Chicky says, quick to his defense, *it was a fluke.
A cytokine storm. That's when they first mentioned autoimmune
issues, but Mom was in denial.*

Right away, Chicky landing in the hospital after a punching match with Prince is reframed as Lois's failure to respond
properly. But, to her point, our mother was in denial about
much of what happened in our childhood. Denial was her
coping mechanism. She loved Chicky, and didn't want her to
be seen as weaker than the rest of us. And Prince was her only
son, which is a big deal in Jewish families. Chicky often refers
to him as the "prodigal son," but the story of the prodigal son
is that he leaves home, reckless and wasteful, and returns home
repentant, a changed man. Prince never left Michigan; the girls
did. I always had one foot out the door, and it wasn't just that I
liked to travel. It was more like escape fantasies: a commune in
Washington, a bass player in Los Angeles, Boston on a whim.
Lois reveled in what she saw as my adventurous spirit. But that
would be her missing the point again. I wasn't looking for fun.
I was looking for something better than what I'd experienced
growing up. It was self-preservation, not wanderlust.

"Anyway," I say to Chicky, "you think you aren't part of the
dynamic, but you are. I'm just saying, there is no neutral. Neutral

is complicit. It's like when people say they vote Republican because they're fiscally conservative, ignoring the social justice issues that are bundled into the conservative package. Trading women's rights for tax cuts. We need to look at the total picture, not just what impacts our personal bank account."

Chicky says something like, *OMG, Marcelle, I'm not going to cancel Prince. He's my brother, not a politician!* It occurs to me that I don't even think of him as a brother anymore. I think of him as a cartoon villain like the Joker: comic yet dangerous.

In writing this book, I have discovered that a lot of my girlfriends had difficult brothers. Brothers who belittled them. Dragged them across the floor. Dislocated their arm. Screamed at them. Threatened to sue them because he didn't like the way they were handling their aging mother's affairs. Took control of their mother's finances and stole money from the trust. Tried to silence them, and didn't even offer them the one hundred thirty grand hush-money payment. I found one such brother in a few stanzas of a book of poetry written by a woman whose daughter went to school with my kids.

"I grew up in a house that sprawled across acreage
but spent most of my time alone
Terrorized by an older brother
the refuge of my room became my captivity
When it came to my siblings my mother was a horse
with blinders"

I recognize my mother in that poem. This is not a book about abuse. It is, however, a story about the intersection of being Jewish and female. Try as I might to sidestep it, there it is, on the page, because abuse is part of the lived experience for way too many girls. Statistically, girls are at greater risk of abuse, generally by an older brother. Over 40 percent of children have engaged in physical aggression toward a sibling, and 85 percent of children have engaged in verbal abuse. Even "teasing" is considered harassment, which is a form of abuse, *if it is not welcome*. It's so common that it is often normalized. Typically, it is the younger sibling who is targeted, the youngest being the most vulnerable.

Full disclosure: I'm not speaking to Prince right now. I'm not speaking to Prince because he's not speaking to me. Or vice versa. Hard to tell. We're not speaking to each other. Let's leave it at that.

"I don't know," Chicky says, sounding weary. "I just wish you two would talk. He really loves you, Marcelle."

Yeah, that's what Mom always said, I think to myself, putting Chicky on speaker so I can empty the dryer and fold the clean clothes. I enjoy doing the laundry. I like how all the dirt, sweat, and stains get washed away. I would bleach my whites if it weren't so bad for the environment. Instead, I use a chlorine-free powder and white vinegar.

Left. Right.
Siloed.

THE DAY AFTER

They're like flowers, I thought, stepping back to admire my work. I was cleaning my kitchen and had placed the container of cooking utensils in front of the cutting boards, *just so.* White, plastic, rectangular, in two different sizes, which gave a double-matted look to the still life: *Kitchen Utensils in Ceramic Jar.* The simplicity of it. The way a kitchen counter properly appointed can lend an air of everyday beauty that projects peace and calm. There was a teabag next to the stovetop. *Honey Lavender Stress Relief.* I was going to make tea but forgot to boil the water.

I was stoned.

No makeup, my hair a mess. It was way past noon, and I was still in my jammies. I don't usually get high. Sure, I drink wine, take the occasional Xanax, swallow chocolate-covered melatonin balls at night and chase them with CBD oil. "Relief

Tincture," to be exact. That had been my 2016 pre-election maintenance program. I was in post-election crisis mode. This called for the big guns. CBD *plus THC.* Watermelon Sour Gummies. They were sugar-coated and kicked in fast. Soon, I was cleaning the kitchen with purpose: sweeping the floor, wiping the counters, scrubbing the stovetop. The "purpose" was more about what I was *not* doing. I was not watching MSNBC, not listening to Steve Kornacki explain the map, or Nate Silver explain how the polls could be both accurate and useless. Overnight, my friends had become Electoral College experts. My phone was on fire with group texts. Everyone I knew was frantically hand-wringing and texting wildly.

How did this happen?

But she won the popular vote!

It's official, the U.S. is more misogynistic than racist.

Ping! Ping! Ping!

I was still admiring the utensils in the vase-like porcelain container. There were wooden spoons mixed with metal ones in varying sizes: one soup ladle, a whisk, and several spatulas. It was beautiful—like a diverse ecosystem on my kitchen counter. Cooking tools existing in harmony, except for one bright red rubber spatula, which I considered tossing in the trash. But Harry would think I was crazy, and he's the cook.

The dryer beeped.

I was also doing the laundry. I was multitasking while democracy teetered. *How could people vote for this guy?* And just like that, a political thought punctured my bubble. *Quick,* I thought, *turn on some music to block it out!*

"What's Going On" or "Where Is the Love?"

Marvin Gaye vs. The Black Eyed Peas.

Dilemmas.

I went with Marvin Gaye because it was an entire album versus just one amazing song. Then I was hungry, so I pulled my election-night leftovers from the fridge. Chinese takeout. My friends Al and Lee went Mediterranean, and Pinky went with Pinot and pasta. Harry went to work that morning, as usual, as if it were any other day, and I was all alone, eating cold sesame peanut noodles for lunch. I debated a good long time over bowls—an earth-tone speckle-glazed and textured ramen bowl vs. a slick ceramic pasta bowl with a brightly hued abstract floral design, considering the choice from all angles before deciding. Chinese food is closer to Southeast Asian cuisine and would therefore make sense in a ramen bowl, but noodles are more like pasta, so I went with the pasta bowl.

Decisions.

It really shouldn't have been that difficult to choose between an uber-qualified woman and an unhinged man. I get that they were both imperfect candidates, but if you were stumped, I mean, if you really weren't sure what to do (as opposed to, say, being misogynist and racist), couldn't you just vote for the person with the most experience? The one who wasn't filled with hate.

"Alexa, play 'Where Is the Love?' by The Black Eyed Peas."

I glanced at the still life, my jar of cooking tools, sparkling, the light from the kitchen window reflected on the oversized metal spoons. It calmed me. Out of nowhere, a random thought popped into my head: *This will not be good for Jews.* Moments later a second thought, not random, very much connected to the first, came into my consciousness: *This is no time to be lollygagging around in my husband's WASPy last name.* That's when I opened my laptop, logged on to Facebook, and updated my name to Marcie Blumberg Maxfield.

It was a snap decision. It only took a few minutes to change my name on Facebook. Maybe it took longer, time is stretchy when you're stoned. For years, well, more like decades, I had been living, working, *being* Marcie Maxfield. Passing on paper and in the digital world. In a matter of minutes, certainly less than half an hour, I dismantled my whitewashed social media presence. One might think an action like this would be monumental, that it would hit me like a thunderbolt, crack open my psyche in some profound way. In truth, reclaiming my family name on social media was little more than a symbolic gesture.

On the other hand, writing this book is like coming out of the closet. It has me worried on many levels, not the least of which is how the Jewish community will react, but also how People of Color will receive a white-skinned woman refusing to check the box "White." And I can tell, having workshopped the hell out of this book, that it's going to annoy some people, because there has been blowback already. But the goal isn't to piss people off, it's to express my truth in ways that shed light on the subject. Call it instinct, but I knew Trump would be dangerous for Jewish people.

Jewish people.

Like we are one homogenous group, we're more like those cooking utensils on my kitchen counter. We come in different shades and colors. Some vote blue and some vote red; some practice Judaism religiously, others not at all. The only time Jewish people become a homogenous "we" is when other people start talking about us.

THE BIG WE
The spectacle of Trump becoming president energized me in ways that I hadn't experienced since my youth. As a kid, we

marched *on* weekends, *against* war, *for* teachers. *Fuck the system!*
While a student in Ann Arbor, I participated in the Black Action
Movement (BAM) that occupied the Student Administration
building for three days. I have a vague memory that one of their
demands was that the university provide tutoring for affirmative
action students. It seemed to be a reasonable request. We didn't
use the word "ally" back then, but I showed up and sat in, adding
my body to the count. One could dismiss us as fun-seeking college kids, crashing the administration building, rifling through
drawers, pilfering office stationery. But also, just our being
there, white-skinned students, made the idea of arresting all of
us a bad PR move, and in that way, bolstered security for BAM.
After graduating from college, work and life became all-con-
suming. My ideas about social justice didn't shift so much as my
free time disappeared. I had a career to manage, rent to pay, kids
to raise. Then came Trump's electoral victory, and I found myself out there protesting again—this time around, dragging my
kids with me, teaching them how to stand in opposition. I went
to DC for the Women's March on Washington along with several women I had known for years; women in my personal and
professional network, including one whose daughter had gone
to preschool with mine, another who had hired me at three different magazines, and a woman with whom I had worked at
those publications. It seemed like everyone was going to DC:
my niece in New York, my college roommate from Ann Arbor,
and the women I volunteered with, teaching creative writing
and mentoring youth in detention. We stood there in the cold,
wearing pink pussy hats, watching female icons take the stage to
talk about women's issues, resistance, and politics. It felt monumental. The sheer number of people flooding the streets in DC
and around the country was widely reported to be the largest

single-day demonstration in American history, which makes sense when you consider that women hold up half the sky. For those of us who participated, it was inspirational, a watershed of sisterhood, not to mention great protest signs. *If you're not angry, you're not paying attention.* That was one of the slogans scrawled, printed, blown up, everywhere. If *Women's Rights Are Human Rights* and *We Are All Human,* then *Black Lives Matter.* Basic social justice signage algebra. Women united in outrage took to the streets, their voices augmented by protest signs and pussy hats. It was a people-have-the-power moment. The old guard showed up. Angela Davis and Gloria Steinem.

G-L-O-R-I-A.

Glooooooreeeeuh!

Onstage, actresses shared personal stories of sexual assault and abortion. There were MomsRising and Indigenous peoples reminding. Marginalized voices talked representation. America Ferrera pointed out that the president is not America, *we* are America. All of us, standing in the streets, making our voices heard, demanding to be seen. *This is America!* For one day there was pure joy in a sea of pink pussy hats. Knitting stores experienced an economic surge. It was *banners only* in DC, where *sticks* in the hands of a bunch of pissed-off women worried the police. Jumbotrons broadcast heartfelt speeches about choice and women's rights; men and dads with toddlers on their shoulders marched as allies. In the biting cold of January, a mass of bodies lit up the streets, smiles blazing, fists pumping, keeping each other warm. I started snapping pictures of protest signs:

The Future is Female.
This Is What Democracy Looks Like.
Stay Loud.

Returning to L.A. all fired up, I decided to harness the power of these images and teamed up with a friend to turn photos taken at the marches into postcards, which we sold at subsequent events. A friend in Georgia sent us a picture of legendary congressman John Lewis at the March in Atlanta and it felt like winning the lottery! Photos were pouring in, we were printing cards and coordinating postcard parties—*write your representatives in Congress, they work for* you! Whatever (minuscule) profits we made were donated to organizations in support of women's issues. It wasn't about the money or the viability of postcard politics. We just felt like we had to *DO* something. My big idea, which never came to fruition, was to publish a coffee-table book that would document and celebrate visual messaging from the marches.

THE LEADERS

A Muslim, a Black activist, a white lady, a Latinx social justice reformer, and a Jew walk into a bar. No, this is not a setup for a joke. This was an intersectional wet dream. Radical inclusivity. That is, until they ousted the Jew, saying: *you people this, you people that, you people hold all the wealth, you need to own your slave-trading history.* That's the sound of Jew-bashing at an executive meeting for the Women's March. Nothing is as renewable or as predictable as pin-the-blame-on-the-Jew. The remaining gang of four used the Women's March to amplify diverse voices—Women of Color, LGBTQ, Cis, Trans, hijab-wearing, plus-sized women—all marching for gender, racial equality, health care, and environmental protection. (Note: All religions were welcome, but some religions were more welcome than others.) The leaders of the movement crafted a statement of "Unity Principles," which said: "We must create a society in which all women—including Black women, Indigenous women, poor women, immigrant women, disabled women, Muslim women, lesbian, queer, and trans women—are free."

This was my first introduction to the concept of intersectional politics and how Jewish women are left out of the conversation. After eleven Jewish people were gunned down at a synagogue in Pittsburgh, the Women's March had to acknowledge the existence of antisemitism. Not in theory, not just on the far-right, but in their organization, among their leadership. The Black activist got caught on tape sitting front row at a Nation of Islam event, then she doubled down and called Louis Farrakhan the GOAT—The Greatest of All Time. This is a man who conflated the words "semites" with "termites" in one infamous (now-deleted) tweet, setting off a media frenzy. A movement in tatters, having accomplished nothing tangible for women's rights, a Muslim, a Black activist, and a white lady exit the scene, leaving behind one Latinx social justice reformer and a big mess to clean up.

But really, what went down?

Near as I can tell, and as reported in *The New York Times, The Washington Post, CNN, ABC News,* and other news outlets within days of Trump's first election, a woman from Hawaii named Teresa Shook created the first Facebook page proposing a Women's March. Shortly thereafter, Vanessa Wruble, a Jewish woman from Brooklyn, took Shook's idea and ran with it. Understanding that the March needed to be inclusive, Wruble put feelers out for Women of Color to join the organizing team. Enter Tamika Mallory, a Black gun control activist, and Carmen Perez, a Latina criminal justice reform activist. They, in turn, brought Linda Sarsour, a Palestinian

American activist, on board. Bob Bland, a white female fashion designer, managed the Facebook page for the March and became one of the event's leaders.

From there, things got complicated. There was a meeting where the "role of Jewish women" was discussed. This is not in dispute, although the exact tenor of that conversation is subject to interpretation. Then, shortly after the first March, Wruble was allegedly pushed out; she maintains that her Jewish identity played a role in the decision. Mallory and Perez dispute that accusation, but Mallory's connection to Louis Farrakhan blew up in the media, especially after she appeared on ABC's daytime talk show *The View* and refused to disavow her support for Farrakhan, a controversial leader in the Black community known to be vehemently antisemitic. Organizations pulled their financial support of the Women's March, and many people called for the remaining co-chairs to resign. The leadership team (minus Wruble) refused to step down but agreed to participate in antisemitism sensitivity training, and they amended their Women's March "Unity Principles" to include Jewish women. By way of apology, Mallory stated that, "Since that conversation, we've all learned a lot about how while white Jews, as white people, uphold white supremacy, ALL Jews are targeted by it."

I call this Orwellian doublespeak because the language used disguises the truth. It leads with this concept: Jews uphold white supremacy—linking Jewish people to white supremacy three times before acknowledging that ALL Jews are targeted by white supremacy. I have no issue with the concept that Jewish people are both privileged and persecuted. My problem is that by the time Mallory's statement acknowledges that "ALL Jews" are targeted by white supremacy, it's an afterthought. At least she used all caps. Still, I question whether this statement reflected a newfound sensitivity to the precarious space that Jews inhabit, or whether she had a gun to her head. And that gun was in the shape of a public relations disaster. There was so much news coverage about antisemitism in the Women's March, specifically in response to Mallory's appearance on *The View*, the pressure was on to course correct.

Mallory's refusal to denounce Farrakhan on national TV effectively said, *I'll ignore what he thinks about Jews because of what he does for the Black community.* This strikes me as the definition of being complicit—to overlook Farrakhan's antisemitic diatribes because he satisfies your own community's interests. I'm torn here. On the one hand, I don't want to supply oxygen for the multitude of hate Louis Farrakhan has spewed about Jewish people, but also, it needs to be substantiated. In my mind, he's antisemitic in the way that Trump is a liar. He doesn't just tell a few lies; lying is his entire strategy. He calls the Jewish people Satan and blames them for slavery, for normalizing sexual degeneracy, and for Jim Crow laws. He preaches that Jews are the architects of white supremacy—controlling media, entertainment, banking, publishing, sports, and medicine, and that all doctors and lawyers are Jewish.

I have a lot of doctors. My internist is Indian, as is my rheumatologist. My orthopedist is Black. My eye doctor is Asian. My skin doctor is gay. My chiropractor is Vietnamese. My dentist is possibly Persian, which could mean Iranian Jewish. I've never asked. Four of my doctors are female. That's progress. The medical field, like our country, is diverse. Gone are the days when a claim like *all doctors are Jewish* can be taken seriously. And yet I do take Farrakhan seriously because, like Trump, he has a significant number of supporters. By conflating Jews with termites and saying that Jewish people "infected the world," Farrakhan is attempting to dehumanize Jewish people. That was Hitler's strategy, so that, ultimately, good white Christians could look the other way when the gas showers were turned on, because by then, Jews were considered a different species. Vermin. If this sounds like Trump 2.0, that's because it's no different than what is happening now, in the U.S. Our government is labeling immigrants as rapists and murderers and "disappearing" them to prisons in foreign countries, never to be seen again.

BUT FIRST

There was Charlottesville. This is when antisemitism came out from under a rock and marched into the streets of Virginia in broad daylight. It wasn't encrypted, coded, or dog-whistled. It was on blast: *Jews Will Not Replace Us*. Fringe groups from all over the country showed up in force, waving Confederate and Nazi flags. The stated organizational goal of this event was unification of the white nationalist movement. It's interesting to note that on both the progressive left (Women's March) and the far right, the term "unity" or "unification" was used, and that neither side included Jewish people in their umbrella concept. The *Unite the Right* rally was comprised of a variety of groups, including alt-right, neo-Nazis, neo-fascists, Klansmen, and far-right militias. What started as a protest over the removal of Confederate monuments morphed into a racist/antisemitic march that erupted in a clash between protesters and counter-protesters. Both sides were armed.

Tragically, one female counter-protester was run over and killed. Her name was Heather Heyer. A paralegal and civil rights activist, she had reddish hair, pink cheeks, and a Chihuahua named Violet. She has been described as strong and sweet, a late sleeper, and good enough at her job, so committed to the cause of helping the disenfranchised that her boss rearranged *his* work schedule to accommodate *her* sleep preferences. I don't want to gloss over this woman as a statistic on my way to finishing this story. Heather was only thirty-two years old when she was run over by a twenty-two-year-old white supremacist who revered Hitler's policies, about whom one of his high school teachers said, "A lot of boys get interested in the Germans and Nazis because they're interested in WWII, but James took it to another level."

Another level. As if there's an acceptable level of Nazi appreciation but this kid just went too far. I knew a boy like that when I was growing up, and I also made excuses for his Nazi fascination. It seemed harmless at the time. A stupid boy phase. But I was a teenage girl, not an educator.

I have children now, understanding that our primary job as parents is to raise good humans. When I recall the stupid phases our son went through as a high school boy, at the top of the list would have to be his obsession with the online card game *Magic: The Gathering*. I thought it was "stupid" because it seemed like a huge waste of time, but let's be clear: it was otherwise inoffensive. It may even have been more worthwhile than I gave it credit for in terms of developing strategic thinking skills, building community, etc. Overall, harmless play. But it shouldn't have come as a surprise to a high school teacher that the same kid who was obsessed with Nazis in high school ended up at the rally in Charlottesville a few years later, injuring multiple people and killing Heather Heyer. Nazi fascination is a red flag, not a behavioral stage.

I recall being in an elevator with my kids—Sasha was in preschool and Sammy was in a stroller—when a total stranger got on the elevator with us. I don't remember a thing about her, where we were, what she was wearing, or even how old she was, other than that she was older than me. Instead of cooing at the baby, she addressed me: *You fix the things that were wrong with your childhood, but along the way, you'll make other mistakes.* It was an odd piece of unsolicited parenting advice that not only have I never forgotten, but I took seriously. It became my parenting baseline. I was raised by a mother who embraced a boys will be boys attitude about a spectrum of "boy" behaviors that are, theoretically, *not okay* by today's standards, but it would be a misnomer to pass it off as a generational glitch. America's tolerance for aggressive and/ or aberrant behavior in boys has not abated. You need look no further than mainstream Republican politics. The President[15] is an adjudicated sexual abuser; his first pick for attorney general[16] was under investigation for statutory rape; his defense secretary[17] has faced allegations of sexual assault and has body tattoos that are typically associated with far-right neo-Nazi groups. Skeletons in your closet like these would have been career-ending not long ago, but now they are openly flaunted in the manosphere.

Many people associate Charlottesville with the President's comment *There were very fine people on both sides.* For me, though, that comment was nothing compared to the ominous chant *Jews Will Not Replace Us.* This was straight out of Hitler's playbook. Dressed in combat fatigues, armed with semi-automatic rifles, marchers walked past Congregation Beth Israel on their way to the rally, chanting "Sieg Heil" and "Blood and

---

15   Donald J. Trump
16   Former Congressman Matt Gaetz
17   Former Fox News host Pete Hegseth

Soil." Members of the congregation were instructed to exit through the side door to avoid violence in the street.

A little background information on terminology. "Blood and Soil" originated in Nazi Germany. "Blood" refers to the goal of a "pure" Aryan master race defined as Nordic/Germanic white non-Jewish people. "Soil" conjures a special relationship between Germanic people and their land. It was codified into law under Hitler and used to seize property from Jews. Replacement Theory suggests that there is a plot designed to undermine or "replace" the political power and culture of white people living in Western countries with immigrants. Not only is that the basis for the chant *Jews Will Not Replace Us*, but also the reasoning behind the deportation of immigrants. This notion of "white genocide" has been around for a while. It was a foundational part of Nazi ideology in Germany, which considered Jews to be the single most dangerous threat to white civilization.

"I knew a Trump presidency would not be good for Jews," I said to Chicky in one of our long-distance catch-up phone calls. My tone of voice conveyed a sense of smugness at how prescient my knowing this was. She laughed and said, "No shit, Sherlock." I imagine her on her comfy beige couch, feet tucked under one hip, sipping chamomile tea. We started to bandy about options.

"We could move to Portugal," I suggested.

This was before the pandemic, before working from "home" came to mean "from anywhere"—a bungalow in Brazil or a café in Nice. Now, everyone and her sister has discovered Porto, driving rents and real estate prices up. At the time, though, Portugal seemed doable. Safe. Friendly. Affordable. Chicky pointed out the irony of moving to Portugal to escape antisemitism. Jews were burned at the stake in Lisbon during the Spanish Inquisition. I countered that the Spanish Inquisition happened almost four hundred years ago and there must be a statute of limitations. Plus, they remained neutral during WWII. Chicky conceded my point, which doesn't often happen. She's my older sister and infinitely (four years) wiser. Chicky floated the idea of getting European passports. Grandpa Joe was Hungarian. So was Harry's grandmother. But Hungary? They're as bad as the far right in America. Chicky dismissed my concern, insisting that once you get a passport, you can live anywhere in the EU.

"What about Spain?" I suggested.

Chicky and I have a soft spot for Spain. We both studied at the Universidad de Salamanca, but not at the same time. "I heart Salamanca," I said, my voice melting with memories. Plus, it would be easier to brush up on Spanish than to learn Portuguese. We could stroll the Plaza Mayor and stop for coffee. Chicky reminded me she doesn't drink coffee. I chose to ignore that comment. Chicky doesn't understand blue-sky thinking. Still fantasizing about cobblestone streets, fresh olive oil, and bicycles as a means of transportation, I mentioned that we could buy a house in Italy for only ten thousand euros.

"They're selling them online!" I exclaimed.

Chicky said, "Yeah, but they want babies." That's why real estate is so cheap in Italy. They want to promote population growth."

"We'll bring the kids with us," I offered. *They'll make many little Italian babies.* Neither of my kids was married or had kids, so this seemed like a brilliant idea to me. Not to mention, a slap in the face to Mussolini.

Chicky: You realize, we're talking about leaving the country because we're Jewish.

Me: It's just a Plan B. In case things get worse.

Chicky: Worse than Nazis marching in the streets in Virginia?

Me: How do you know when it's time to go? Will someone send us a heads-up memo?

Chicky: By the time you get the memo, it'll be too late. Heads-up, Marcelle. It may be time to pack and go.

Me: You always think the sky is falling.

SNOWFLAKE

The first thing I noticed was that my digestion, which had always been a thing I didn't notice, became a thing I couldn't avoid. I was bloated, gassy, uncomfortable. My stomach felt like it does after a transatlantic flight, only I hadn't been anywhere. I had been sitting on my couch, glued to the tube, watching the Trump era unfold. My internist referred me to a gastroenterologist, who put me on the FODMAP elimination diet. The idea was to determine what foods were irritating my gut. I ran out to the grocery store and stocked up on rice, rice cakes, rice pasta, gluten-free bread, and nightshade vegetables. But I didn't stick to the diet long enough to figure out which foods were bad for me because I was pretty sure food wasn't the problem. It was the steady diet of Trump everywhere, all the time: on the news, on my Facebook feed, popping up in my inbox, on late-night television.

MAGA was messing with my digestive system, and probiotics were not going to cure it.

These days, I treat the news like the sun, limiting exposure. But, at first, it was kind of an addiction. Every time some politician said something outrageous, especially about women or Jews, I felt a stabbing pain in my belly. At some point, bloating turned into the opposite of bloating. I was running to the toilet five, six, ten times a day. If anyone noticed, no one said a word. It's not the kind of thing one brings up in polite conversation. In my head, all I could think about was managing my stomach, but on the surface, everything appeared normal. I was working, volunteering, printing postcards, hanging out with people, and going to the movies. A friend from London sent me a link to an indie film about Holocaust survivors produced by a friend of hers that was playing in L.A. Although it's not the type of film I typically attend, I wanted to show support, so I bought two tickets and invited my friend Deb for her birthday. She knows several survivors, or descendants of survivors, so I thought she'd find it interesting.

SIDEBAR

I don't know any survivors. My family left Europe before WWII started. *They got the heads up.* Or, if they didn't, they didn't get out at all—like my Grandma Molly's European relatives. Chicky says that as a young girl, our grandmother used to visit Budapest by ship, crossing the ocean with a steamer full of store-bought American clothes that were whisked away and replaced with beautiful frocks made by Hungarian dressmakers. Maybe her relatives were seamstresses? I know so little about them. I didn't even think to ask. Grandma Molly is long gone, and I rely on what Chicky says. She's the family historian. Chicky says our Hungarian relatives were well-to-do and that, leading up to the war, they wrote Molly letters begging her to visit, mentioning that they had "gifts" for her. But her father wouldn't let her go back to Europe because it was too dangerous. Years later, Grandma Molly told Chicky she felt guilty for not going; she lived with regret for not saying goodbye to her aunts and uncles and cousins. She was sure they had wanted to give her their jewels to smuggle out of Hungary.

In May 2023, Christie's had a sale of jewelry that grossed over two hundred million dollars, making it the most valuable single-owner jewelry collection ever to be sold at auction. The jewels were from the estate of Heidi Horten, an Austrian heiress, whose husband, a Nazi sympathizer, made his fortune by acquiring companies for pennies on the dollar from Jewish families that were pressured into selling short during Nazi persecution. This process of transferring wealth from Jewish enterprises to non-Jews was called "Aryanization." Upon his death, Horten left his estate to Heidi, and she invested in jewels and art. Lots of it. I don't know why I link these two things in my mind. Heidi's jewels weren't my ancestors' family jewels, and my family's jewels may not have been worth anything more than sentimental value. But for me, on some level, it's all connected. Heidi's gain is predicated on my loss, if only symbolically—not just my family's loss of property, but my loss of family in Europe. Subsequently, there was an uproar over the Horten auction and Christie's canceled further sales of over 300 additional jewels "due to intense scrutiny" surrounding the origins of Heidi Horten's estate.

My sense of outrage at an estate sale built from the ashes of Jewish lives provides some insight into how Black Americans must feel about not receiving their fair share of wealth. This suggests that American Jews and Black Americans have more in common than what Louis Farrakhan preaches.

SNOWFLAKE CONTINUED

Deb and I drove separately and met up at the theater on Wilshire Boulevard to see the movie about Holocaust survivors. As soon as we sat down, I started to feel anxious. The houselights were low, the movie hadn't started, Deb was talking about her daughter's boyfriend, that they were moving in together, how expensive washing machines are. Her lips were moving, but her voice was coming from somewhere else, and it was loud. So loud, I had to fight the impulse to cover my ears. I wanted the movie to begin so she would stop talking, but when it started, the feeling of being bombarded by sound escalated. I closed my eyes so I wouldn't have to watch the grainy images of concentration camps, but the sound, a composite voice-over narration by multiple survivors, was unbearable. So, I snuck out to go to the bathroom on the balcony. Then, I sat on the stairs between the balcony and main floor. This was an old-time Hollywood theater, a bit tattered, but the remnants of its heyday remained in design touches, such as velvet drapes and ornate Art Deco lighting fixtures. The stairs had plush, not industrial, carpeting—soft to the touch. Fishing my earbuds out of my purse, I plugged into an Oprah/Deepak Chopra meditation about creating peace from the inside out. When it was over, when I was done inhaling and exhaling, breathing slowly, rhythmically, and had regained some sense of calm, I could not make myself go back into the theater. Instead, I texted Deb my apologies, got in my car, and drove home.

"*You* invited *me!*" she texted back, sounding annoyed. "It was my birthday celebration! We were planning to go out for a bite afterward, and you ditched me!"

She didn't understand, and I couldn't explain; I couldn't tell anyone what was going on. The FODMAP diet was useless. I didn't have food allergies. I was a snowflake, my system too delicate for the barrage of hate that was spewing in the world. The constant thrum of Trumpism, the disruption of norms, the concept of "alternative" facts, the tweets, the dog whistles, the outright aggression against Jews, the impending reality of *The Handmaid's Tale* about to be unleashed in the United States. It was all too much for me.

THE BREAKUP

It was hot and sunny in Los Angeles when I grabbed my kids and took them downtown to the *Day Without a Woman* protest. Teach your children well. A Latinx woman took the stage. She was fired up, the crowd was fired up, everyone was whooping and cheering, and I was right there with them, until she said this: "We don't need suburban women in yoga pants."

"She's talking to you," Sam snickered, pointing at me. He was wearing white jeans and a T-shirt with a logo from a pizza parlor in Santa Barbara. I wasn't wearing yoga pants, although I often do, and not just when I practice yoga. I wear them around the house because they're comfy, and sometimes, also, to run errands. In the Valley. Valley Glen. Formerly known as Van Nuys. It's not the city, but it's not exactly the suburbs, either. Still, I felt called out and canceled.

"Well," I replied. "If I weren't a writer, I couldn't be here on a Wednesday afternoon attending this protest rally." And if my kids weren't cobbling together part-time jobs, neither could they. More to the heart of the matter, "suburban women in yoga pants" is just another dog whistle for a catchall of identity descriptors: white, middle class, privileged. I had this crushing sense of being unwanted in a movement that I had jumped into with both feet, marching in DC, in L.A., listening to speaker after speaker after speaker, heartened by the collective sense of 'we' in the air. But right here, in my adopted city, at an event organized by the Women's March, a woman onstage was saying, in no uncertain terms, *we don't want you.*

I'm all about women from communities of color leading the women's movement this time around. I know well the history of how Women of Color and LGBTQ voices were marginalized in the women's movement of my mother's generation. I'm happy to be an ally. Not to lead, but to lend support, to add my physical presence to the cause and demonstrate strength in numbers. But to be told not to show up, that infuriated me. I was done. When the Women's March sent me a message on Facebook about their next event, I posted this: "Sorry, I can't attend the March, I'm busy being Jewish that day."

It was snarky, I know. That's often how I deal with difficult situations. It's a coping mechanism. The next day, there were tons of comments. For a moment, I experienced the heady rush of being a social media influencer or at least sparking a conversation. Refreshing my cell phone every few minutes, checking the feed, until, boom, this comment hit me like a gut punch: *Why don't the Jewish girls get their own March?*

And there it was: a social media wake-up call. I'm not one of them, no matter who 'them' is. Not white. Not of color. Siloed. As a Jew, I had been uninvited to the intersectional party. I slammed my laptop shut fast as if recoiling from an electric shock. Later, when I attempted to show Sam the comment, I couldn't log on to the FB page, discovering that, adding insult to injury, I had been banned from the Women's March page for twenty-four hours.

"You're a troll, Mom!" Sam exclaimed, using a tone that communicated surprise, sarcasm, and some degree of admiration, as if he didn't know I had it in me.

I was still reeling from the comment about Jewish women getting their own March. Being cast out of my chosen cause increased the stress on my body. My digestive system careened out of whack. At Starbucks, when I asked for the bathroom code, I meant, *now!* I'd had panic attacks before, when I was moving or changing jobs, or that time at the movies with Deb, but this was different. The Women's March betrayal catapulted me into generalized panic disorder. Next step up the rung of anxiety is agoraphobia, which now I understand, because you're afraid to leave the house in case you lose your shit. In public. My blood pressure was sky-high, my nerves rattled. This is way too personal. You don't want to hear it. How Donald Trump ripped the country wide open, and the Women's March failed me, and how I may never feel that sense of belonging to something bigger than myself again.

BOOKENDS

I awoke with the song "Let It Be" in my head. Once again, it was the morning after a U.S. presidential election. This time, an unqualified white man had beaten a qualified multiracial woman; only now, he's a convicted felon, and he's been held liable for sexual abuse. The first time Trump won, I was in shock, my faith in American institutions shaken to its core. I was shouting to the rafters, RESIST! Fat lot of good that did. This time around, I was listening to "Let It Be" on re-peat. Suspended in wait-and-see mode. I love my daughter's reaction, which was a bit tongue-in-cheek, but also hopeful. I rang her The Morning After, and Sasha said, cheerfully, "He promised to fix all our problems, and in four years I will be able to buy a house!" *Yeah, right. Peace, baby! Fingers crossed.* These days, I find myself googling Claudia Sheinbaum Pardo, Mexico's new president. *A Jewish Woman!* And I write that with all the inflection of a Jewish bubbe. Sheinbaum is an academic, an environmental scientist, and the former mayor of Mexico City. *She* is a champion for children and healthcare, women's issues, and renewable energy. She has the potential to redefine Mexico's future by focusing on critical domestic issues, such as crime and public safety. Just saying, I'm not ruling out crossing the border in the other direction.

Privilege

AROUND THE TIME OF COVID and the Black Lives Matter protests, I joined an anti-racism book club on Zoom. We read books on white fragility, white power, white rage, woke racism, and something called *Dear White People*. Books by Toni Morrison and James Baldwin. Books about racial bias and conspiracy theories. Islam and gender. One book that compares racism in the U.S. to Nazi Germany and the caste system in India. Another that conjures the perilous journey undertaken by immigrants from Central America and Mexico as they attempt to cross the border into the United States. We watched a film about Muhammad Ali and Malcolm X and went to the theater to see a play about race, sex, power, and generational trauma. And we read *Minor Feelings* by Cathy Park Hong—a collection of essays that explore the Korean American experience. My copy of that book is marked up and dog-eared. Read and reread. If chewing the pages—literally digesting her words—had enabled me to spit out *JewGirl* with anywhere near the beauty, grace, humor, and anger of Hong's writing, I would have done so. After reading *Minor Feelings,* a book about dissonant feelings, one woman in our book club commented that if she, meaning the writer, was so unhappy living in America, why didn't she just move back to Korea?

SHE WAS BORN HERE! I wanted to scream.

It's like asking why I don't go back to Hungary. Russia. Ukraine. Lithuania. Countries where my ancestors lived, died, and/or fled. But I didn't scream, I commented in my normal speaking voice, because I'd come to appreciate this group, and we all say the wrong thing occasionally. That's the point of the book club: to confront and process our understanding of racism in a safe space, without judgment.

Early on, as in the first book discussion, I verbalized my belief that any "privilege" I had was mitigated by being Jewish, female, and a survivor of sexual assault. "You have skin privilege," the group leader, a college educator on race, schooled me. You may experience prejudice or gender-related trauma, but you benefit from systemic racism. Then she said, "Can you imagine how much worse it would be if you were Black?"

Shamed, I backed down immediately. "Yes," I said. "Of course. So much worse."

Part of the misunderstanding stemmed from the fact that I didn't have the appropriate language to discuss racism. I still understood the word "privilege" to mean economic advantage. I didn't understand the nuance between the words "prejudice" and "racism"—that white people can experience prejudice, but only People of Color experience racism, because prejudice implies discrimination, and racism indicates systematic power backing up discrimination. Part of the leader's response stemmed from the lack of credence paid to antisemitism in the United States. This is especially true on college campuses, where the narrative of Israel as an oppressor/colonizer is prevalent, erasing the history of oppression Jewish people have experienced and ignoring the complexity of the Israeli-Palestinian conflict. A big part of the issue is that while Black history is a critical piece of the American narrative, antisemitism is not distinctly American, because so much Jewish history happened somewhere else. Antisemitism—and, more specifically, Jewish people being at risk of annihilation—is viewed as a 20th-century European problem. Yet, Jews are still at risk at any moment in time, somewhere in the world: in France, in Russia, in Israel, and the United States.

I backed down because I understood that Jews don't count when talking about racism in the United States. For one thing, Jews are an ethnoreligious group, not a race. But especially now, at a time when the U.S. is confronting its history of racism against Black people, throwing Jews into the mix is just too much wrongdoing for people to absorb.

Our book club comprised six white women, raised Christian, and me. I found myself having a singular experience while discussing these books. I was nodding my head, *yeah, I get it.* Whenever I brought up the similarities between the Jewish experience and People of Color, the other members of the group seemed surprised, as if they knew nothing about the history of antisemitism in America. Neither the degree to which it existed, nor the specifics: redlining and exclusionary practices, nor the scope of antisemitism simmering in white power groups. Even I knew nothing about the widespread and powerful support for Nazi Germany that existed in the United States leading up to WWII until we read Rachel Maddow's book *Prequel: An American Fight Against Fascism.* After the press picked up JD Vance's statement about childless cat ladies, one woman in the group said it was the first time in her life that she had ever felt targeted, illustrating the significant gap between her life experience and mine, even though, on the face of it, we appeared to be a homogenous group: white, middle-aged, college-educated women. It would be easy to dismiss these women as clueless, but that's not fair; they just didn't know. Antisemitism is something they'd never had to think about.

I didn't register the same measured horror and outrage after reading these books on racism that these women did. Having experienced antisemitism, I connect to struggles around racism in a different way. But I stayed in the group, month after month, poking the bear, refusing to identify as white, insisting that white privilege is about more than skin color, that it's connected to Christianity. I kept telling my stories, waiting for one of them to suggest reading a book about antisemitism in America.

"Why don't you suggest a book on antisemitism?" a friend of mine asked.

"Because I want them to come to it on their own," I said. I hate being the only Jew in the room. I know how people sometimes perceive me. Loud. Opinionated. Pushy. Or the class clown, irreverent. The women in my book club wanted to read about racism, but didn't even see, acknowledge, or want to discuss antisemitism. It took a while, but eventually someone suggested reading *Antisemitism: Here and Now* by Deborah E. Lipstadt—a fictionalized academic approach to the current up-tick of antisemitism on college campuses. Silly as this sounds, that simple gesture, a book selection, made me feel validated. Then, because the ice had been broken, I felt comfortable suggesting *The Plot Against America* by Philip Roth, a novel that imagines an America if Roosevelt hadn't won a third and un-precedented election, if instead, Nazi-sympathizer Charles Lindbergh had become president in 1940, turning America into a fascist country. The chaos that ensues is frightening, pre-scient, and disturbingly relevant in today's America.

A word about my privilege. When I moved in with Harry, he was living in Koreatown, near Beverly and Vermont, in Los Angeles. It was a 1930s apartment in a not-yet-gentrified neighborhood. We were not yet in our thirties. We had roaches in the shower, and a roommate who slept in what was intend-ed to be the living room. Retail strips lined Beverly Boulevard: a convenience store here, a liquor store there, a Guatemalan bakery, and a Korean-owned video store.

The video store had a banner hanging from the roof that said, FREE MOVIE RENTAL. I drove by it all the time and never stopped, but one Friday after work as a receptionist at a radio station, I decided to surprise Harry. Movie Night! I parked right under the banner and went inside. The guy be-hind the desk explained that I had to join their video club first, for I don't remember how much. Fifty dollars? A hundred dollars? Twenty-five dollars would have been too much money for us back then. We were barely scraping by, and besides, his banner said FREE. I argued with him a bit about false adver-tising before leaving the store empty-handed.

In a flash of frustration about everything—being broke, how hard it was to get ahead in L.A., working as a receptionist at a radio station despite having been the assistant director of promotion at a radio station in Detroit, a guy named Flame who hired me, insisting that answering phones was a fast-track to the promotion department, my sense that this was a path for girls only, that a guy would bypass this "foot in the door" opportunity, false advertising, impervious store managers, men, the roaches in our shower—I climbed onto the hood of my car and yanked the FREE MOVIE banner down.

I only lived a few blocks away, but there was a cop on my tail almost immediately. The officer pulled me over and asked to see my license and registration, citing a retail complaint. "Officer," I countered, "the banner said 'free,' and they wouldn't give me a free rental!" He wasn't interested in my explanation of bait-and-switch advertising, he was busy writing me a ticket for something—another detail I can't quite remember—possibly "defacing private property." Here's what I do remember: I was mad as hell. I think, perhaps, he asked me to get out of the car, or maybe not, but I do know that I intentionally opened the door as hard as I could, slamming it into the officer's knees.

If I hadn't been a white girl, my head would have been slammed into the hood of my car, my hands cuffed behind my back, and I would have been taken downtown. If I had been Sandra Bland (a Black woman), most likely I would have been arrested. Sandra was twenty-eight years old, about the same age as I was at the time of this incident. She was starting a new job at a university in Texas when a state trooper pulled her over for failing to signal a lane change. She'd had the audacity to light a cigarette while speaking to the officer, and the encounter escalated from there, leading to her arrest.

I have no idea what happened to Sandra during the three days following her arrest for failing to signal a lane change. I only know that she died by suicide in jail. At least that was the official cause of death. Another thing I know is that I have gotten away with behavior that a Woman of Color might not have survived. My white skin is like water. It's the world I swim in, so ubiquitous that sometimes I don't even notice it unless I make a conscious effort to examine my privilege along with the antisemitism that I am hyperaware of, along with the gender inequalities I have experienced.

That comment, *my skin is like water,* comes from a cult-classic commencement speech at Kenyon College given by David Foster Wallace called *This Is Water* that I return to over and over again, like some people go to temple or church, an ashram, or yoga retreat, always getting either new understanding or a basic brush-up from the text. It begins like this: "There are these two young fish swimming along and they happen to meet an older fish swimming the other way, who nods at them and says 'Morning, boys. How's the water?' The two fish swim on for a bit, and then one of them looks over at the other and says, 'What the hell is water?'"

Standard analysis of this short but monumental lecture about the value of an education centers on default settings—the importance of acknowledging one's natural biases, one's ability to choose to step outside of his or her default setting, and that the ongoing task in life is not *going* to work, it's *doing* the work to remain conscious, even while driving a car or standing in line at the grocery store, or yeah, while arguing with a Korean video store manager. Who may have had as hard a day as I did. Likely, longer. And probably had mouths to feed. That banner was his hope of attracting new business, staying afloat, paying the rent or feeding the kids, and I came along and ripped it down because I couldn't see his struggle. Only mine. In the words of David Foster Wallace, "The point of the fish story is merely that the most obvious, important realities are often the ones that are hardest to see and talk about."

Old Jew

HARRY AND I WERE in his car when the phone rang. "Hi, Claire," he said. "You're on the speakerphone. Marcie and I are on our way to …"

It didn't matter where we were going, it sounded like a preemptive move. Heads-up: The wife's in earshot.

She said "hi."

I said "hi" back.

Harry and Claire have known each other forever. Friends from college. Full disclosure: Claire and I have never been close. There was an incident a long time ago that disrupted any simpatico feelings we might have developed. The three of us were out to dinner when Harry asked Claire how work was going. It was a benign question, like *How's life?*

Claire launched into a long-winded complaint about her assistant, who had recently returned from maternity leave. "She calls the nanny from her desk just to make sure the baby is okay," she said, her tone dripping with dissatisfaction. *Oh, the problems of being a professional woman and managing unreliable, uncommitted staff.* She felt awful because this woman had worked for her for years. Nonetheless, she was probably going to have to let her go.

And I kind of blew up. I was pregnant with Sasha, my belly button popping through my maternity top, struggling with how I was going to manage a baby and a full-time job, the commute across town, all of it. So, I blasted her right there in Killer Shrimp. Told her she had a lot of nerve talking shit about working mothers in front of me. I used to have a quick temper. Plus, the shrimp was really spicy.

A few years later, when Claire got married, she didn't invite us to the wedding. She said she didn't think we'd come because we were living in Paris at the time. As if there weren't planes that flew non-stop from Charles de Gaulle to LAX, or it was an unfathomable distance to travel for a wedding *with kids.* Like we'd be crossing the Atlantic by boat. She acted as if she were being considerate when, in fact, *we just weren't invited.* Harry sent her a wedding gift anyway because he's a nice guy and doesn't dwell in the land of insults and slights like I do. I would have sent her a knife to sever the cord, but they have a close relationship; he thinks of her as a sister.

Their relationship is nothing like mine with my sisters. We're all up in each other's grills. *She did what?* Phone calls that go on for hours, fights that last for days, not weeks anymore. Life is too tenuous. We're getting older, which brings me to the reason Claire called. Harry's mom has dementia and Claire (now an assisted living consultant who specializes in finding placement for aging parents) was helping Harry navigate the situation. Nan was living in a memory care facility near us in the desert.

Poor thing.

No one wants to end up like that, but as those places go, Happy Abode wasn't bad. She had a private suite, with free roam of the building and the enclosed outdoor patio. Sadly, Nan was beyond appreciating life's little luxuries like having your own toilet or freedom to roam. Most days she wore random travel T-shirts and stained sweatpants, her long gray hair hadn't been cut or styled in years. She was ragged and stringy. She was also punchy. She got into a fight with a guy in a wheelchair, grabbed his *LA Times* right out of his hands, accusing him of stealing her paper. Then, when one of the other residents tried to retrieve the paper from her, she whacked him with it! Started a brawl at the old folks' home. As a result, Happy Abode was demanding round-the-clock care, which cost an arm and a leg.

That's why Claire called Harry, and he put her on speakerphone. She was sure it was the facility's fault. Also, I suspect, she blamed me because I had found Happy Abode on my own, without consulting her. Claire thought Harry's mother belonged in a fancier place, one that served better food. I was thinking *Claire hasn't seen Nan in a long time. Nan's apt to pour milk over a tuna fish sandwich, smush it flat like a pancake, happy as a clam.*

"Jeremy is moving," Claire informed us. Jeremy was the uncle of a friend of Claire's who retired in Palm Springs and was living at the same place as Nan, but now Claire was moving him to a better facility.

"Hey, what does Jeremy look like?" Harry asked.

"An old queen," Claire replied.

I didn't say a word. Neither did Harry. We didn't even exchange looks because he was driving the car, but my ears perked up and I was in observation mode. Claire hadn't seen the stain on the saggy bum of Harry's mom's sweatpants. She had no clue how Nan was doing compared to this guy named Jeremy. Harry wanted to know what shape Jeremy's pants were in, so to speak. In other words, was he lucid? Was he still showering, combing his hair, and wearing clean clothes? Harry wanted to check this guy out the next time he visited his mother, so he repeated his question. "What does Jeremy look like?"

This time she said, "An old Jew."

I'm just going to put this out there: Calling someone "a Jew" is like saying the N-word. You really shouldn't say it unless you are Jewish. That's why I can call myself *JewGirl*. From my lips, it's like taking back the night. But out of someone else's mouth, someone who isn't a member of the tribe, like Claire, it sounds harsh. I'm going to stop short of saying it sounds antisemitic because then people get their panties all in a twist. *But I'm not like that!* Maybe not, but still, when a non-Jewish person says *Jew*, I hear a silent *dirty* before the word. Claire said *Jew* as if she were talking about a gnat she flicked off her arm.

What does an "old Jew" look like anyway? Fat, thin, tall, short, bald.

White?

But that's not what I was thinking when she said it. What I was thinking was that she knew I was on the speakerphone, and she said it anyway.

If one of my friends had said this, I would have jumped down their throat, but I have learned to moderate my tone when talking to Harry's friends and family. Besides, I couldn't very well jump on Claire for the *old Jew* comment after letting the *old queen* comment slide. So, she got away with it. She's probably been getting away with it her whole life. Straight blonde hair, blue eyes. Entitled. When you look like that, the world treats you like you're something special. There are no barriers to entry. You're not carrying around a Jewish name, or some other ethnic "tell" or identity marker like POC or LGBTQ. You don't follow news cycles covering your tribe as a target of hate crimes and demonstrations; the subject of congressional hearings; university professors backed into a corner, losing their jobs for not defending the rights of your people. You have no clue what it's like to be a topic of conversation on the nightly news.

Later, I thought about that poem "First They Came" by Martin Niemöller, a German Lutheran pastor in Nazi Germany. I'm paraphrasing: *First they came for the Communists, and I did not speak out, because I was not a Communist. Then they came for the Socialists and then the trade unionists, but I did not speak out, because I was not a socialist or a trade unionist. Then they came for the Jews, and I did not speak out because I was not a Jew.*

But I am a Jew, and I didn't speak up in the moment. In my defense, this was a conversation between Harry and his oldest friend. I was just listening in. It was Harry's place to correct Claire, not mine. I'd already been down that road before, when I was pregnant, and lambasted her for not being more supportive of working mothers. My response had been deemed out of line, given her relationship to Harry. After that, I made it a policy to stick to pleasantries with Claire and leave the difficult conversations to Harry. But I have never once heard them disagree, let alone fight, or call each other out for bad behavior.

Here's what bugs me about Harry letting those comments slide. We have many gay friends. I'm Jewish. Our kids are Jewish. Half of Harry's relatives, even on *his* side of the family, are Jewish. It shouldn't be up to me to school his childhood friend. He should have spoken up, and because he did not, not only did she get away with it, but she may not even have known how offensive she sounded. Not speaking up is just as bad as what Claire said, maybe worse. It's passive acceptance, and passivity supports the status quo. In the short run, Harry avoids having a difficult conversation with an old friend, but in the long run, he's doing her a disservice. He's cruising along Highway 111, loose as a goose; he's got one arm on the wheel, and it's another sunny day in the desert. She's out there dropping homophobic and antisemitic comments like it's just another day in her white Christian world.

And I am left to shoulder the uncomfortable feelings.

"I know, I heard it," was all Harry said after he hung up the phone with Claire. Meaning: *I don't need a lecture.* To which I replied, "The least she could have done was say an old *Jewish man.*" I focused on semantics, avoiding the bigger conversation, which we would have later, when I could collect my thoughts and control my temper, because Harry is my partner, the father of my children, a good guy, who just needs to be reminded to step up sometimes.

My father was short, a bit stocky, barrel-chested. He had light eyes and dark hair, streaked with silver as he got older. He warmed considerably as he aged. He smiled and told stupid dad jokes. There are pictures of the two of us walking arm in arm, sitting shoulder to shoulder on a couch, smiling. Did he look Jewish? I think so. Did he look like Jeremy? I have no idea.

What do you see when you think of a Jew
Do you see me?
A writer. A mother. A sister. A wife.
Or do you see your shadow
That mythical other
Some shady character who's ruining your life,
Counting their money and pulling the strings.
A cartoon figure with a big nose
Or a woman dripping in designer clothes.[18]

Bear with me because I'm going to ramble a bit. I used to cook a bird every Sunday, so I could feed my dog homemade chicken with rice and carrots and then make broth for myself from the bones. We were so healthy. Cooper was a solid, muscular French bulldog who liked long walks and socializing at the park. If I tried to take him home before he was ready, he'd refuse—planting his front paws on the grass or street, standing his ground, as if to say, *no way*. I'd have to give him another fifteen minutes of playtime or take him for an additional lap around the block, because there was no way I could drag or carry that dog home. Then, in the middle of COVID, my knee swelled up and I could barely walk. Cooper sat on the floor next to me for months while I did physical therapy exercises. Didn't complain when I was too stiff to take him for a walk, just went in the yard and did his business. Afterwards, he'd come back inside and curl up next to me on the couch, as if comforting me was his job.

At first it was my knee, then my ankle, then my shoulder, and then I knew it was the family curse: autoimmune disease. (Chicky said, *I told you so!*) I quit PT and got a rheumatologist

18   Inspired by the song 1001 Nights by Saint Levant

instead, and as soon as I was better, out of nowhere, Cooper got sick. One day he was chasing gophers and bunnies, begging for table scraps, and the next day he was thirsty, so thirsty, it was like he was dying of thirst. More to the point, he had a tumor in his throat that he was trying to wash away. He took to lying on the wood floor next to my desk for hours, so I'd get down there on the floor with him and read a book, just to keep him company. Toward the end, I'd drive him to the park; we'd sit on the grass so he could enjoy familiar smells. His body weak but his nose taking it all in—other dogs, kids, discarded food scraps. It broke my heart. All that baloney about the Rainbow Bridge, that's a bunch of horseshit. Your dead pooches are not hanging out on some bridge in heaven, lapping up water from a rain cloud. Like that's supposed to make you feel better, anyway. Believe me, your heart's going to break.

Mine did.

On the other hand, I felt nothing when my mother-in-law went into assisted living. Okay, that's a lie. I didn't feel "nothing." It's more like I didn't feel sad. I felt obligated to visit her. When I didn't go, I felt guilty for not going, and when I did go, afterwards I felt as if I deserved some kind of pat on the back. A gold star for good behavior. But the truth is, I was closer to my dog than I was to Harry's mom. Hell, I was closer to my dog than I was to my father. But when I visited Nan, when I was squeezing her hand, when I was sitting right next to this fragile shell of a human being and she lit up at the sight of me, I did feel a tinge of regret, which is kind of how I felt about my father—that I didn't try harder. No, that's not it. It's that I didn't *forgive* harder. I'd stare at Nan's hands; the veins bulging, skin thin, knuckles swollen. Her wedding band stuck on her ring finger, permanently lodged between two joints, her fingers having morphed into tree roots, entwined around the thing that mattered most to her.

Love.

Funny that it should be me, of all people—the daughter-in-law she didn't get along with. There she was nearing the end of her life, and the only person visiting her was me. Her husband deceased, her daughter living in the South of France, her son working in China, and it fell on me to be the person who showed up at this godforsaken place. We had to move her after that brawl over the newspaper, and the new facility was not nearly as nice as Happy Abode.

She spent her days in the memory prison, lying on the couch like a sarcophagus, hands clasped together on her chest, waiting. Oblivious to her surroundings—buzzers and iron gates, locks on the doors, a waif-like old woman floating around barefoot in a flimsy nightgown, a decaying old man slumped in a rolling chair, the television a low hum in the background. Sometimes I'd bring our new puppy, Rue Bader Girl, with me. My mother-in-law liked to rub her ears and scratch her fur. She'd smile from the tactile pleasure, her lips puckered, as if trying to say, "nice doggy" or "so cute," but she could no longer string two words together.

I don't think of her as Nan anymore. The dementia has robbed her of all that Nan was—the good and the bad, the perfect hostess, the mother-in-law from Hell. That's all gone. A while ago, I gave her my moss-colored zip-up fleece jacket from Lululemon. I liked that jacket a lot, too. I wore it to the dog park, to the gym, on hikes. I hesitated for a moment before giving it to her. It was cozy, my favorite shade of green, and it fit me perfectly. But here's what I care about more: not lugging guilt around with me.

After that Christmas dinner punctuated by the JAP joke, when I kicked Nan out of our house, I never gave her another chance. But I gave her my favorite jacket when her caregiver said she was cold. *Yeah, she's cold,* I thought. She was cold and calculating—that JAP joke was not an off-the-cuff blunder. It felt pointed and premeditated. I can be cold, too; it's not something I'm proud of. At any moment in time, if we had been able to talk about the issues between us, we may have been able to repair the relationship. Instead, I put up a protective barrier between the two of us. We talked on the phone; I sent photos of the kids; we exchanged gifts on the holidays. We visited occasionally. But none of it was heartfelt. I can't rewind and fix that. All I can do is sit with her now and then.

Guilt

THE IDEA FOR THIS book began in a blood bank with my refusal to check the box "White." It didn't seem such a big deal at the time to choose "Other" instead of "White."

Who cares?

But I have gotten pushback from all sorts of people— Jewish, non-Jewish, and People of Color.

"Well, yeah," Carlo, my dog park buddy, said, nodding his head while we were discussing the whole checking-the-box thing. "Black people are having a moment. They don't want you riding their wave, and they for sure don't wanna let you skate on the skin issue."

"I'm on my own wave," I protested. *We're having a moment, too*, I thought. *Only, not a good one.* My Jewish friends are more nervous now than they've ever been. Even before the war between Israel and Hamas, just in general, things had not been trending well for Jews. Since then, antisemitic incidents in the United States have increased substantially. Carlo just kept nodding as if deep in thought, sporting a modern mohawk, head on tilt. He's a DJ of some renown. He's also South American and French, and, like me, a person who rejects the box system.

"Fuck that." Those were his exact words.

This issue continues to confound statisticians. More people checked the box "Other" than "Black" in the 2020 U.S. census. I like to think it's a movement—all of us "othered" people in one box together, embracing diversity. The government, though, is concerned about the rise of the "Other" category, which is why the next census will ask: What is your race and/or ethnicity, expanding the previous list of options to include Hispanic/Latino and Middle Eastern/North African (MENA). Some Jews will fall under the MENA umbrella, but as an Ashkenazi Jew, I'll be holding my ground, still checking the "Other" box. People can pooh-pooh that, as they already have, and most likely will continue to do so.

I'm used to it.

One of my freewrites about this issue was labeled "dangerous" by a Black woman in my writing group. Three times. Her voice emphatic, the verbal equivalent of writing in all caps. DANGEROUS. DANGEROUS. DANGEROUS. Freewrites are a form of generative writing—loose, unedited, beginnings of story ideas. Writing classes run the gamut from uploading text online in relative anonymity to what this class had become for me: a writers' community.

Or, at least what felt like a community.

We met every Thursday on the east side of Los Angeles at Sarah's place. Her apartment was layered and textured in vibrant colors; shag rugs, walls filled with art—multicolored elephants and abstract canvases in variations of pink. Sarah was Barbiecore before it was even a thing. She wrote positive, uplifting messages in Sharpie on her mirror in the bathroom. Things like *Be Strong* and *Smile*. We bonded fast and talked on the phone all the time. I was somewhat intimidated by the rest of the group, many of whom were actors, because they read their pieces with theatrical flair and, sometimes, even tears. I read mine with no hint of emotional content whatsoever, as if to say, *it's there, in the words, on the page, in between the lines, pay no attention to the messenger or her delivery.*

I had no clue how to connect with a live audience.

The first time I ever read one of my own stories out loud in a writers' group, the teacher stopped me one paragraph in. "Start over," he said. His name was Chaz. He wasn't a big guy, but his voice was commanding. "You're reading too fast," he bellowed.

I started over from the beginning.

He stopped me again, this time interrupting me mid-sentence. "Slower," he insisted, like he was an acting coach, not a writing teacher. The room was dead silent. I could sense pity or possibly fear in the other students' faces. His criticism flowed like a run-on sentence. "You're still rushing, you need to pause, breathe, your delivery has no impact, do you have something to say or not? This may be interesting, who can tell, it's like you're reading the phone book."

I started over, focusing on pronunciation.

"Again," he said, interrupting me. "From the beginning. This time with feeling."

I started from the beginning, over and over, slowing my words to the verbal equivalent of a crawl, to what felt like a remedial pace. English as a second language. It was maddening, embarrassing, and frustrating all at once, but I did not cry. I refused to break. I don't know how many times he made me start over, or how long it took, only that at some point I was allowed to finish reading my piece. When it was over, I experienced a huge sense of relief and an even stronger sense of pride that I hadn't burst into tears.

He seemed pleased with himself. He had used me to make a point: the importance of dramatic delivery. But to me, it felt like he was just another man surfing the line between constructive criticism and bullying. I considered walking out of the class, but he came with such pedigree; he had devotees, and this being Hollywood, I knew not to burn bridges. When it was over, he complimented my writing. The next week, he did the same thing to Sarah while she was reading a piece about a guy who had physically threatened her.

"How did this make you feel?" he wanted to know, his voice full throttle. "Are you angry? Sad? Scared? I'm not sensing your reaction. You're holding back. Start over. Go deeper." He was pacing back and forth in front of her. It looked like he was stalking her: She was fidgeting in her seat, pulling the hair at the nape of her neck, blonde and shaggy, her voice shaky, almost as if she were being re-injured; it was uncomfortable to witness. Sarah and I bonded after that class. That's when we decided to start our own writers' group at her place with a new teacher named Benny.[19]

Benny ran our class like clockwork. We read in the order in which we arrived, five pages, double-spaced, and we were allotted twenty minutes each. He used an egg timer. When it rang, your time was up. It always seemed that we were mere mortals struggling to bring story to life, laying our pieces at

---

19   Setting and characters fictionalized based on real events.

the altar of Benny, who was some sort of literary empath, with the ability to uncover deeper meaning from words on the page than most of us recognized or even intended. Sometimes we would bring fragments to class, like offerings, and say: *I'm not even sure what this is.* Benny would tell us exactly what it was, where it belonged, and how it fit into our overall theme or the hero's journey. He'd nod with approval, pleased that our subconscious had delivered a gem in the form of a scrap of paper we'd written on just before we fell asleep the night before class, not knowing where it came from or what it meant. Sometimes he'd push, and there would be tears. It's crazy how easy it is for actors to cry, but not me. I might get angry, shut down, or withdraw, but I never cried.

Well, not because of something Benny said, anyway.

We'd been together for over a year, meeting every week, sharing our work, cheering each other on and providing helpful, insightful feedback. There was one session, around the time of Mardi Gras in New Orleans, when we played Jon Batiste, and everyone got up and danced. We had become friends, invested in each other's stories. Cheerleaders without the pom-poms. So, it caught me off guard when Amira called my work DANGEROUS.

Before I get into what happened *after* Amira commented on my piece, I want to share what was said by everyone else *before* she spoke up, not because I'm patting myself on the back, but because it provides context for what followed.

Sarah smiled, saying: *You nailed it, girl!*

Catrina called it powerful.

Michael high-fived me.

Jerry said, *I feel you and I don't even like Jews.* Jerry did standup, so it needs to be said that we all laughed at his comment.

Then came Amira's rebuttal. I could barely process the gist of her comments, which centered largely on me ignoring my privilege, questioning this fundamental concept that I don't check the box "White" because I'm Jewish. This trips people up a lot. For me, it's simple. I acknowledge the privilege that comes with white skin. That said, I reject the box system because it does not encompass the whole story about race and ethnicity, specifically as it relates to Jewish people. American Jews have been othered and are increasingly at risk, regardless of skin color. We do not have a shared history with white Christian America. That's what led me to express that I do not feel responsible for, nor do I feel guilty about, slavery in the United States, because *my* people were roaming the desert, out of Egypt, running around the Middle East, Asia, Africa, Europe, and Russia, from one bad situation to another, for 2000 years, trying to avoid being enslaved: the Spanish Inquisition, pogroms, concentration camps, and the gas chamber.

That's why Amira called my piece DANGEROUSx3.

What followed felt like an avalanche of support for Amira.

Sarah put her hands on her heart, looked straight at me, and said: *I love you, but Amira has a point.*

Catrina fell in line, saying that just because someone is Jewish doesn't mean they aren't white.

Michael said something about how we all benefit from American slavery.

Jerry said he feels guilty every time he pays $6 for a cup of coffee. But seriously, yeah, there's no "get-out-of-guilt-free" card for Jews.

It felt like a velvet course-correction. The only writer in the group who had my back was Fran, and she, too, was Jewish. Everyone else deferred to Amira.

Later, it would occur to me that Amira's comments might have been less about what I had read in class that day and more a commentary on what she thought of my ideas in general but that she'd held her tongue all year long. Later, I would consider that it might have been difficult for a Woman of Color to speak her truth in opposition to mine. Later, Benny would accuse me of blowing up his class, and I would feel bereft at losing his guidance. Later, I would ruminate on everything that went down that day, especially losing my cool. By the time the buzzer had rung, my turn was over, and I was in tears. My public persona, that caustic, sarcastic, wry, funny girl had crumbled like volcanic ash. While I've blocked out most of what happened in that class, I am pretty sure it would be accurate to say that my inner Karen surfaced. And she did not shine, she whined.

I felt hurt, misunderstood, and confused. These were my colleagues. They had always supported my writing until one woman put the kibosh on me. Whatever Amira may have said or meant, this is what I heard: *Girl, you have no fucking clue what it's like for a Black woman in the real world. So, stop your sobbing. You have it so good you should be thanking the gods, the Nina, the Pinta, and the Santa Maria, all of them that brought you here on a ship, above deck, not chained in the bowels of the boat, grateful to have been born with white skin. Shout "Hallelujah" and stop pissing and moaning about not checking the box "White" already.*

Here's how I wish I had responded: "As a woman whose rights are under attack, a member of a minority that is targeted, and a survivor of sexual assault, I have a hard time being lumped in with white privilege. Because when we speak of white privilege, we're talking about white *and* Christian. If you want to talk about power in this country, it's white, Christian, and male. You have only to consider the demographic portrait of American presidents: all male, all Christian, all white, with one exception: President Obama. No women, no Jews. My point is that, while I acknowledge my skin privilege, I also have gender and ethnic struggles. As a Jew, I don't have a shared cultural history with nativist white Americans who can trace their heritage back to the Revolution, or if not the Revolution, at least to slavery. My ancestors, part of the largest wave of Jewish immigrants coming to the U.S., arrived after the Civil War and before the Second World War. Although I am American, my sense of shared history is with the Jewish Diaspora.

Unfortunately, I don't think I was that eloquent.

When I recounted what had happened in my writers' group to my son, he remarked that if they wanted to prove that I was a white privileged Karen, they did, but also, they proved that my thesis holds—that it's white Christians *and* People of Color vs. Jews. That wasn't my thesis, though, because not everyone who isn't Jewish is antisemitic. However, we *are* at a point in time where antisemitism on the progressive left is accelerating to catch up with the antisemitism on the far right in this country.

Up until that moment, everything I had written had a sharp edge, almost as if I didn't even feel the enormity of my subject matter, as if I were an objective reporter, detached from the girl who was othered in middle school for being Jewish, the swastika on my dorm room door, the JAP joke delivered by my mother-in-law on Christmas, the animals massacred at my kids' preschool, finding my family name on the wall of an internment camp in China, the betrayal of the Women's

March. The weight of it all, the reality of the situation being revealed by my personal experience, came crashing down on me in that workshop. It appeared that lines were being drawn, sides chosen, and I was not alone. *We were alone.* Fran and I, the two Jews in the room. Here I was, writing *about* being othered and experiencing *being* othered, both at the same time.

That this group no longer felt like a safe space hit me like a tsunami. *Nazis are marching in Nashville! It may not be safe for Jewish people anywhere in this country anymore. I have nowhere to go.* Portugal was a pipe dream, a fantasy. The reality was that I had no affiliation larger than my family and my tribe. And I'm not talking about the family I was born into, either. My world had shrunk to the size of the family I had created—my chosen family: my husband, kids, and core best friends.

It's like my mother always said: Antisemitism never goes away; it only lies dormant.

What happened after that class can best be described as an email guilt fest. Everyone in the group had guilt to share. They felt guilty about Rwanda, the Armenian genocide, Darfur, in addition to slavery and the Holocaust. Guilty for being blonde and pretty, about having a nice apartment and a stocked fridge when food insecurity and homelessness were an epidemic in Los Angeles. About benefitting from rent control, gentrification, and film residuals. It felt as if my writing had been the catalyst for a floodgate of feedback, and Amira's comments released feelings that had been sitting there, just under the surface. The situation was so intense, Benny suggested an after-class session the following week to talk about what was going on. I worried that what they really wanted to do was talk about my bad ideas, which made me think of the Cultural Revolution in China when students denounced family and friends.

At first, I responded with self-deprecation. I sent a group email saying that part of me wanted to lighten the conversation by saying something funny, because that is my survival skill: an ability to inject humor into uncomfortable, difficult, and painful situations. But that is a skill I use in writing, not always in life, and I was feeling emotionally raw after that meeting. I had not planned on attending class the following week, or ever again, for that matter. Then I thanked everyone for making it clear that dropping out was not the right response.

In hindsight, it would have been wiser to have skipped the next class.

When we stayed after class the following week, I tried to take a logical approach, asking Amira if *she* felt guilty about the Holocaust. I was trying to set up an equivalency between the Holocaust and slavery, only and specifically in terms of our respective responsibilities for, and subsequent feelings of, guilt. I figured that a Black American woman wouldn't feel responsible for the Holocaust, so she'd understand my saying that I didn't feel responsible for slavery. But she replied that, yes, of course, she felt guilty about the Holocaust. This makes no sense to me, not then or now. I don't understand why anyone who wasn't involved in the Holocaust should feel guilty about what happened. Sad, outraged, and embarrassed to be human, all things I feel about slavery in the United States—an unresolved stain on our country's history that bleeds into the present experience of all Americans, especially the Black experience.

But guilty?

The only way I can wrap my head around a Black person feeling guilty about the Holocaust is that they are human, and human beings committed atrocities. But that is so broad a definition of guilt as to render it meaningless. Sometimes I wonder if this whole mess was nothing more than a semantic issue. Perhaps the idea of collective guilt should be reimagined as collective empathy.

In that follow-up session, the one Benny suggested because he thought we needed space to express ourselves outside of critiquing each other's work, Amira extended a gracious apology for having called my writing dangerous. She was calm and controlled. Her apology may even have been genuine, but her delivery seemed flat. It didn't bother me that the situation had spun so far out of control that she might have felt obligated to apologize. I was willing to accept her apology with equanimity and put the whole incident behind us. Then Sofia, the social justice lawyer who lives, works, and breathes on the frontlines of immigration battles, jumped in, spitting mad, saying that Amira had nothing to apologize for because everything she said was fact. As in, the truth.

Not *her* truth. *The* truth.

I point this out because, as writers, we understand there are many truths. In a way, writing, especially memoir, is the digging at one's truth in the hopes that it will strike a more universal note. I, on the other hand, had struck a nerve, and so had Amira. From there, it all fell apart. This time, instead of whining, I was angry. It was an anger that had been building for decades, centuries—an anger so deep I hadn't consciously known it was there. Denial is what enabled me to write about being Jewish and antisemitism without having an emotional breakdown in the process, because I had suppressed those feelings my whole life. When they came out, it didn't even sound like me. My voice sounded foreign—feral and guttural—as if

I were channeling a wounded animal, caught in a trap, lashing out. It was an explosion of pent-up rage. I have little recall of the specifics of what was said, only that, once again, the only person who had my back was Fran. The only reason I remember what she said is that she was the first person to speak, and I hadn't yet fallen apart.

Fran pointed out that in the entire time we had been writing together, no one had ever commented on the politics of anyone's story, that our role in providing feedback had always been to share what we heard, what we connected with or didn't understand, what we liked, what might be missing, and suggestions on how to improve or expand the work. That calling someone's writing "dangerous" was outside the accepted norms of feedback. Then came Amira's apology, followed by Sofia's claim that Amira's truth was *the* truth, and that's when I lost it, practically growling at them. I live in fear that somewhere out there is a recording of me having a total hysterical meltdown. Embarrassed by my lack of emotional control, I sent out a slew of apologies, shut down my computer, and planted myself on the couch. Meaning, I was on that couch for weeks on end. Harry was overseas on assignment, so I didn't even bother to shower. I curled up on my gray couch with the pink furry throw pillows, wearing my pink and gray camo pajamas, and watched TV.

"You got shrapneled," my friend Pinky said. I love her for always having my back, but nothing anyone said made me feel better. Not even Harry's constant refrain, via FaceTime from another country, that controversy is good. I hadn't set out to be controversial; I was just writing about the intersection of being Jewish and female, having no idea how controversial that would be.

Punching Up

I WAS STILL ON the couch ruminating about the demise of my writing group when Dave Chappelle hosted *Saturday Night Live*. This was shortly after Kanye West said he was going to go "*death con 3 On JEWISH PEOPLE,*" which sounds like a line from an action movie; that moment when our hero, machine gun in hand, ammunition strapped across his chest, shouts *Charge!*

Only Kanye didn't shoot anyone. Instead, he just tweeted some inflammatory nonsense before going to bed. His tweet referenced a military term used to describe the level of readiness for action—a range between 1 and 5, with "1" being the readiest. So, Kanye was only middling ready, ready-*ish*. Also, it's DEFCON, not "death con," but still, I got the message. (So did his fans who stood on the 405 freeway overpass in Los Angeles, holding a banner that said: *Kanye is right about the Jews,* raising their arms in a Nazi salute.)

A month or so later, Dave Chappelle hosted *SNL* and tried to create some wiggle room for Kanye.

Chappelle was in good form, smart and funny, riffing close to the edge, that line between what you can and cannot say, which is where great comedy lives. He had some throwaway jokes about confusing Sha Na Na with Shabbat and asking why some Jews dress like Run-D.M.C., then he said something about Kanye getting into so much trouble that Kyrie got into trouble. I didn't know who Kyrie was, but I laughed anyway.

Laughing felt good.

Five minutes into his monologue, Dave Chappelle said: "I know Jewish people have been through terrible things all over the world, but you can't blame that on Black Americans. You just can't. You know what I mean ... cuz, Kyrie Irving's Black ass was nowhere near the Holocaust. In fact, he's not even certain it existed."

I know it was five minutes in because I have watched and rewatched that monologue so many times, I can almost deliver it myself. The first time I saw it, I was in a depressive stupor, lying on the couch, my bare feet canoodling with the dog, a glass of wine on the armrest, potato chips on the coffee table next to a spoon inside an empty ice-cream container. Frozen non-dairy, coconut flavor. This was months into my post-writing group pity party.

What did he just say? I wondered through the fog of my salt and sugar binge. Slowly coming back to life, I sat up and rewatched Chappelle's monologue. And there it was again: He said you can't blame the Holocaust on Black Americans. Then, I got to thinking, *Now why can Dave Chappelle say that on network TV when I was criticized by my writing group for saying pretty much the same thing in reverse?*

Well, for one thing, Chappelle did take some heat for that monologue. He courts heat. Heat is his energy source. He's not just telling jokes: As a standup comedian, Chappelle leans into controversial subject matter. For another, he can stand the heat. That guy is worth something like sixty million dollars. And he didn't get where he is by being politically correct. Probably, though, it has more to do with punching up, not down. This idea that in comedy, it's okay to have fun at the expense of people who are in a position of privilege. In effect, to use comedy to deconstruct power.

Although I personally (and pretty much every Jewish person I've ever met) have way less money and power than Dave Chappelle, Kanye West, or Kyrie Irving, Jewish people as a demographic group are perceived as having *too much* money and power. Chappelle gets away with joking about Jews because, when *he* does it, it's perceived to be punching up. The comedy rule applies to systemic privilege, not personal net worth. And I get it. I may not have that kind of money or power, but I do benefit from white privilege, and white privilege dovetails with this concept of collective responsibility, blame, and guilt. That's why I got slammed by my writing group for saying I don't feel guilty about slavery, because it was perceived as an attempt to wiggle out of my whiteness, even though *my* ancestors' white asses weren't anywhere near the United States during slavery or Reconstruction. They were getting their Jewish asses kicked all over Europe, the Middle East, Asia, and Russia.

That monologue woke me up.

It was as if Dave Chappelle had reached through the screen and slapped me across the face. *Get up off the damn couch, girl!* It was a soft touch, though—a metaphoric slap. Just clarifying, because I do not want to get into more trouble by accusing Dave Chappelle of physical abuse, even in my imagination.

I've already been counseled not to mention Dave Chappelle at all, given that he's been semi-canceled by the LGBTQ community for allegedly being transphobic. I watched his controversial Netflix special *The Closer,* and I think the problem is that he broke the comedy rule about punching up, not down, because the trans community has less power than Dave Chappelle, even if he is Black. That said, despite all the controversy surrounding Chappelle, I am referencing his monologue on *SNL* because it impacted my life.

"Impact" is not quite strong enough. Dave Chappelle saved my life.

Nah, that's too strong.

Dave Chappelle's monologue resurrected this book.

The first thing I did after I got up off the couch was reboot my computer and read what I had written to date. It was a slow recovery; my guard was up. I was afraid of my voice and the problems it might get me into. Then, baby steps, I began the process of editing what was already written. Still, I was blocked, unable to face a blank page, and my book needed a new ending. The piece I had taken so much heat for in my writing group was intended to be this book's ending. It was a layered, lyrical essay meant to convey how *over* antisemitism I was, titled *ENOUGH ALREADY*—a play on words taken from a Passover song called *"Dayenu,"* meaning, *It would have been enough*.

"Dayenu," traditionally sung on our spring holiday, acknowledges everything the Israelites were thankful for during their exodus from Egypt: the parting of the Red Sea, the gift of bread, and surviving forty years in the desert. Stanza after stanza recounting the miracles that led the Jewish people out

of slavery to freedom. After each event, we say in unison, *It would have been enough.* Only, my version was more like a bitch list; a summation of micro aggressions from life experience connected by the words "The time" as in, *the time* this or that shitty thing happened. It went something like this:

The time our neighbors built a fence between our two houses—not a line in the sand, but a partition in the driveway, a demarcation between them and us. Then they lobbed antisemitic slurs across that fence. I wasn't sure what a *kike* was or why they called us "dirty" Jews, but our parents ignored it, so we did too. It wasn't as if they were throwing rocks at us. We were kids. Our credo was: Sticks and stones will break your bones, but names will never hurt you.

The time, traveling in Europe with my children, we saw a swastika spray-painted on the banks of a river, the words *Die Jew* next to it, scrawled in graffiti, and I had to explain antisemitism to my grade-school kids, which is about the same time my parents had to explain it to me. But really, what explanation is there? Other than that, *it exists.*

All the times my in-laws offended me, told a JAP joke at dinner, intentionally mangled the Hebrew word *bar mitzvah,* remarked that my voice was *so nasal,* and I never confronted them, not once. Instead, every time I called them on the phone, before I spoke, I would take a deep breath and try so hard to sound like a WASP.

The time, years later, a friend of the family, on Harry's side, sat in our living room with a glass of wine and tried to reframe my mother-in-law's antisemitism as "snobbishness." Don't take it personally, he said, she has a lot of ANTI-isms. She didn't like People of Color, either. When I asked what she had to be such a snob about, he responded that she read *The*

New Yorker, implying that she was sophisticated. I'm not sure how reading *The New Yorker* magazine makes a person somehow better than the writers who are published or reviewed in it. Ta-Nehisi Coates. Isabel Wilkerson. Haruki Murakami. Jhumpa Lahiri, Jonathan Safran Foer, Junot Díaz ... the list goes on. But I didn't argue the point. All I could think was, *Thank you. Thank you for admitting what has been denied all these years, from the moment Harry and I were engaged. Making me feel gaslit, as if it was all in my head. Or I was being too sensitive, creating problems where there were none, when my being Jewish was the problem.*

All the times this or that happened. A vendor accused me of trying to *Jew him down*; the eye doctor suggested I get my hair straightened; a stranger asked me if I was from New York because to a lot of people, New Yorkers and Jews are indistinguishable. Because my voice is nasal, maybe. Probably because my voice is like a solid handshake, strong and opinionated. The time a friend invited me for a ride on someone's boat, and while we were standing on the dock, she turned to me and said, *You'll like him, he's Jewish,* as if all Jews like each other. I stared at her, our entire friendship flashing across my mind. We had been roommates, confidants, pranksters, best friends, and all that time, I was just her JewGirl friend. I glared at her, my face hidden behind dark sunglasses and a floppy hat. My first reaction was to turn around and go home, but I was her houseguest. My suitcase was at her condo, she had the car and the keys, so I got on the boat.

I don't even like motorboats. They pollute the water.

I think about all the times I didn't want to make a scene or ruin a friendship. Instead, I let it go, sucked it up, or backed down. Backing down was my go-to response. A silent glare became my preferred form of resistance. It has been my whole life, ever since middle school when I was singled out for being the only Jewish girl in the class. I learned this strategy from my mother. Without even consciously deciding how to react, I had internalized Lois's worldview: People are antisemitic; *it is what it is*. Until one day it was just too much, and I fell apart in my writers' group. Slit a vein and let it bleed.

Dayenu

I'M MORE COMFORTABLE WITH observation than confrontation, expressing my feelings old school, with pencil and paper, journaling my outrage on paper. By the time my thoughts get past my notebook, into the computer, they've been diffused. Cherry-picked. Plus, there's the backspace/ delete option, which is harder to pull off in conversation. The process of writing this book exposed an elephant on the page: my reluctance to confront antisemitism head-on.

This lightbulb moment of self-awareness came to me while reading *Bury My Heart at Wounded Knee* in our anti-racism book club. A member of the group suggested that we consider a tandem read, one that identified Israel as a settler-colonizer nation engaged in the displacement of Indigenous peoples comparable to the United States' treatment of Native Americans. This is a point of view that has gained traction on college campuses and is closely aligned with antisemitic rhetoric. My immediate response, my knee-jerk reaction, was to drop out of the book club. To avoid conflict, yes—but more specifically, to avoid a repeat of what had happened in my writing group. I lived in fear of difficult conversations, of not being able to control my emotions. Afraid the discussion might become contentious. So, before I had time to overthink it, I shot off a private email to the group leader notifying her that I was dropping out of the book club.

Relief was immediate. Crisis averted.

I would not have to risk another day, week, or month on the couch, covered in shame, ruminating about what had transpired. Pleased with my decision, I went to bed. The next morning, I was awakened by the sound of my index finger tapping against the headboard. To be more precise, it was my knuckle. Thud. Thud. Thud. Our headboard is solid wood. The knocking was not just persistent—it was loud. My subconscious was banging my corporeal self awake. Mentally catching up with the incessant finger-tapping, I knew the moment my eyes opened, in a flash of conscious awareness, that I could not sneak off and drop out of our book club via the back door or a private email. I had to show up for the discussion. It wouldn't matter what they thought, whether their opinions were valid or not, whether I agreed or disagreed with them, or even whether the other members of the group supported me or not. It wasn't a popularity contest. I just had to show up and stand my ground without losing my cool. I had to rewrite my own story. Not the Jewish story; there are millions of Jewish stories. *My* story. My story that no longer had an ending. *This* book, without an ending, because I had thrown *ENOUGH ALREADY* in the trash, afraid it was toxic. Radioactive. DANGEROUSx3.

Eventually, my idea for this book's ending shifted into a life-affirming Passover Seder at our house in the desert, surrounded by my handpicked tribe of friends and family—Harry, Sasha, and Sam, and all the people who have joined us on Passover throughout the years. It's an ever-changing cast of characters: The Men with French Wives and their kids, Sasha's boyfriend, Sam's girlfriend. Jewish and non-Jewish friends representing diverse ethnicities and multiple countries[20]. This image of us all at the Passover table—wine, food, and laughter. Welcoming and belonging.

My chosen family.

Our table used to be Harry's workbench in the garage—a repurposed oak slab that seats twelve. He sanded it, oiled it, surfed the internet for steel legs to support it. It's a labor of love, that table. On Passover, it is filled with people who love and support each other.

We often fool around with the *Haggadah,* the holiday script that tells the story of the Israelites' liberation from slavery in Egypt. One year, when the kids were little, I gave them mini toy insects and animals to represent some of the plagues that befell our oppressors: Frogs, Flies, Lice, Locusts, Livestock. Typically, though, we just dip a finger in red wine as we recite the plagues. Another time, when the kids were older, we sat on the floor, to be more like our ancestors, reclining on cushions, while contemplating the essential question: *Why is this night different from all other nights?* My personal all-time favorite Passover is the Bob Marley Seder because I like how reggae music is so closely aligned with Israel and the Hebrews. I made a killer playlist, but Sam won't let me use that *Haggadah,* either because he doesn't like reggae, or he thinks there's better reggae music than Bob Marley.

Sam prefers listening to music no one has ever heard of. He considers it a badge of honor to be one of the few followers

---

20   Canada, El Salvador, England, Egypt, Ireland, Jordan, France, Morocco, and Russia. If I've left anyone out, I apologize!

of an obscure indie band that only five people in Sweden know about. He's the same way about film. On the other hand, Sasha is all about mainstream artists. They used to fight about this. Sasha would accuse Sam of being elitist, and Sam would act as if his tastes were more sophisticated than Sasha's. Her feelings would get hurt, and then I would have to intervene, or at least I felt the need to referee—something my mother never did.

Then, miracle of miracles, my combative teenagers grew into a support system for each other. They still don't share the same taste in music or film, but they've developed into amazing gift-givers. Sam works in the design industry, so Sasha gave him a subscription to the trendiest, most obscure design publication on the planet. For her birthday, Sam gave Sasha a vase by Houseplant, Seth Rogen's pottery brand. The vase is iridescent blue, the color of her eyes. Along with the vase was a pair of tickets to see Rogen perform at the Hollywood Bowl, and this makes my heart swell: Sasha invited Sam to the concert as her date.

I'm reminded of that stranger in the elevator who said to me all those years ago, about parenting, *You fix the things that were wrong with your childhood.* I had no idea what she was talking about at the time and considered her to be a random stranger, possibly a bit wacky, but now I understand her words to have been a prophecy. She was delivering a message: It is within your power to *not repeat* the mistakes your mother made. The second half of her message, *along the way you make other mistakes*, I guess that's to be expected. Moms aren't perfect.

On this particular Passover, both kids helped prepare the meal. Sasha made sweet'n'salty matzah topped with melted chocolate, nuts, and candy. Sam acted as my sous chef because he's more organized than me in the kitchen. I tend to dive into a recipe without reading it first. No prep, but great music. My favorite cooking playlist is Kitchen Swagger on Spotify. When the song "Hell N Back" by Bakar came on, I started dancing.

"OMG," Sasha said, laughing, as she tilted her head and rolled her eyes, as if to say, *there she goes again.* Her hair pulled up in a ponytail exposing the *Chai* tattooed on the back of her neck, in a softly diffused, washed-out ink, the color of a peanut. The Hebrew symbol for *life.*

"Mom!" Sam pleaded. "C'mon, focus. Matzah ball soup." His sleeves rolled up, ready to work. I noticed that he'd lost that lanky teenage-boy look, becoming more solid.

"Just this one song," I insisted. *It'll all come together. It always does.*

The only dish I prepare for the Passover Seder without any help is the charoset, which my Grandma Molly taught me to make as a child. Chop the apples and nuts. Add cinnamon. Mix in the wine. Sometimes I get fancy and make a Sephardic charoset with dried fruit and nuts. On this Passover, the one I was going to end my book with, we used a Humanist Haggadah inspired by the teachings of my rabbi in Detroit, Sherwin Wine. For the first time in my life, I led the Seder, starting with *Kiddush,* the blessing over wine.

I raised my cup and looked at the faces of friends I'd known for decades, the mix of generations at the table spanning multiple decades, recalling the time my father told me family is everything; everything else (or did he say *everyone* else?) is shit. It freaked me out when he said that. *You mean to tell me that this family that I was born into is as good as it gets?* I smiled to myself, thinking how wrong he was, and how lucky I was to have created my own sense of family. My best friend Pinky. Al and Lee, and their two kids. My husband, Harry. Our son and daughter, siblings who broke the chain of generational trauma.

But I never got around to writing that ending. It seemed cheesy, and I wanted to say something more profound. Like this: Almost two years after I began this project, at another doctor's office, filling out yet another intake form, there in black and white, was a new checkable box: "Multicultural." The list of box options was growing. It's a complex, dynamic endeavor to categorize humans. Whispering that word "multicultural" to myself felt satisfying. It was like finding the correct answer in a crossword puzzle. Unlike the word "other," it doesn't imply that I'm different. On the contrary, it implies abundance. That my essence can't be distilled down to one thing, which makes perfect sense. I'm white *and* Jewish. It's not a binary choice—white or not white. I don't have to check "other" to assert my Jewish identity, and I can't deny my white skin or the privilege that comes with it.

But even that seemed too spot-on.

Instead, I decided to resurrect the last paragraph from my never-to-be-published workshop piece entitled, "Enough Already." The one that caused me so much *tsuris,* a Yiddish word meaning "woe." It may be the only part worth saving.

The Passover Seder, like the Jewish religion, is mutable. While the basics remain the same, including the story of Exodus, the Four Questions, the plagues, the copious wine, the hiding of the matzah, the Seder plate, and the ritual place setting for Elijah, there is room in the Jewish religion for interpretation and change. And so, pouring a cup of wine for the prophet

Elijah, *in case he shows up*, has come to symbolize an act of unconditional hospitality, no matter who shows up at your door. The specific story of the Jewish people escaping slavery is seen in a larger context, through the universal lens of persecution and human suffering. Adding an orange to the Seder plate (an item of food that did not used to belong but now does) symbolizes that all people, no matter how they identify, no matter what their gender or sexual orientation, are welcome at our Seder table. In the spirit of change, reflection, and reinterpretation, taking in all the times that this or that happened, the age-old, the history of misogyny and antisemitism, to this soft landing: Find love. It's the only way forward.

Notes

Books

American Dirt by Jeanine Cummins

Antisemitism Here and Now by Deborah E. Lipstadt

Biased by Jennifer L. Eberhardt, PhD

Bring the War Home: The White Power Movement and Paramilitary America by Kathleen Belew

Bury My Heart at Wounded Knee by Dee Brown

Caste: The Origins of Our Discontents by Isabel Wilkerson

Dear White People: A Guide to Inter-Racial Harmony in "Post-Racial" America by Justin Simien

Jews Don't Count by David Baddiel

Lord of the Flies by William Golding

Minor Feelings: An Asian American Reckoning by Cathy Park Hong

Monsters: A Fan's Dilemma by Claire Dederer

People Love Dead Jews by Dara Horn

Prequel: An American Fight Against Fascism by Rachel Maddow

Talking To Strangers by Malcolm Gladwell

The Bluest Eye by Toni Morrison

The Fire Next Time by James Baldwin

They Knew: How a Culture of Conspiracy Keeps America Complacent by Sarah Kendzior

White Fragility by Robin DiAngelo
White Rage: The Unspoken Truth of Our Racial Divide by
 Carol Anderson
*Woke Racism: How a New Religion Has Betrayed Black
 America* by John McWhorter
Women and Gender in Islam by Leila Ahmed

Film

King, Regina, Dir. *One Night in Miami...* Amazon Original
 Movie, 2020

Theater

Slave Play by Jeremy O. Harris

Online References

Boxes

AP Associated Press. *"Jewish people make up 2.4% of the U.S.
 population but are the targets of about 60% of hate crimes
 linked to religion, says FBI director."* Marketwatch.com.
 November 2, 2023. https://www.marketwatch.com/
 story/jewish-people-make-up-2-4-of-the-u-s-population-
 but-are-the-targets-of-about-60-of-hate-crimes-linked-to-
 religion-says-fbi-director-2dd86906

Siegel, Tatiana. *"Hollywood's Israel Divide Intensifies."* Variety.
 December 5, 2024. https://variety.com/2024/film/news/
 hollywood-israel-palestine-susan-sarandon-roger-wa-
 ters-1236208303

Duignan, Brian. *"Replacement Theory."* Britannica. Last
 Updated: Aug 23, 2025. https://www.britannica.com/
 topic/replacement-theory

JewGirl

Gowman, Katherine. *"The Other America"* The-Other-America.com. *2014.* https://the-other-america.com/new-page-3

Sutherland, Callum. *"The Rise of Antisemitism and Political Violence in the U.S."* TIME Magazine. June 2, 2025. https://time.com/7287941/rise-of-antisemitism-political-violence-in-united-states/

Humanism

Edwards, Mark. *"Was America founded as a Christian nation?"* CNN. July 4, 2015. https://www.cnn.com/2015/07/02/living/america-christian-nation

Related

Abcarian, Robin. *"Was it OK for 'The Bear' to use this Jewish slur?"* Los Angeles Times. July 16, 2023. https://www.latimes.com/opinion/story/2023-07-16/the-bear-jewish-ethnic-steretyping-rob-eshman

Boy with the Elastic Smile

Fact Sheet: *"Judaism and Abortion."* National Council of Jewish Women. 2019. https://www.ncjw.org/wp-content/uploads/2019/05/Judaism-and-Abortion-FINAL.pdf

Marcus, Kenneth L. *"Fact Sheet on the Elements of Anti-Semitic Discourse."* The Louis D. Brandeis Center for Human Rights Under Law. ca. 2014. https://www.ohchr.org/sites/default/files/Documents/AboutUs/CivilSociety/ReportHC/75_The_Louis_D._Brandeis_Center__Fact_Sheet_Anti-Semitism.pdf

Department of Veterans Affairs (VA). USASPENDING. gov. September 29, 2024. https://www.usaspending.gov/ agency/department-of-veterans-affairs?fy=2024

"Total women's health funding by the National Institutes for Health (NIH) from FY 2013 to FY 2025." Statista. https://www.statista.com/statistics/713378/total-women-s-health-funding-by-the-national-institutes-for-health

Belew, Kathleen. "White power movements in US history have often relied on veterans – and not on lone wolves." The Conversation. April 25, 2023. https://theconversation. com/white-power-movements-in-us-history-have-often-relied-on-veterans-and-not-on-lone-wolves-200417

"ISD report details rise in 'your body, my choice' and other misogynistic content following the US elections." Institute for Strategic Dialogue. November 13, 2024. https://www. isdglobal.org/isd-in-the-news/isd-report-details-rise-in-your-body-my-choice-and-other-misogynistic-content-following-the-us-elections/

Jewish Geography

Fact Sheet: "Violence Against Women," World Health Organization. March 25, 2024. https://www.who.int/ news-room/fact-sheets/detail/violence-against-women

Fact Sheet: "Rape & Sexual Assault in the U.S." National Organization for Women, NYC. 2019. https://nownyc. org/issues/get-the-facts-take-rape-seriously/

Dederer, Claire. "What Do We Do with the Art of Monstrous Men?' The Paris Review. November 20, 2017. https://www.theparisreview.org/blog/2017/11/20/ art-monstrous-men/

Neumeister, Larry; Peltz, Jennifer; Sisak, Michael R. *"Jury Finds Trump Liable for Sexual Abuse, Awards Accuser 5M."* APNews.com. May 9, 2023. https://apnews.com/article/trump-rape-carroll-trial-fe68259a4b98bb3947d42af-9ec83d7db

Warrior Princess
Haberman, Maggie and Feurer, Alan. *"Trump's Latest Dinner Guest: Nick Fuentes, White Supremacist."* New York Times. November 25, 2022. https://www.nytimes.com/2022/11/25/us/politics/trump-nick-fuentes-dinner.html
Chait, Jonathan. *"Marjorie Taylor Greene Blamed Wildfires on Secret Jewish Space Laser."* New York Magazine. January 28, 2021. https://nymag.com/intelligencer/article/marjorie-taylor-greene-qanon-wildfires-space-laser-rothschild-execute.html
Weisman, Jonathan. *"Robert F. Kennedy Jr. Airs Bigoted New Covid Conspiracy Theory About Jews and Chinese."* New York Times. Updated July 20, 2023. https://www.nytimes.com/2023/07/15/us/politics/rfk-jr-remarks-covid.html
Dickson, EJ. *"'Aspirationally Jewish' Elon Musk Hosts the Most Antisemitic Content on His Platform."* Rolling Stone. January 24, 2024. https://www.rollingstone.com/culture/culture-news/elon-musk-twitter-antisemitic-report-1234953165/
Fact Sheet: *"Antisemitic Attitudes in America: Topline Findings."* Anti-Defamation League. ADL.org. January 12, 2023. https://www.adl.org/resources/report/antisemitic-attitudes-america-topline-findings

Passing

Evans, Greg. *"Ellie Kemper Apologizes for Participation in Debutante Ball with Racist, Antisemitic Origins: Ignorance is No Excuse."* Deadline. June 7, 2021. https://deadline.com/2021/06/ellie-kemper-apologizes-for-debutante-ball-racist-origins-1234770697/

World Jewish Travel Official. *"The Jewish Story of Harbin, China."* World Jewish Travel. December 2, 2021. https://www.worldjewishtravel.org/listing/the-jewish-story-of-harbin

Macro/Micro

Al Tahhan, Zena. *"More than a century on: The Balfour Declaration explained."* Aljazeera. November 2, 2018. https://www.aljazeera.com/features/2018/11/2/more-than-a-century-on-the-balfour-declaration-explained

Fact Sheet: *"Jews and Finance."* My Jewish Learning. https://www.myjewishlearning.com/article/usury-and-moneylending-in-judaism/

Walt, Vivienne. *"Paris Jews Reel After Deadly Kosher-Supermarket Attack."* Time Magazine. January 12, 2015. https://time.com/3663060/paris-terror-attack-jews-kosher-supermarket-siege/

Le Stradic, Ségolène. *"Second Trial in Teacher's Killing Begins in France"* New York Times. Updated Dec. 20, 2024. https://www.nytimes.com/2024/11/04/world/europe/france-paty-beheading-trial.html

(I've Never Been To) Israel

Greenfield, Jeff. *"The Ugly History of Stephen Miller's 'Cosmopolitan' Epitaph"* Politico. August 3, 2017.

https://www.politico.com/magazine/story/2017/08/03/
the-ugly-history-of-stephen-millers-cosmopolitan-epi-
thet-215454/

Shankar, Amulya. *"'Cosmopolitan' is a dog whistle word
once used in Nazi Germany and Communist Russia."*
The World. August 3, 2107. https://theworld.
org/stories/2017/08/03/cosmopolitan-dog-whis-
tle-word-used-nazi-germany-and-communist-russia

"United Nations Resolution 181" Brittanica. https://www.
britannica.com/topic/United-Nations-Resolution-181

Complicit

*"The Sinister Face of 'Neutrality'. The Role of Swiss Financial
Institutions in the Plunder of European Jewry* Institute of
the World Jewish Congress, Jerusalem. 1996. https://
www.pbs.org/wgbh/pages/frontline/shows/nazis/readings/
sinister.html

Lancer, Darlene. *"Sibling Bullying and Abuse:
The Hidden Epidemic."* PsychologyToday.
February 3, 2020. https://www.psychologyto-
day.com/us/blog/toxic-relationships/202002/
sibling-bullying-and-abuse-the-hidden-epidemic

Left. Right. Siloed.

Domonoske, Camila. *"Former KKK Leader David Duke
Says 'Of course' Trump voters are his voters."* NPR.
August 5, 2016. https://www.npr.org/sections/thet-
wo-way/2016/08/05/488802494/former-kkk-leader-da-
vid-duke-says-of-course-trump-voters-are-his-voters

Stockman, Farah. *"Women's March Roiled by Accusations of
Anti-Semitism."* New York Times. Dec. 23, 2018. https://

www.nytimes.com/2018/12/23/us/womens-march-anti-semitism.html

Fact Sheet: *"Nation of Islam"* Southern Poverty Law Center. https://www.splcenter.org/resources/extremist-files/nation-islam/

Yang, Allie. *"Women's March co-president Tamika Mallory discusses controversial relationship with Louis Farrakhan."* ABC News. January 14, 2019. https://abcnews.go.com/US/womens-march-president-tamika-mallory-discusses-controversial-relationship/story?id=60362553

Pildis, Carly. *"Even the Women's March Apology Erases Jewish Women."* Tabletmagazine.com. November 12, 2018. https://www.tabletmag.com/sections/news/articles/even-the-womens-march-apology-erases-jewish-women

Fact Sheet: *"Origins of neo-Nazi and white supremacist terms and symbols."* United States Holocaust Memorial Museum. https://www.ushmm.org/antisemitism/what-is-antisemitism/origins-of-neo-nazi-and-white-supremacist-terms-and-symbols

Stockman, Farah. *"Three Leaders of Women's March Group Step Down After Controversies."* New York Times. Updated Sept. 18, 2019. https://www.nytimes.com/2019/09/16/us/womens-march-anti-semitism.html

Caron, Christina. *"Heather Heyer, Charlottesville Victim, Is Recalled as 'a Strong Woman'"* New York Times. Aug. 13, 2017. https://www.nytimes.com/2017/08/13/us/heather-heyer-charlottesville-victim.html

Bromwich, Jonah and Blinder, Alan. *"What We Know About James Alex Fields, Driver Charged in Charlottesville Killing."* New York Times. Aug. 13, 2017. https://www.

nytimes.com/2017/08/13/us/james-alex-fields-charlottes-ville-driver-.html

Choi, Christy. *"Christie's cancels auction of jewels linked to Nazi-era fortune."* CNN. September 5, 2023. https://edition.cnn.com/style/heidi-horten-jewels-christies-nazi-canceled

Privilege

Treisman, Rachel. *"JD Vance went viral for 'cat lady' comments. The centuries-old trope has a long tail."* NPR. July 29, 2024. https://www.npr.org/2024/07/29/nx-s1-5055616/jd-vance-childless-cat-lady-history

Wallace, David Foster. *"This is Water."* Kenyon College Commencement Speech. 2005. http://bulletin-archive.kenyon.edu/x4280.html

Old Jew

Niemöller. Martin: *"First They Came For ..."* 1946. https://hmd.org.uk/resource/first-they-came-by-pastor-martin-niemoller/

Punching Up

Limbong, Andrew. *"Twitter follows Instagram after restricting Ye's account after antisemitic posts."* NPR. October 10, 2022. https://www.npr.org/2022/10/09/1127732183/kanye-west-instagram-twitter

Chappelle, Dave. SNL Monologue. November 13, 2022. https://www.youtube.com/watch?v=cw4OapDkniA

Da Silva, Chantal; Dasrath, Diana. *"Rise in Antisemitism is feared after banner saying 'Kanye is right' is hung over Los Angeles Freeway."* NBC News. October 24, 2022. https://

www.nbcnews.com/news/us-news/banner-kanye-right-los-angeles-freeway-antisemtic-group-rcna53653

Dayenu
Levin, Sam. *"Suspension of controversial Palestinian class UC Berkeley sparks debate."*
The Guardian. September 15, 2016. https://
www.theguardian.com/us-news/2016/sep/15/
uc-berkeley-israel-palestine-class-suspended-decal

Acknowledgments

Big love to my friends and writers' community, who listened (and listened and listened) to these stories while they were being hashed out, as well as those who read and/or provided feedback on early drafts: Terrie Birndorf, Patty Blumberg, Jone Bouman, Andrew Cohen, Corine Gantz, Janice Gary, Amanda Johnston, Barbara Kinglsey, Mindy Lake, Alex Lerner, Leah Lerner, Janet Lombardi, Courtney Rackley, Richard Rubin, and Susan Sanford. Special thanks to Cynthia Bond, whose online master class provided a safe, thoughtful environment in which to workshop portions of *JewGirl*. I would also like to thank Carolyn Levin for her thorough legal review of the manuscript.

The following people generously provided details where my memory was insufficient: Rabbi Jeffrey Falick, Congregation for Humanistic Judaism of Metro Detroit, and Ruth Shavit, former preschool director, Hollywood/Los Feliz JCC (now SIJCC).

Thank you to my amazing edit/creative team: Nicole Bokat for her notes and encouragement; Melissa Carro, who unflinchingly told me what to cut; Cindy Hochman and Kelly Hartog, both of whom went above and beyond all expectations as copy editor and proofreader; and Danna Steele for the perfect cover art.

A word about my family: I like to think that if my mother were alive, she would love this book. Thank you to Adina Cole for her big heart and to my sisters, who listened to and reviewed countless drafts of the sections about our family dynamic. Hugs to my husband, Richard, who always has my back, and our children, Jade and Jordan, who never complain about showing up in my writing.

A special thanks to all the women who shared their stories with me.

About the Author

MARCIE MAXFIELD is the author of *Em's Awful Good Fortune*, which received the NYC Big Book Award for Contemporary Novel; the Independent Author Network (IAN) Book of the Year Award in Women's Fiction; and the Foreword INDIES Silver Award in Humor. Her play *Girls Together Always* received an ENCORE! Producers' Award at the Hollywood Fringe Festival. From Detroit, Maxfield (née Blumberg) has lived in Europe and Asia and is based in Southern California.

DON'T MISS THE DEBUT NOVEL
FROM AWARD-WINNING AUTHOR

Marcie Maxfield

MARCIEMAXFIELD.COM

NYC BIG BOOK AWARD FOR CONTEMPORARY NOVEL

"*Em's Awful Good Fortune* takes its reader across the world and deep into the heart of its trapped, privileged, suffering, and, ultimately, invincible narrator. Equally funny and brutal, this novel breathes vivid life into a much maligned and little understood 'type'—the expat wife…Maxfield poured her heart into the writing, and it shows: the pages crackle."

—Junot Díaz
Pulitzer Prize-winning author of *The Brief Wondrous Life of Oscar Wao, Drown,* and *This Is How You Lose Her.*